ZERO™ Vol.2

"At The Heart Of I

ZERO

Vol. 2:

"AT THE HEART OF IT ALL"

#6—10

First printed in magazine for

ZERO™

Written by
Ales KOT

Lettered by
Clayton COWLES

Collection designed by
Tom MULLER

Illustrated by
Vanesa R. DEL REY
Matt TAYLOR
Jorge COELHO
Tonči ZONJIĆ
Michael GAYDOS

Designed by
Tom MULLER

Original cover design, graphics and colors by Tom Muller, with Vanesa R. Del Rey, Matt Taylor, Jorge Coelho, Tonči Zonjić, Michael Gaydos, Francesco Francavilla, Nick Dragotta, Cameron Stewart, and Sean Phillips.

Colored by
Jordie BELLAIRE

Vol. 2:
#6—10
"AT THE HEART OF IT ALL"

Image Comics, Inc.

Robert Kirkman — chief operating officer
Erik Larsen — chief financial officer
Todd McFarlane — president
Marc Silvestri — chief executive officer
Jim Valentino — vice president

Eric Stephenson — publisher
Ron Richards — director of business development
Jennifer de Guzman — director of trade book sales
Kat Salazar — director of pr & marketing
Jeremy Sullivan — director of digital sales
Emilio Bautista — sales assistant
Branwyn Bigglestone — senior accounts manager
Emily Miller — accounts manager
Jessica Ambriz — administrative assistant
Tyler Shainline — events coordinator
David Brothers — content manager
Jonathan Chan — production manager
Drew Gill — art director
Meredith Wallace — print manager
Monica Garcia — senior production artist
Vincent Kukua — production artist
Jenna Savage — production artist
Addison Duke — production artist
Tricia Ramos — production assistant

ZERO VOL 2. First Printing. September 2014. Published by Image Comics, Inc. Office of publication: 2001 Center Street, Sixth Floor, Berkeley, CA 94704. Copyright © 2014 ALES KOT. All rights reserved. ZERO™ (inlcuding all prominent characters featured herein), its logo and all character likenesses are trademarks of Ales Kot, unless otherwise noted. Image Comics® and its logos are registered trademarks of Image Comics, Inc. No part of this publication may be reproduced or transmitted, in any form or by any means (except short excerpts for review purposes) without express written permission of Image Comics, Inc. All names, characters, events and locales in this publication are entirely fictional. Any resemblance to actual living persons (living or dead), events or places, without satiric intent, is coincidental. First printed in single magazine format as ZERO #6-10 by Image Comics, Inc. Printed in the USA. For information regarding the CPSIA on this printed material call: 203-595-3636 and provide reference # RICH- 573802. For international rights contact: foreignlicensing@imagecomics.com

CHAPTER 6

HORSE COLLECTORS
Illustrated by Vanesa R. Del Rey

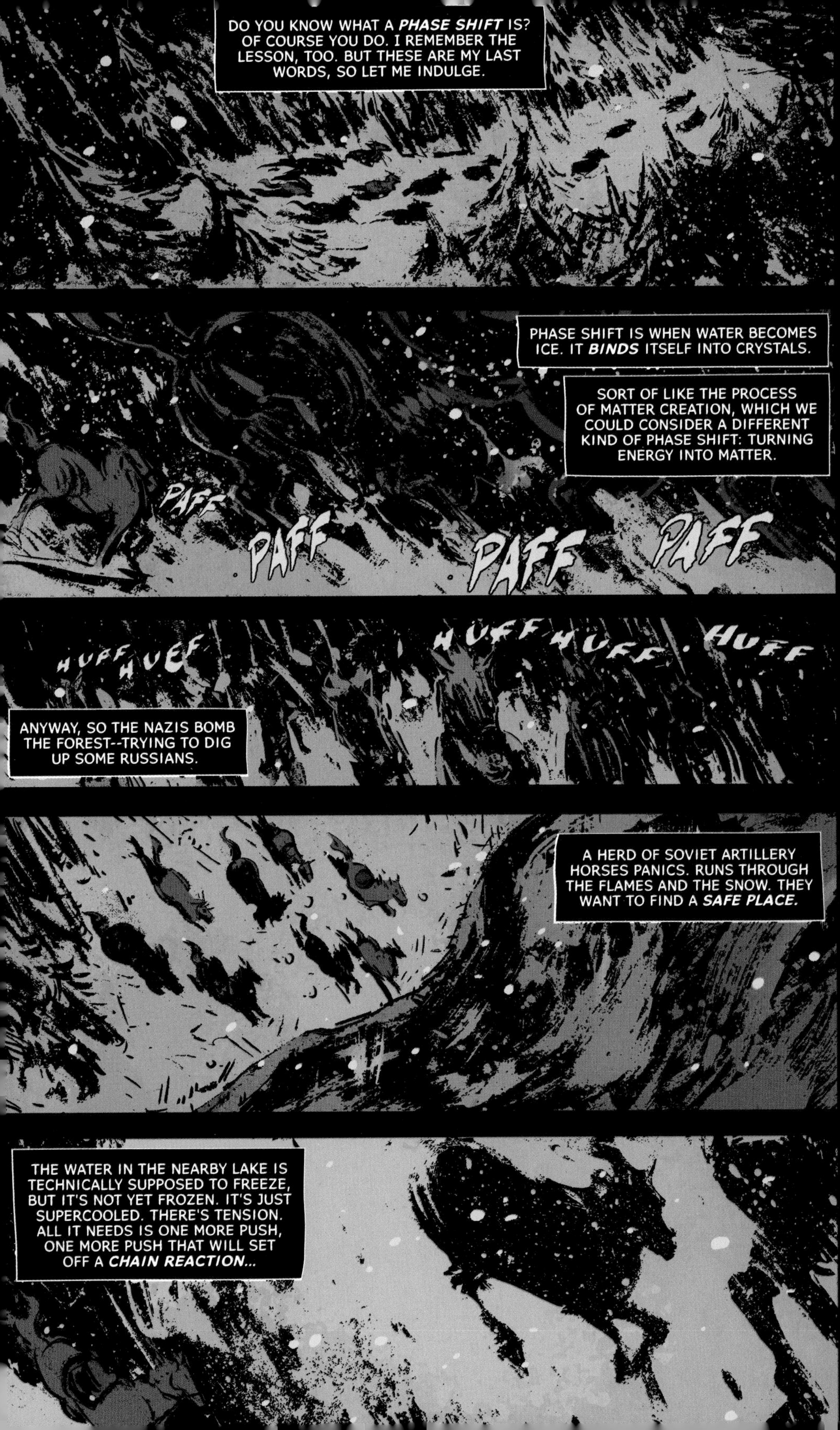
DO YOU KNOW WHAT A ***PHASE SHIFT*** IS? OF COURSE YOU DO. I REMEMBER THE LESSON, TOO. BUT THESE ARE MY LAST WORDS, SO LET ME INDULGE.
PHASE SHIFT IS WHEN WATER BECOMES ICE. IT ***BINDS*** ITSELF INTO CRYSTALS.
SORT OF LIKE THE PROCESS OF MATTER CREATION, WHICH WE COULD CONSIDER A DIFFERENT KIND OF PHASE SHIFT: TURNING ENERGY INTO MATTER.
PAFF
PAFF
PAFF
PAFF
HUFF HUFF
HUFF HUFF
HUFF
ANYWAY, SO THE NAZIS BOMB THE FOREST--TRYING TO DIG UP SOME RUSSIANS.
A HERD OF SOVIET ARTILLERY HORSES PANICS. RUNS THROUGH THE FLAMES AND THE SNOW. THEY WANT TO FIND A ***SAFE PLACE.***
THE WATER IN THE NEARBY LAKE IS TECHNICALLY SUPPOSED TO FREEZE, BUT IT'S NOT YET FROZEN. IT'S JUST SUPERCOOLED. THERE'S TENSION. ALL IT NEEDS IS ONE MORE PUSH, ONE MORE PUSH THAT WILL SET OFF A ***CHAIN REACTION...***

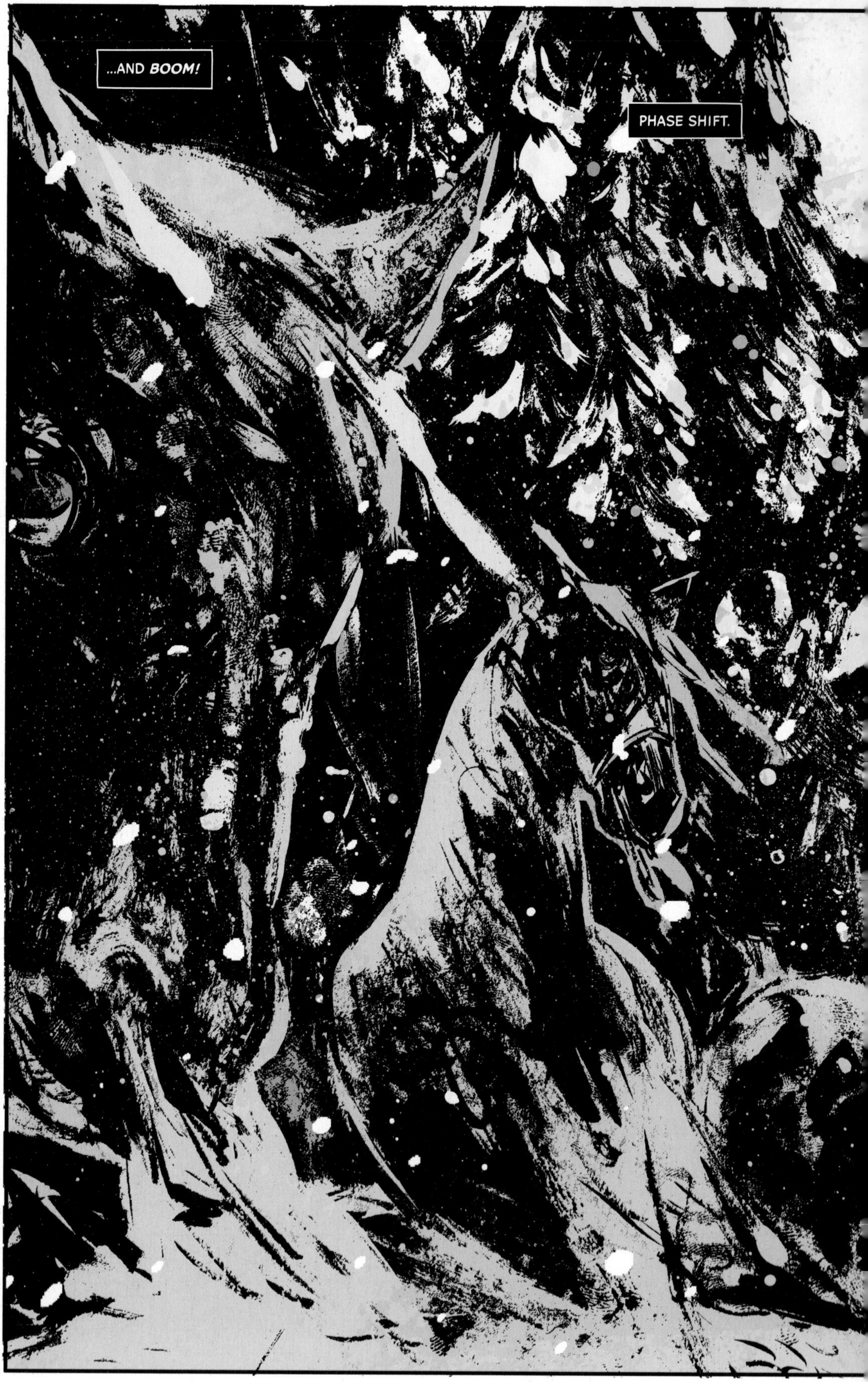
...AND BOOM!
PHASE SHIFT.

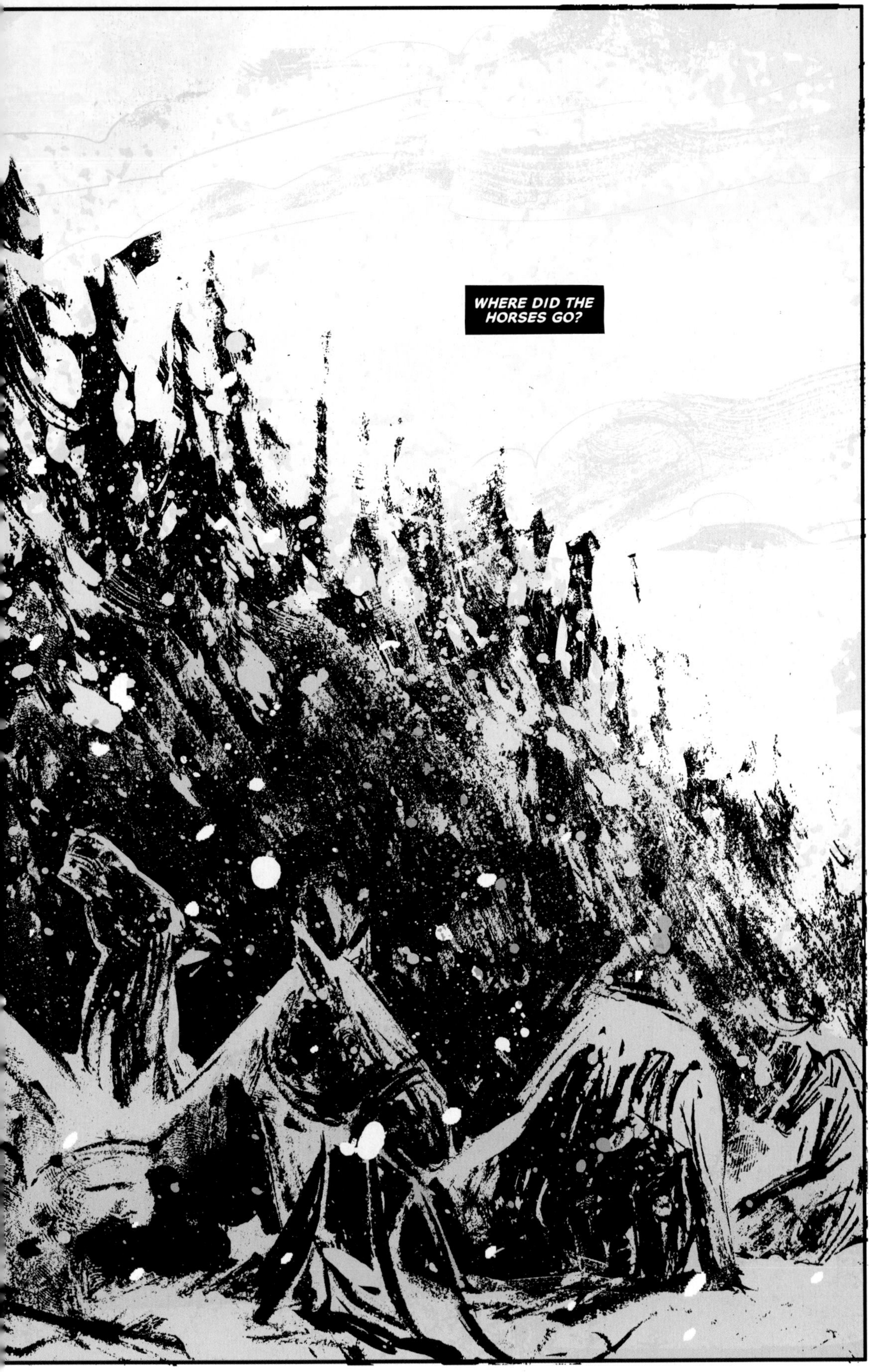
WHERE DID THE HORSES GO?

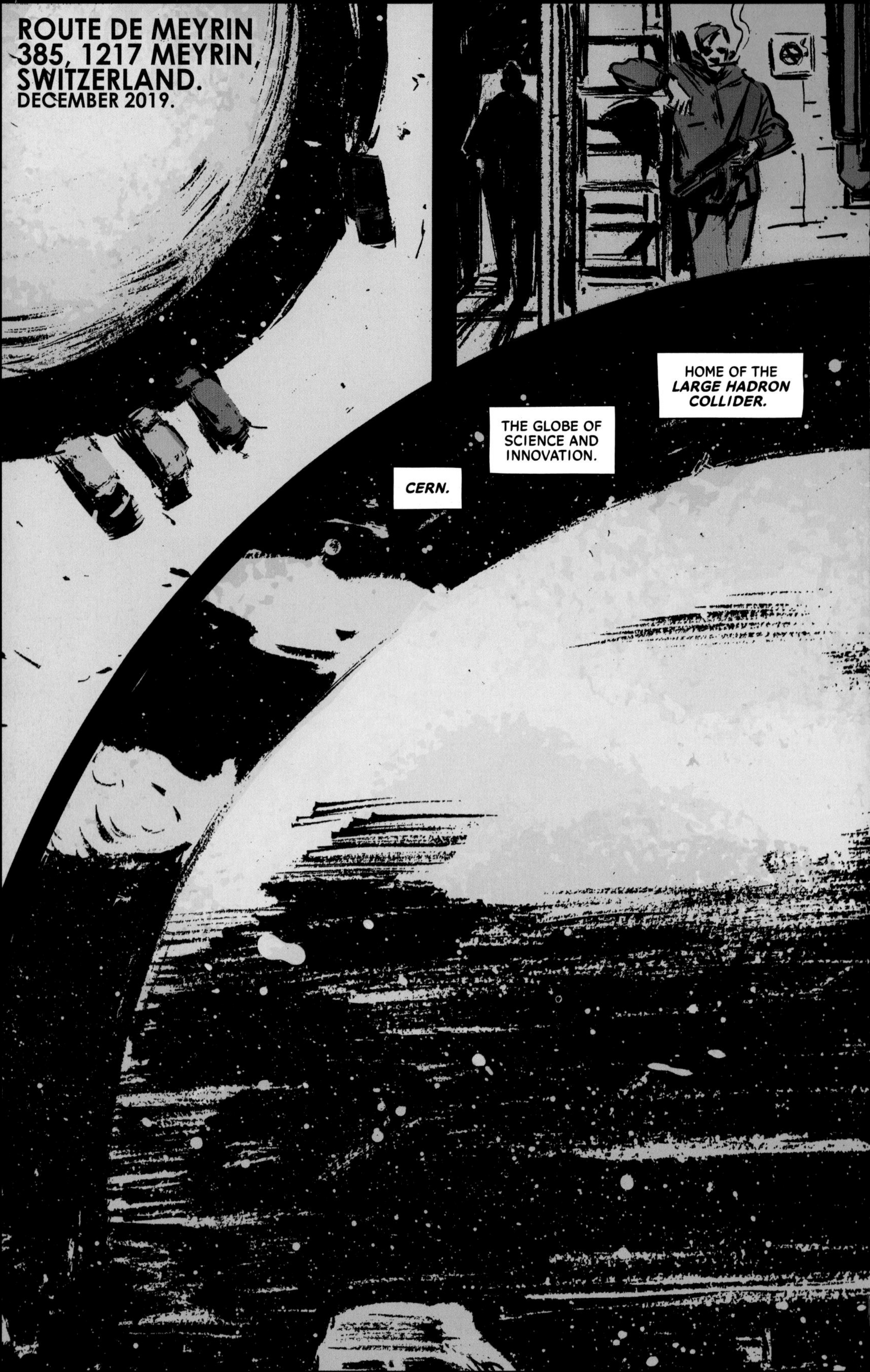
ROUTE DE MEYRIN
385, 1217 MEYRIN,
SWITZERLAND.
DECEMBER 2019.
CERN.
THE GLOBE OF SCIENCE AND INNOVATION.
HOME OF THE LARGE HADRON COLLIDER.

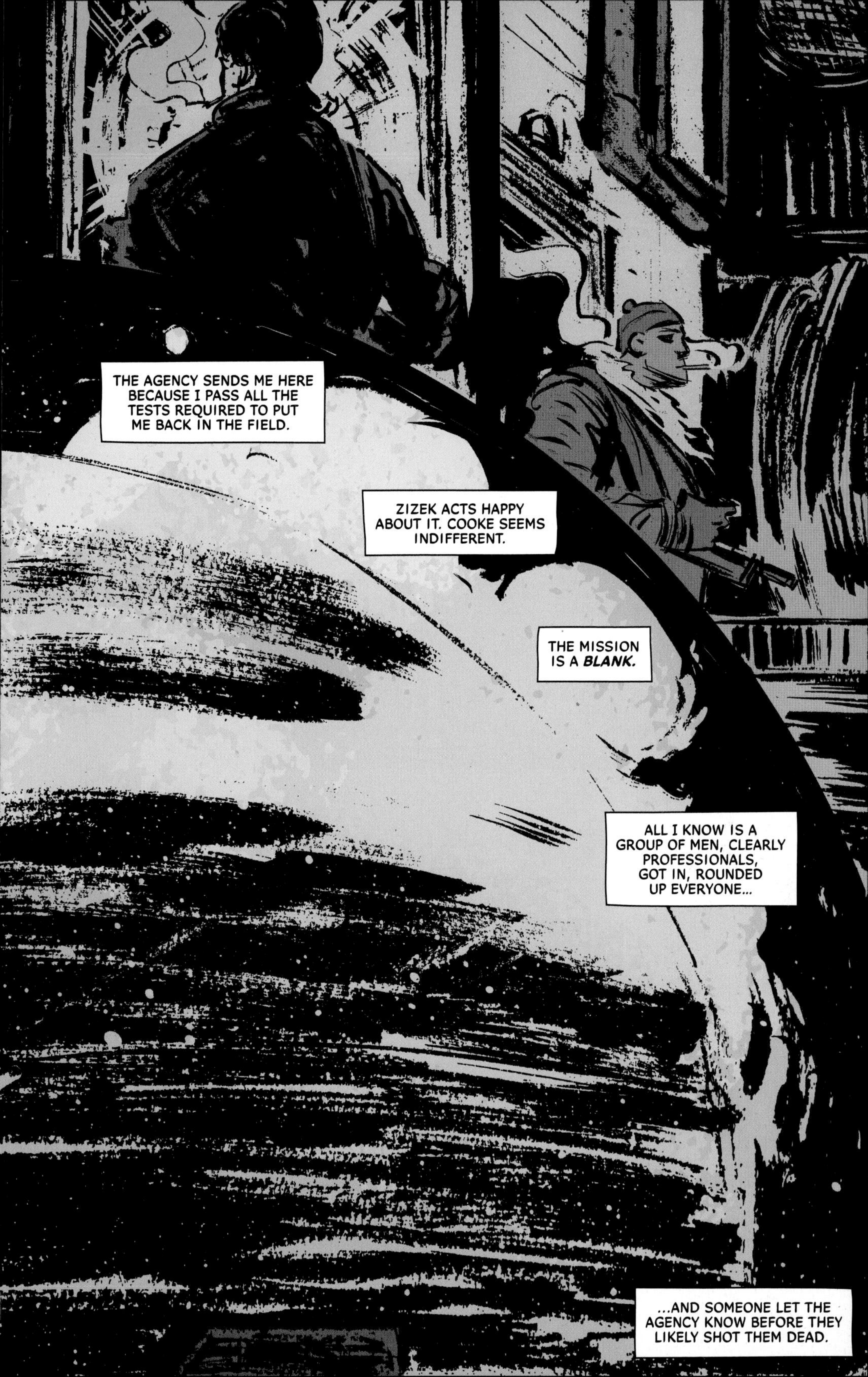
THE AGENCY SENDS ME HERE BECAUSE I PASS ALL THE TESTS REQUIRED TO PUT ME BACK IN THE FIELD.
ZIZEK ACTS HAPPY ABOUT IT. COOKE SEEMS INDIFFERENT.
THE MISSION IS A *BLANK.*
ALL I KNOW IS A GROUP OF MEN, CLEARLY PROFESSIONALS, GOT IN, ROUNDED UP EVERYONE...
...AND SOMEONE LET THE AGENCY KNOW BEFORE THEY LIKELY SHOT THEM DEAD.

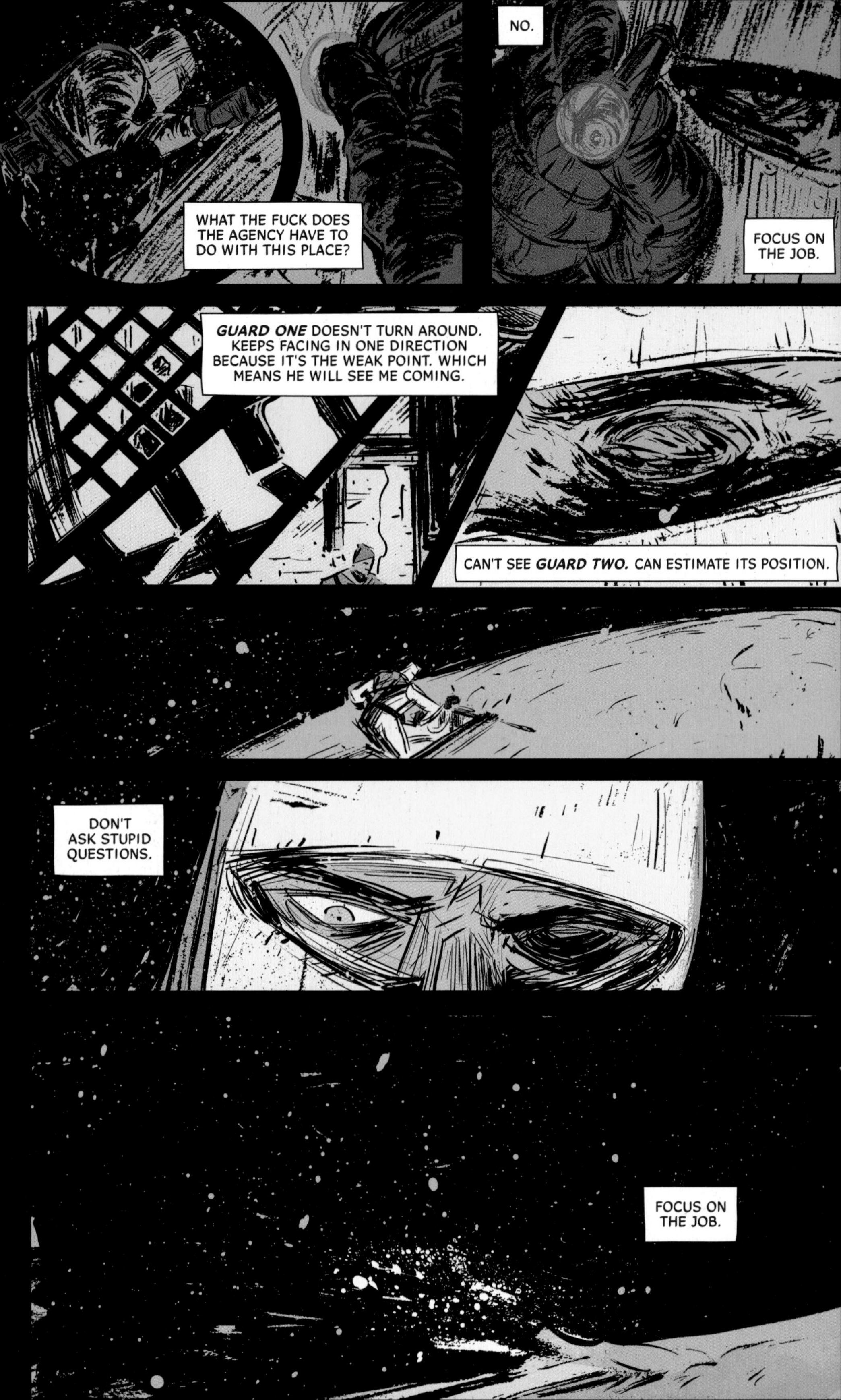
WHAT THE FUCK DOES THE AGENCY HAVE TO DO WITH THIS PLACE?
NO.
FOCUS ON THE JOB.
GUARD ONE DOESN'T TURN AROUND. KEEPS FACING IN ONE DIRECTION BECAUSE IT'S THE WEAK POINT. WHICH MEANS HE WILL SEE ME COMING.
CAN'T SEE GUARD TWO. CAN ESTIMATE ITS POSITION.
DON'T ASK STUPID QUESTIONS.
FOCUS ON THE JOB.

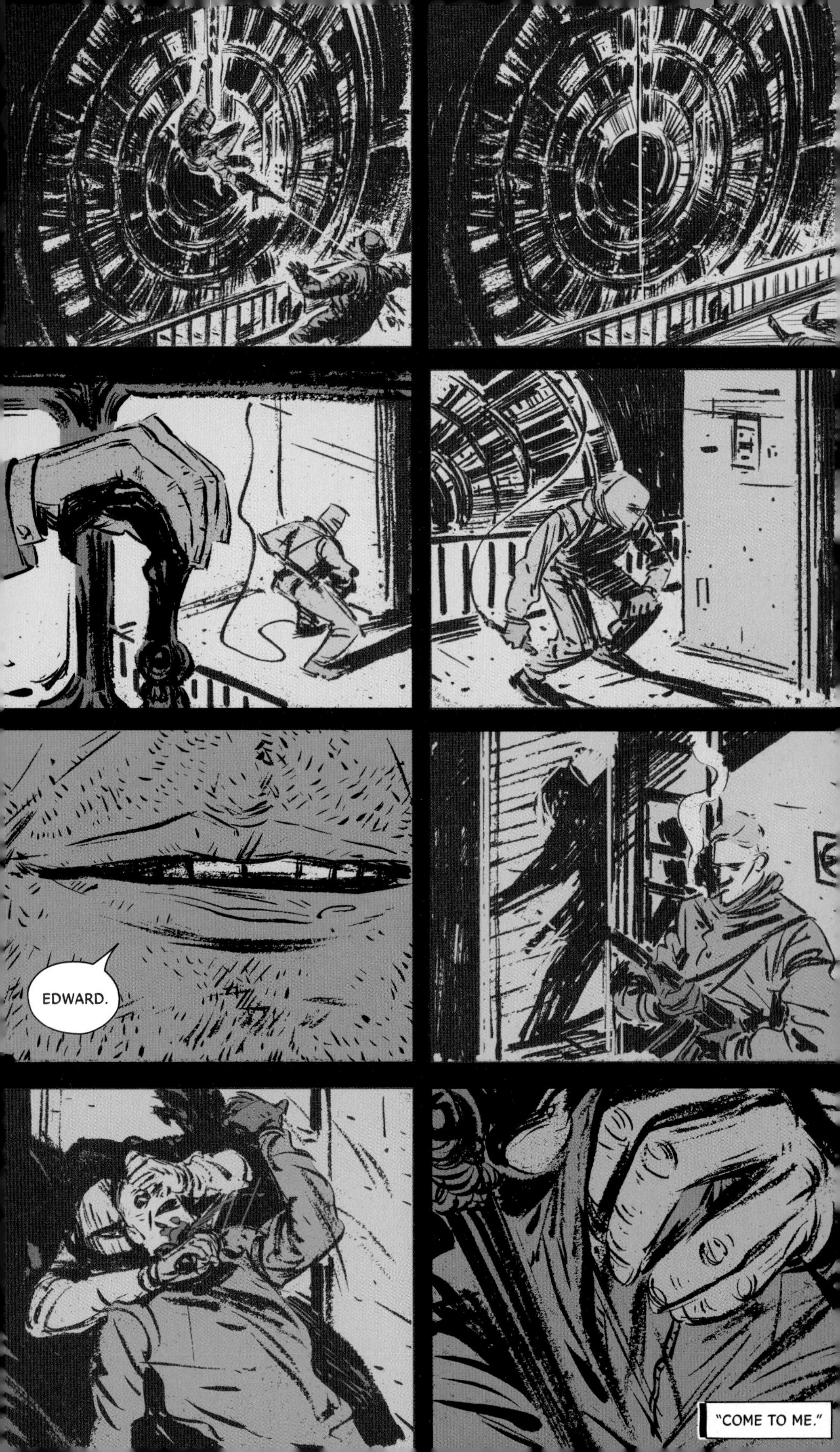
EDWARD.
"COME TO ME."

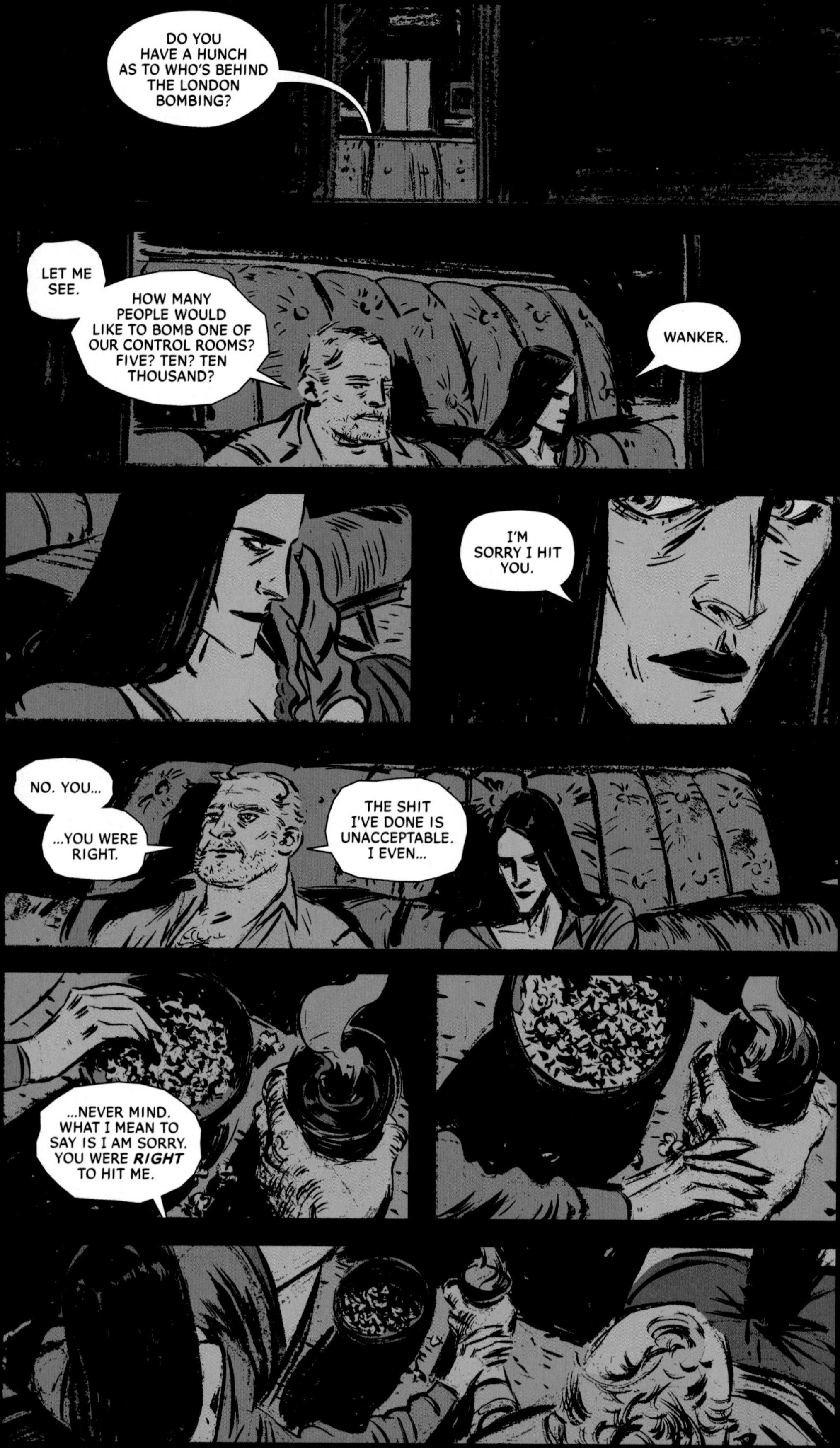

DO YOU HAVE A HUNCH AS TO WHO'S BEHIND THE LONDON BOMBING?
LET ME SEE.
HOW MANY PEOPLE WOULD LIKE TO BOMB ONE OF OUR CONTROL ROOMS? FIVE? TEN? TEN THOUSAND?
WANKER.
I'M SORRY I HIT YOU.
NO. YOU...
...YOU WERE RIGHT.
THE SHIT I'VE DONE IS UNACCEPTABLE. I EVEN...
...NEVER MIND. WHAT I MEAN TO SAY IS I AM SORRY. YOU WERE ***RIGHT*** TO HIT ME.

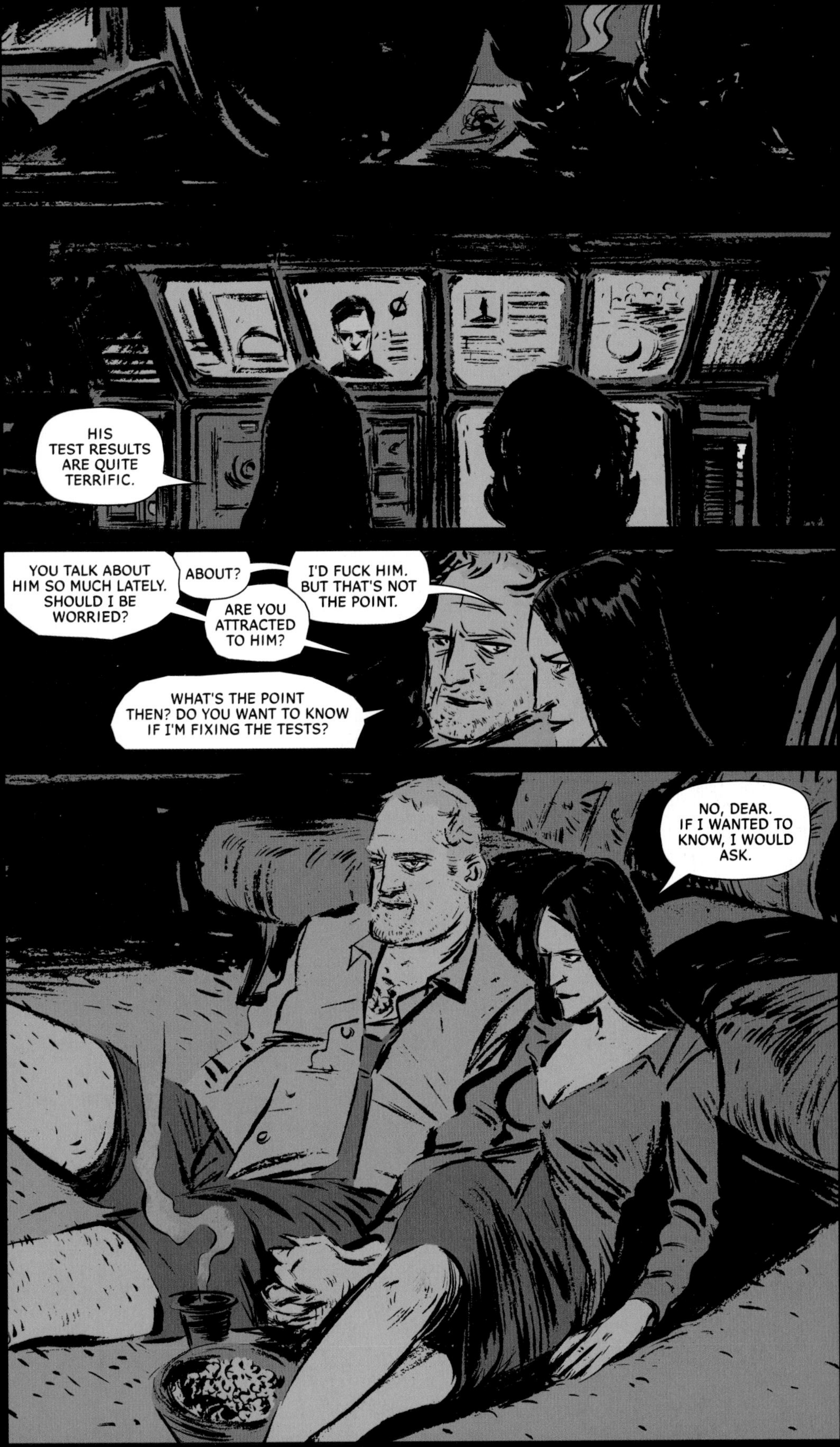
HIS TEST RESULTS ARE QUITE TERRIFIC.
YOU TALK ABOUT HIM SO MUCH LATELY. SHOULD I BE WORRIED?
ABOUT?
ARE YOU ATTRACTED TO HIM?
I'D FUCK HIM. BUT THAT'S NOT THE POINT.
WHAT'S THE POINT THEN? DO YOU WANT TO KNOW IF I'M FIXING THE TESTS?
NO, DEAR. IF I WANTED TO KNOW, I WOULD ASK.

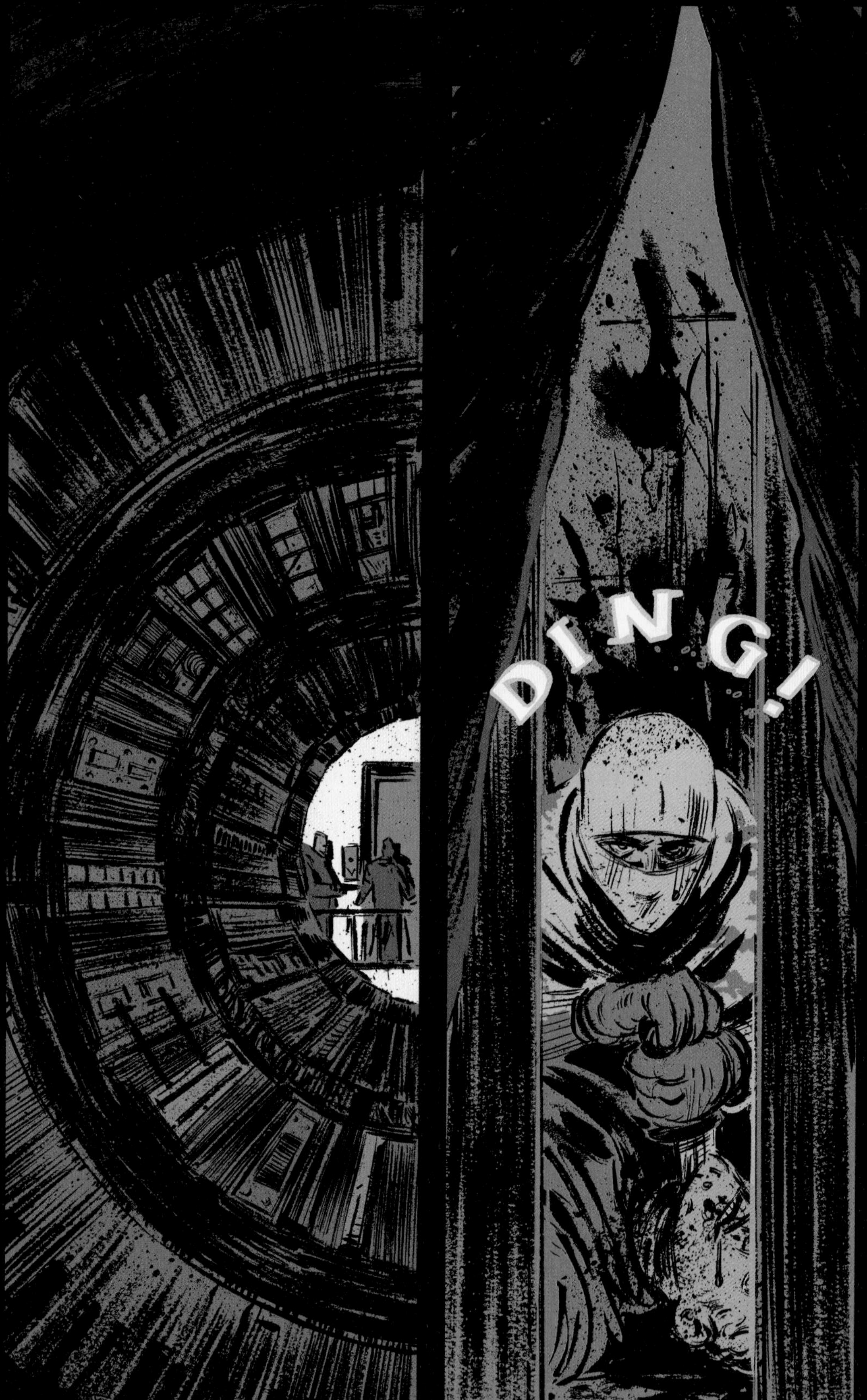
DING!

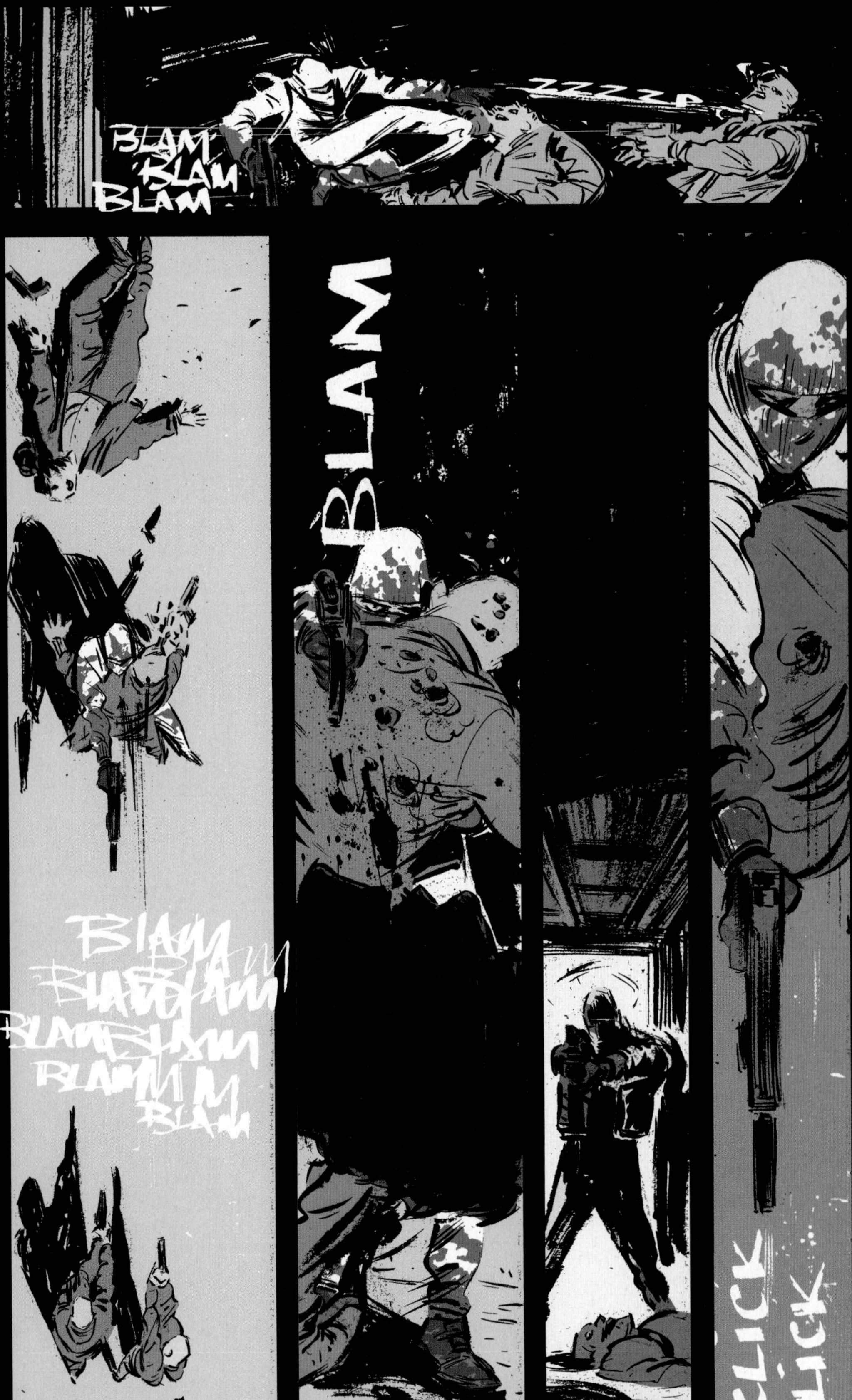
BLAM
BLAM
BLAM
BLAM
CLICK
CLICK

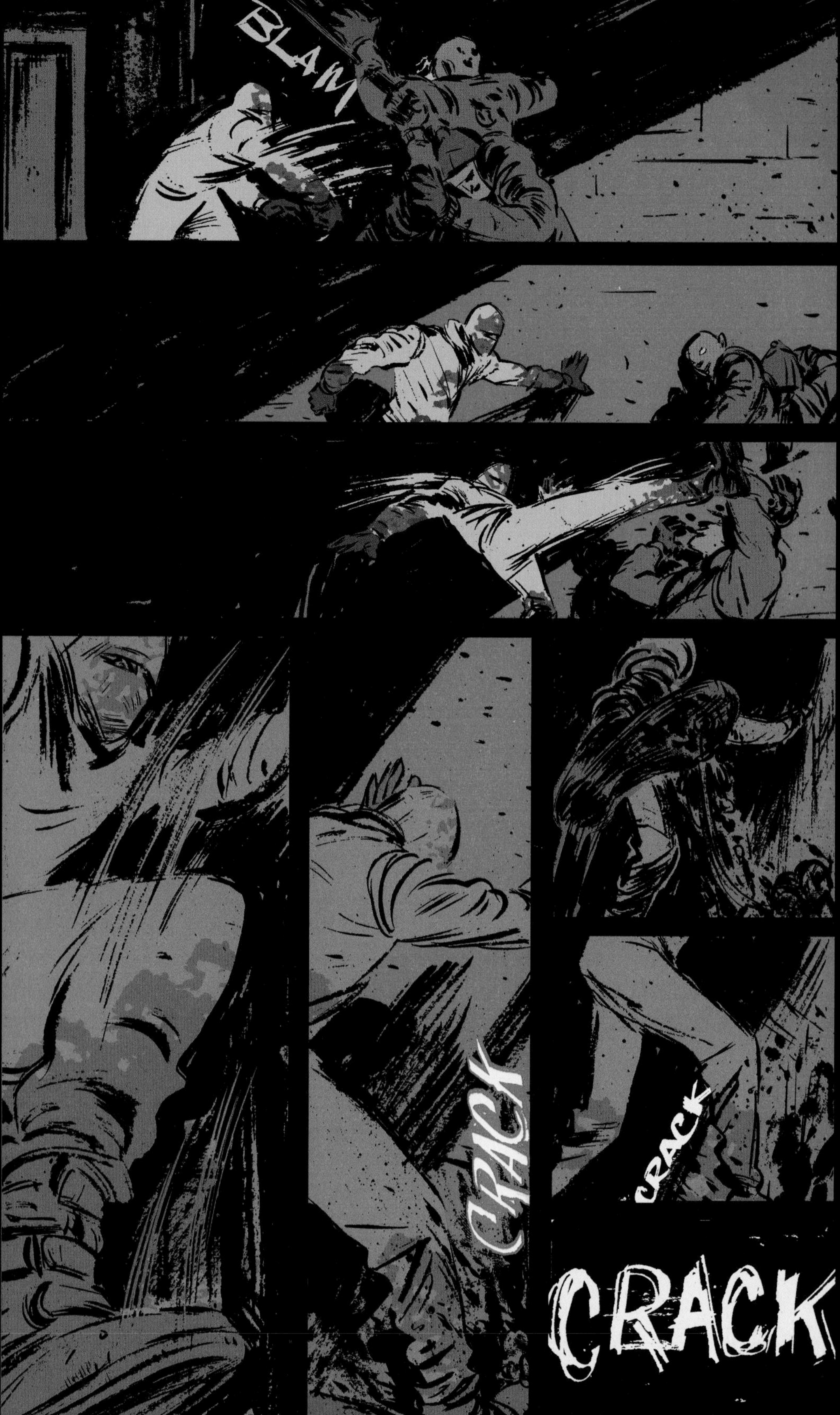
BLAM
CRACK
CRACK
CRACK

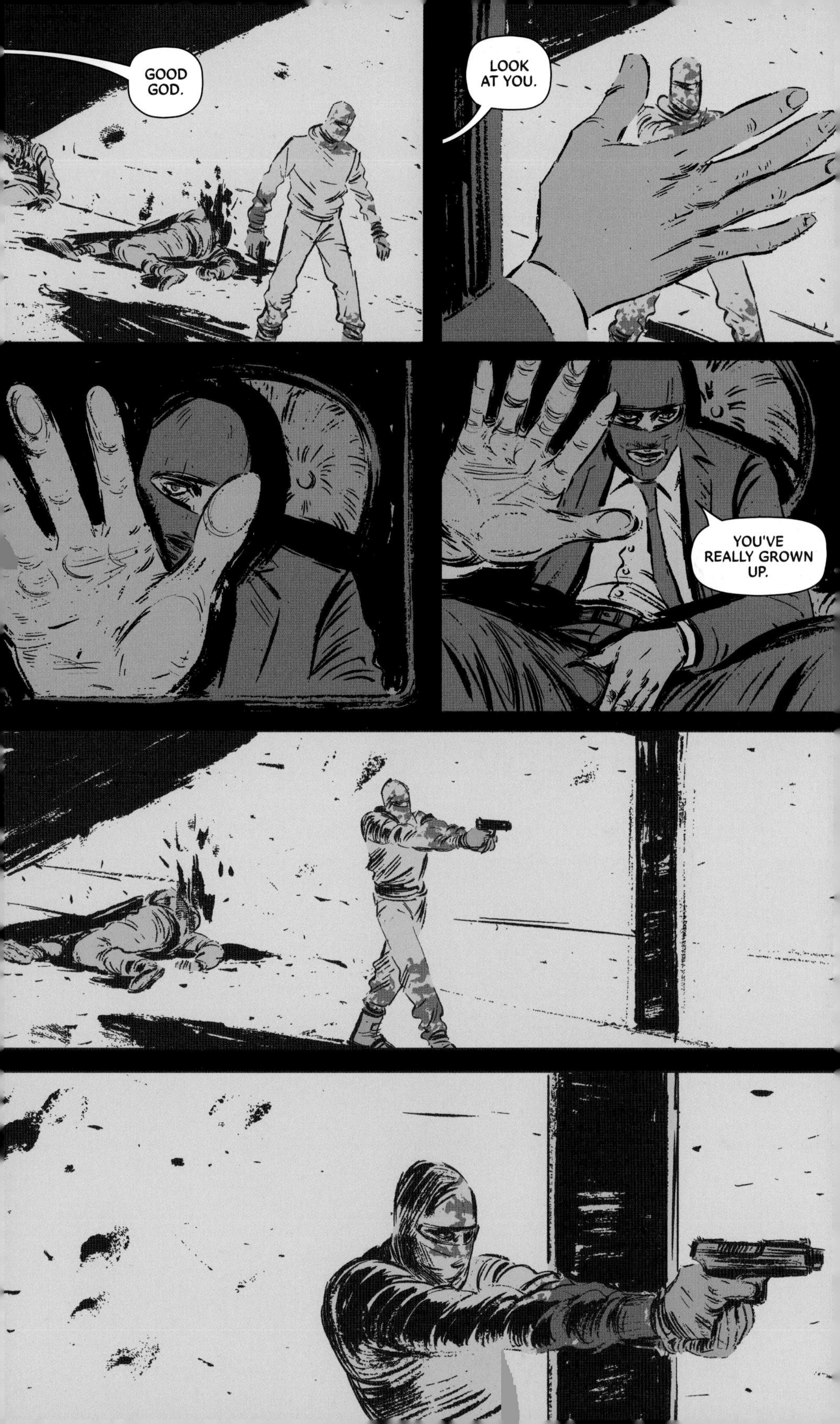
GOOD GOD.
LOOK AT YOU.
YOU'VE REALLY GROWN UP.

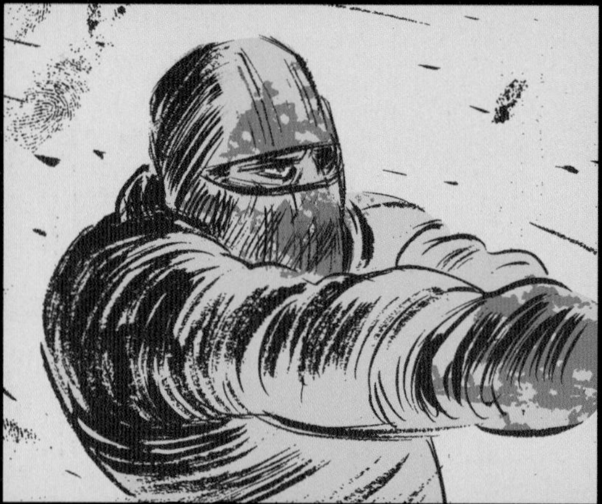

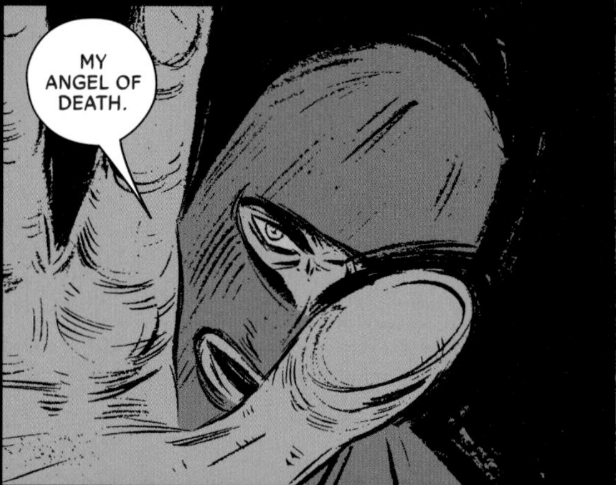
MY ANGEL OF DEATH.

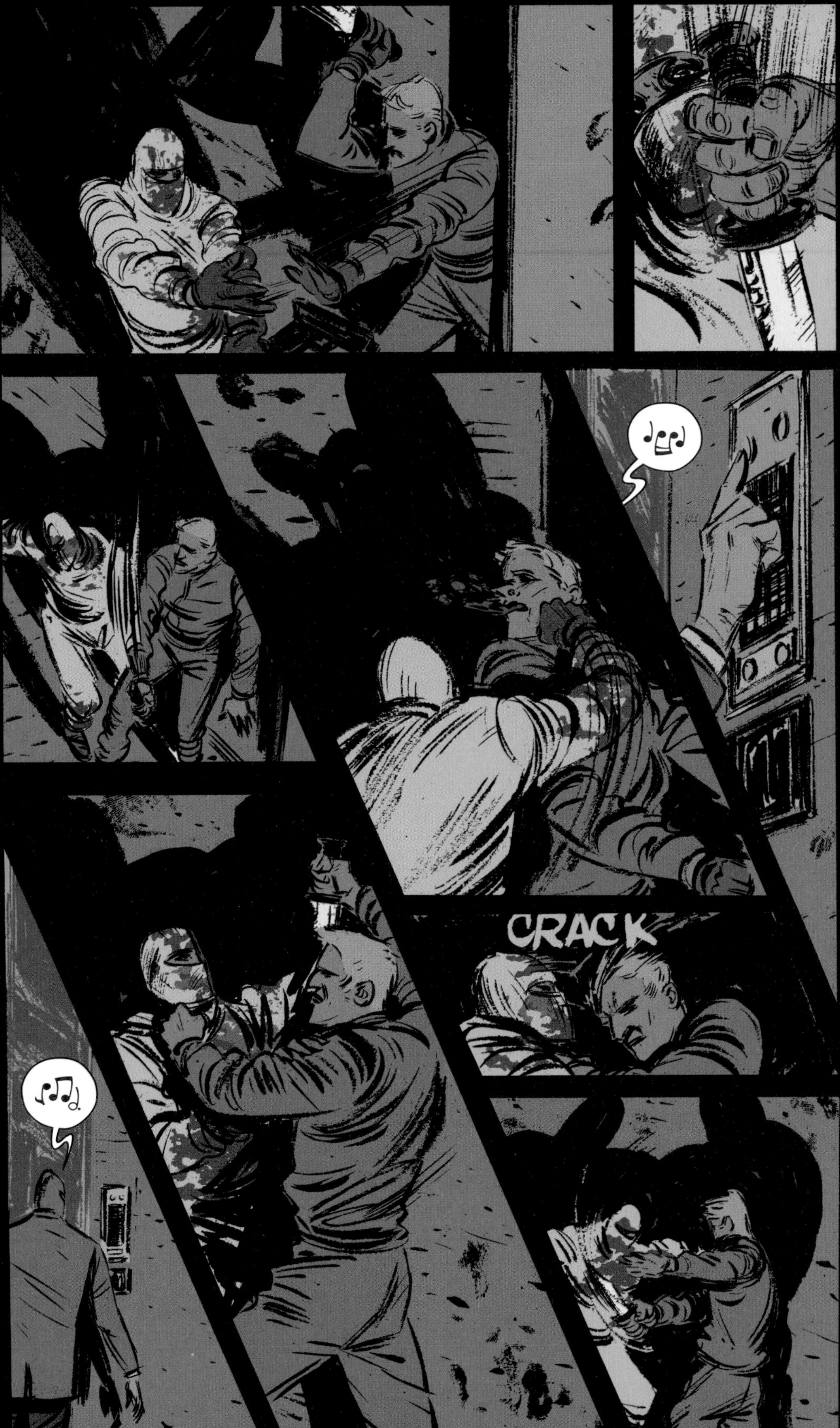
CRACK

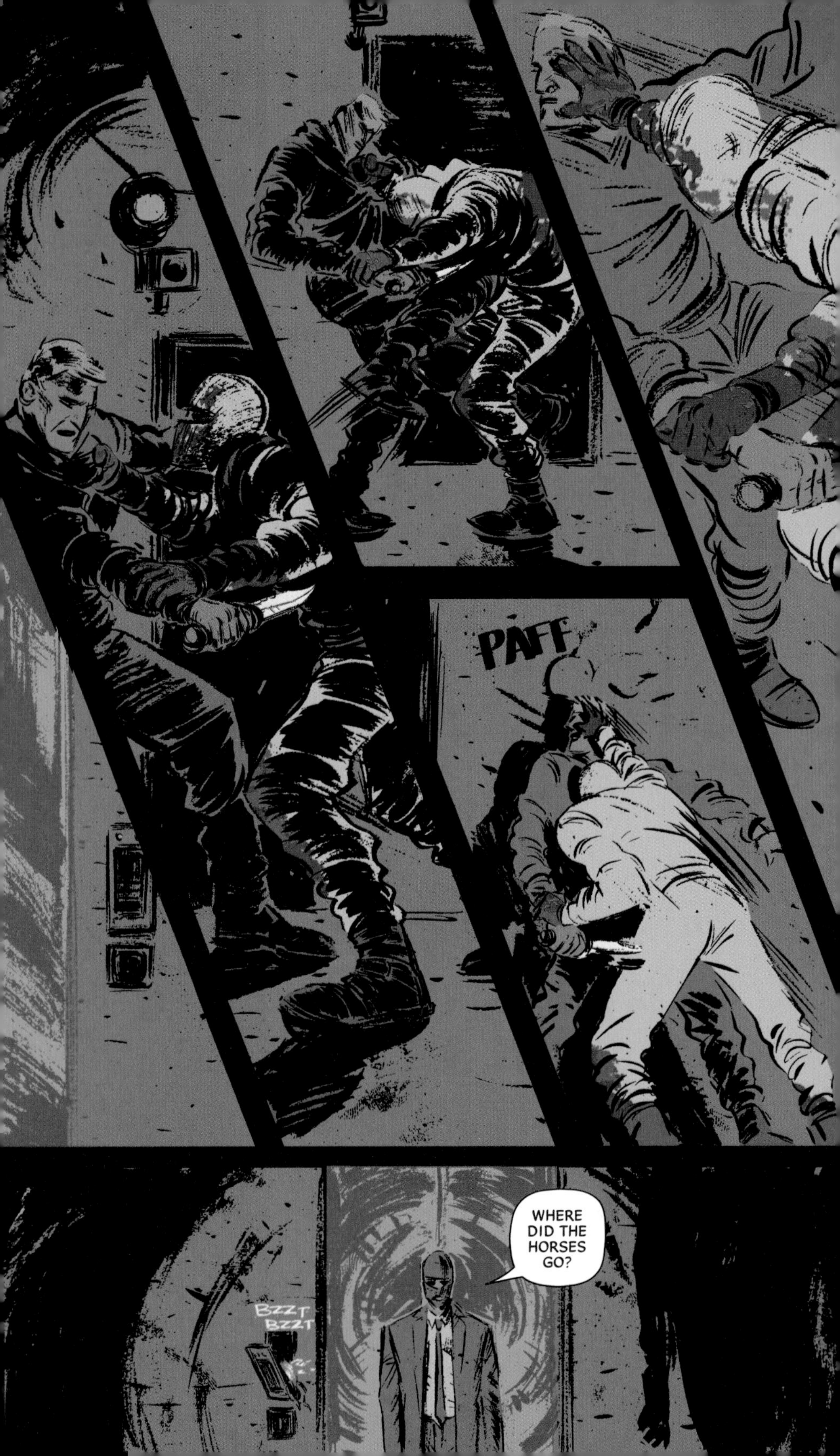
PAFF
BZZT
BZZT
WHERE DID THE HORSES GO?

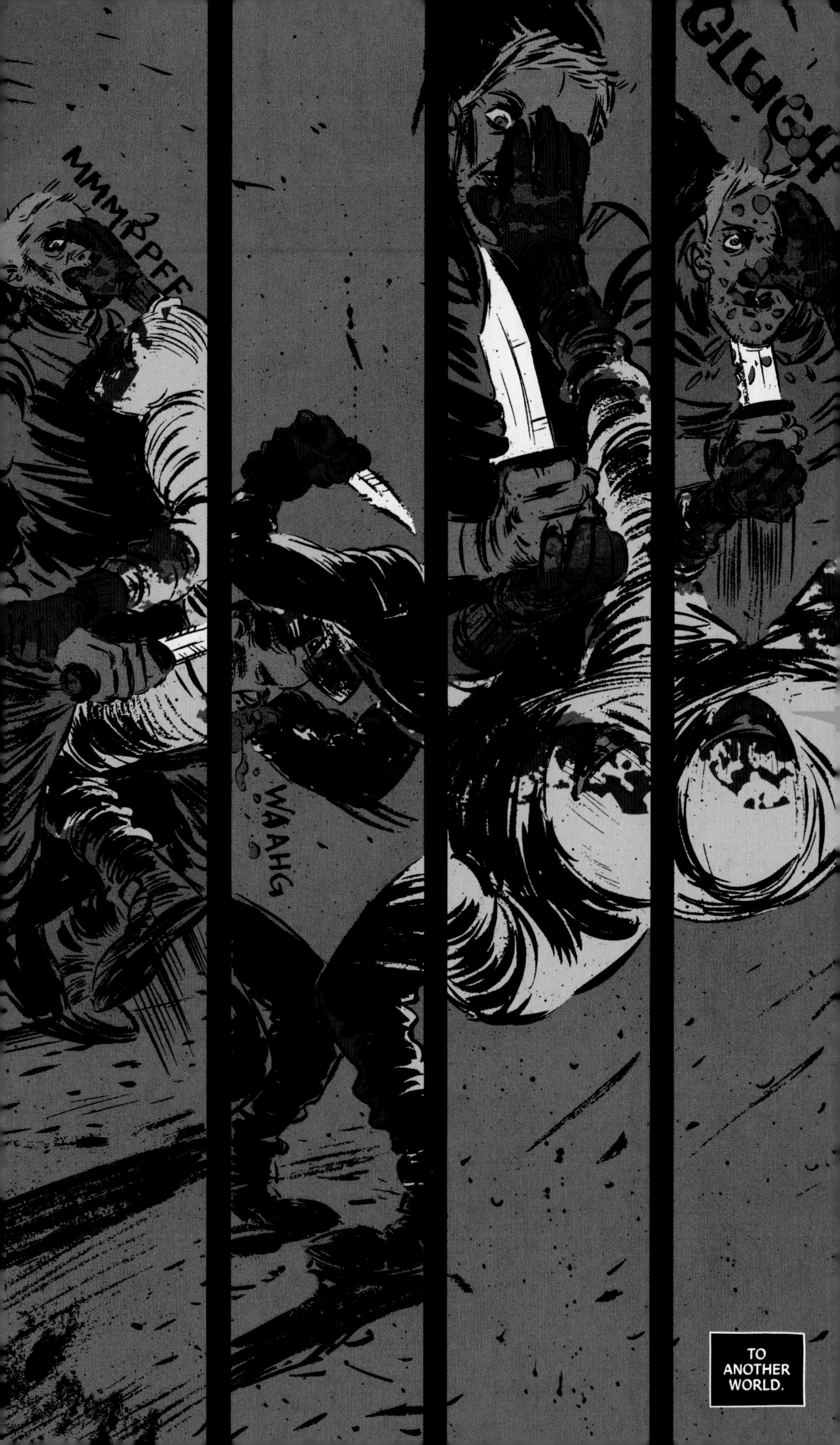
MMMBPFFF
WAAHG
GLHGH
TO ANOTHER WORLD.

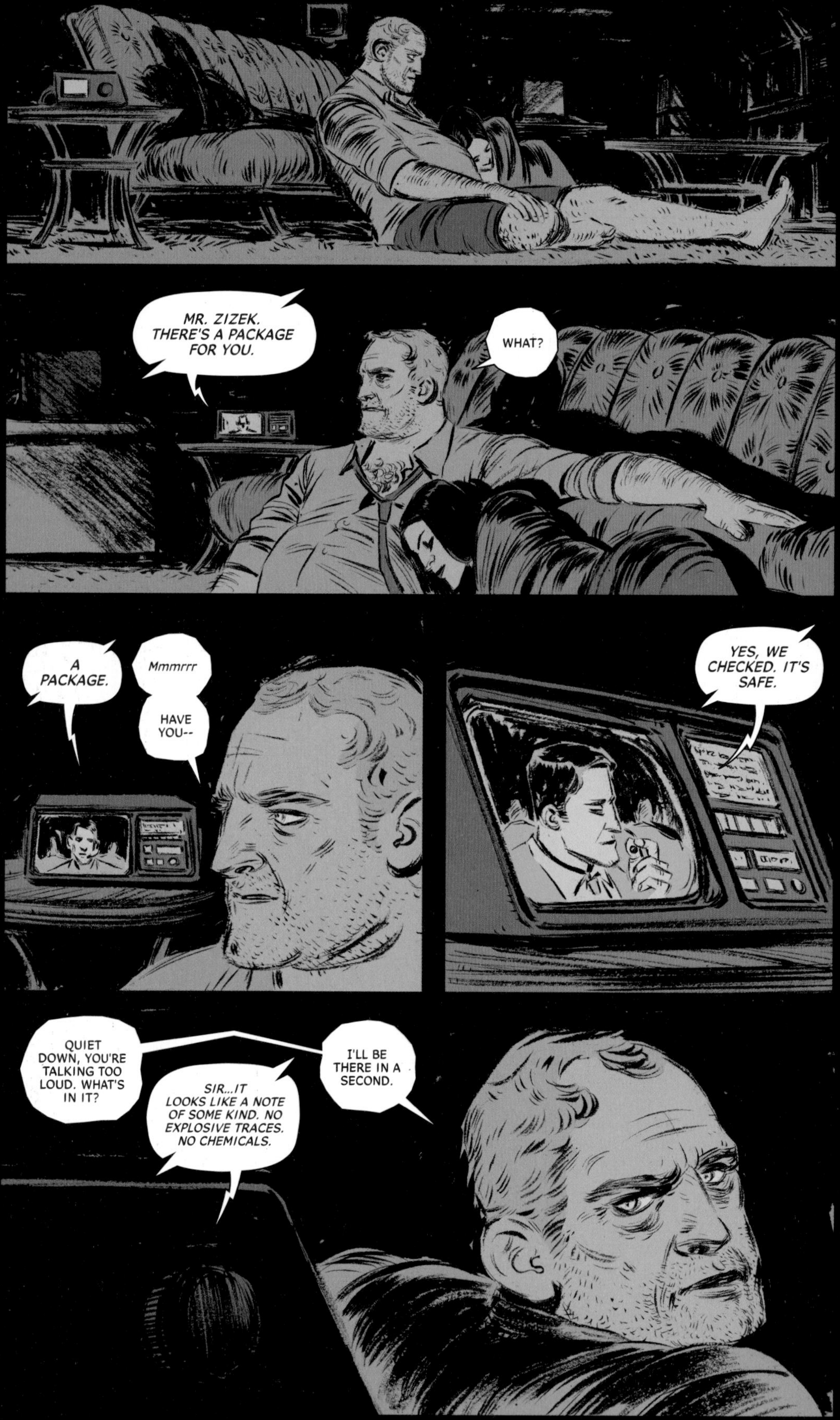
MR. ZIZEK. THERE'S A PACKAGE FOR YOU.
WHAT?
A PACKAGE.
Mmmrrr
HAVE YOU--
YES, WE CHECKED. IT'S SAFE.
QUIET DOWN, YOU'RE TALKING TOO LOUD. WHAT'S IN IT?
SIR...IT LOOKS LIKE A NOTE OF SOME KIND. NO EXPLOSIVE TRACES. NO CHEMICALS.
I'LL BE THERE IN A SECOND.

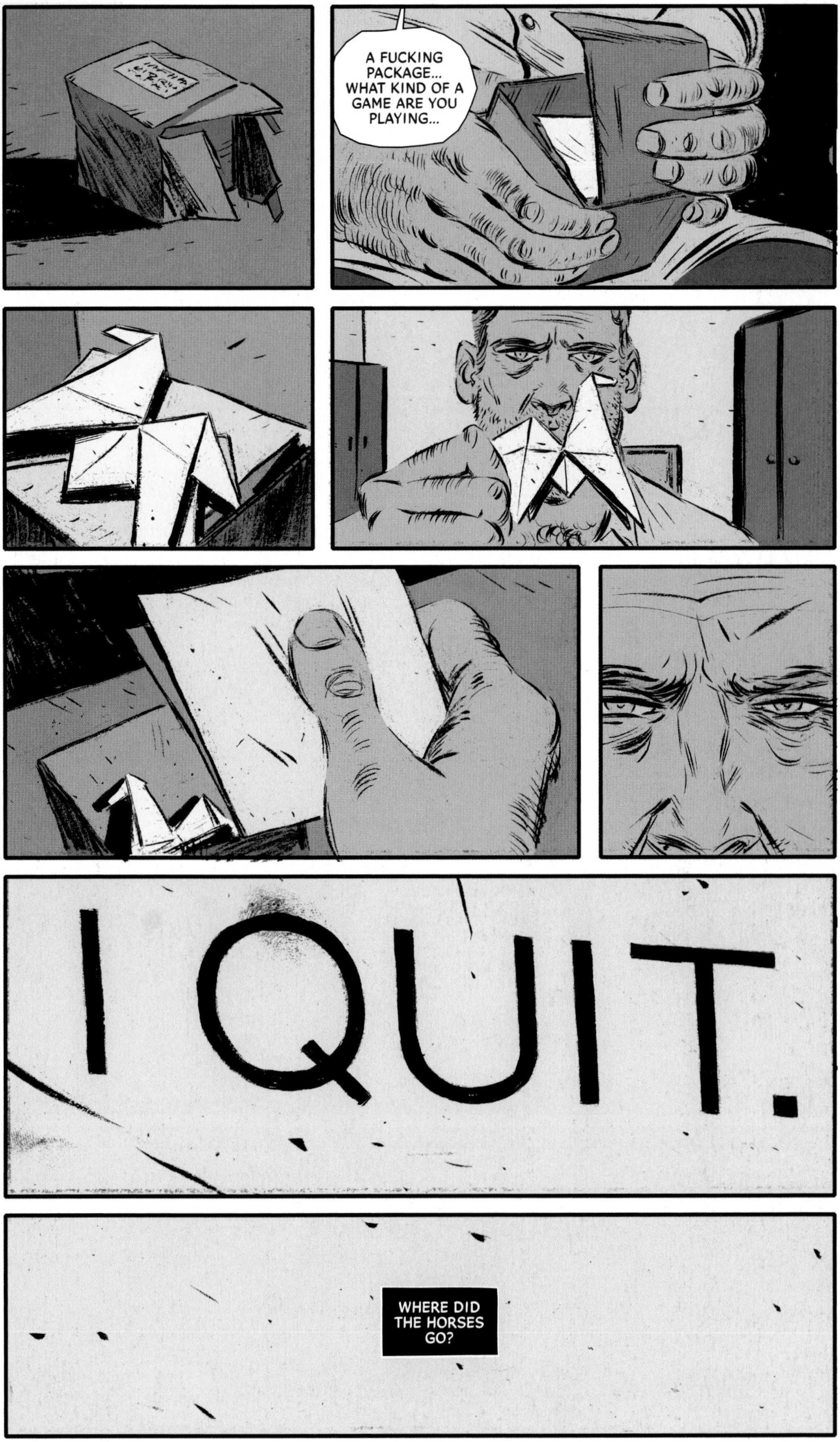

A FUCKING PACKAGE... WHAT KIND OF A GAME ARE YOU PLAYING...
I QUIT.
WHERE DID THE HORSES GO?

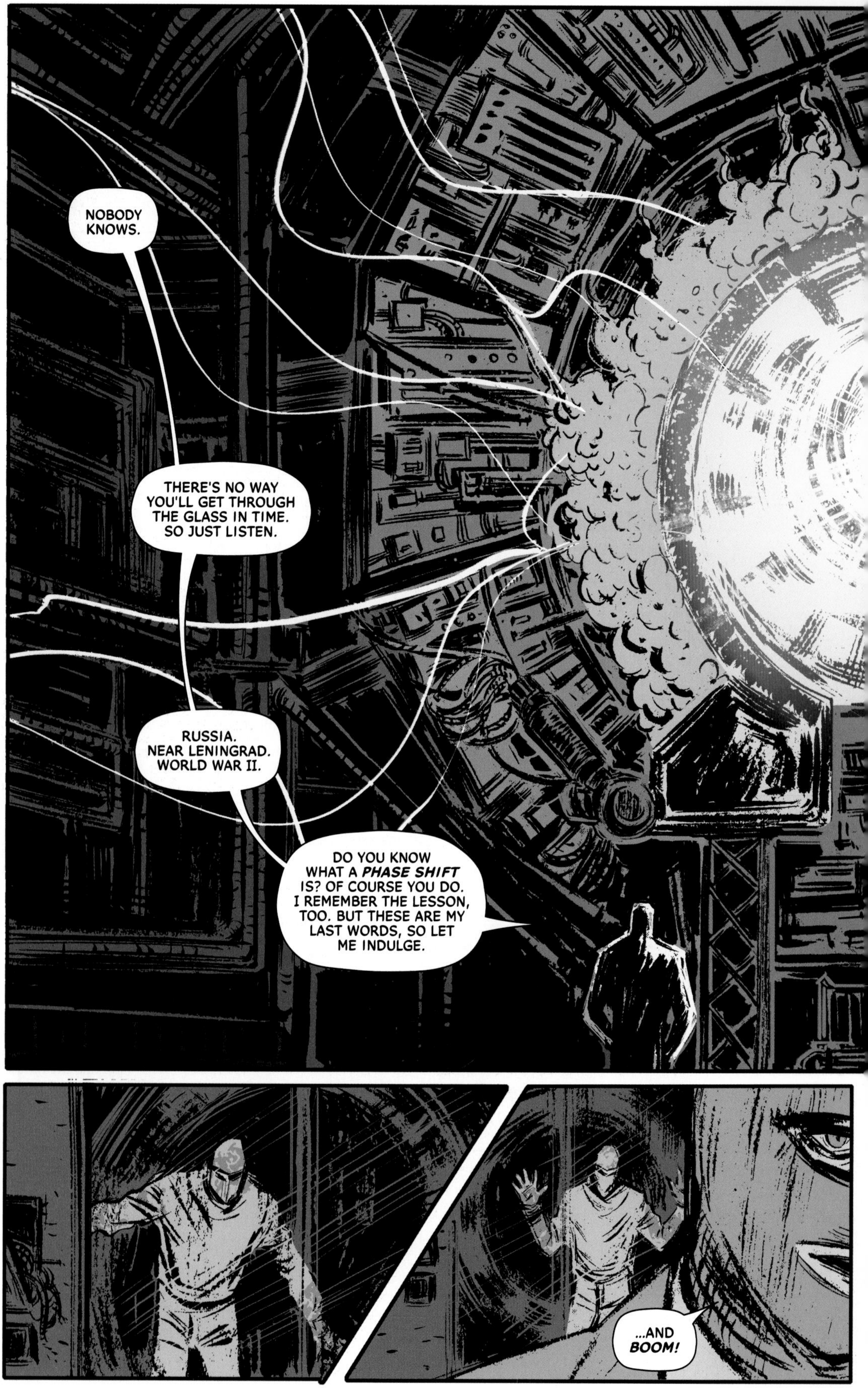
NOBODY KNOWS.
THERE'S NO WAY YOU'LL GET THROUGH THE GLASS IN TIME. SO JUST LISTEN.
RUSSIA. NEAR LENINGRAD. WORLD WAR II.
DO YOU KNOW WHAT A *PHASE SHIFT* IS? OF COURSE YOU DO. I REMEMBER THE LESSON, TOO. BUT THESE ARE MY LAST WORDS, SO LET ME INDULGE.
...AND *BOOM!*

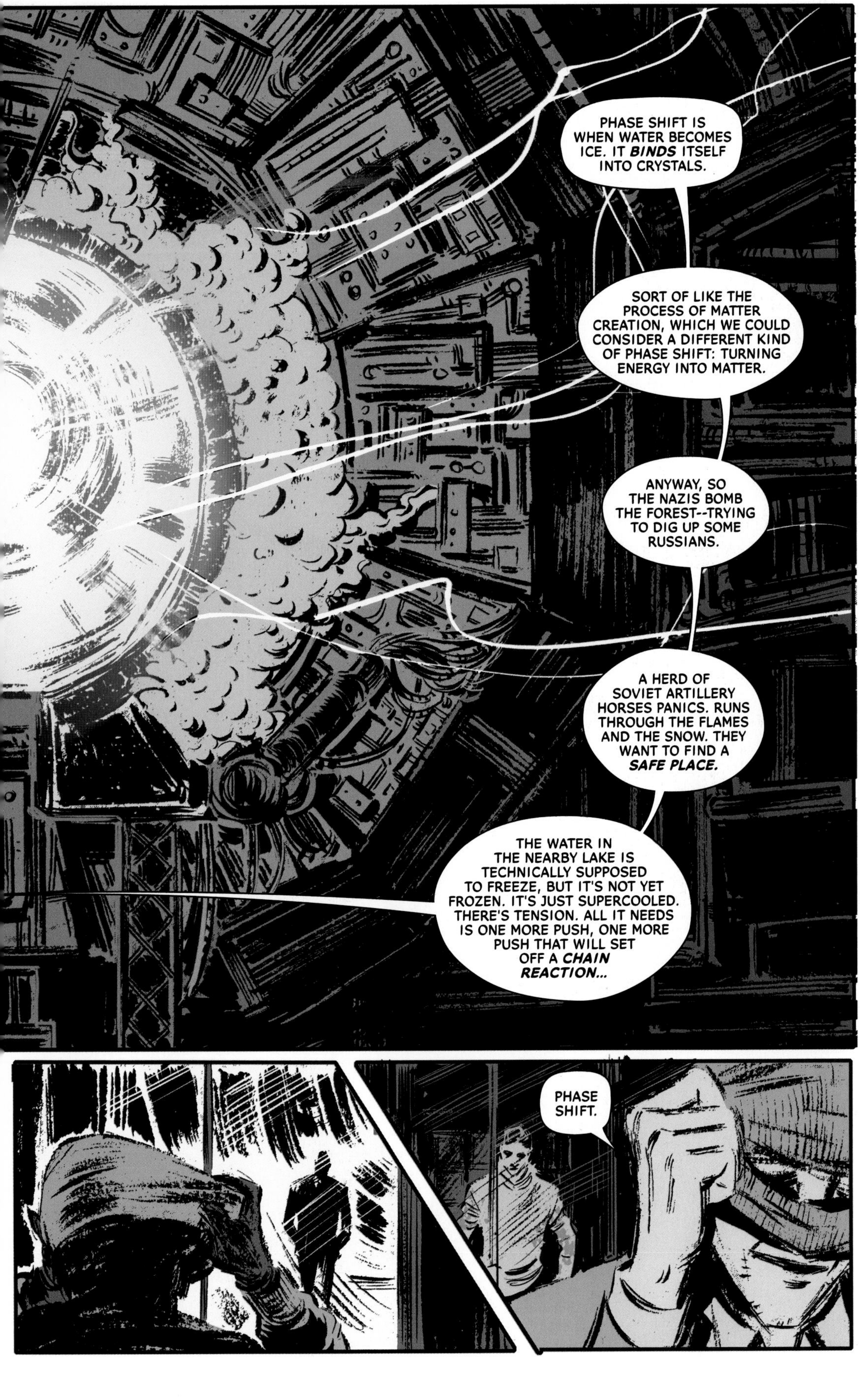
PHASE SHIFT IS WHEN WATER BECOMES ICE. IT *BINDS* ITSELF INTO CRYSTALS.
SORT OF LIKE THE PROCESS OF MATTER CREATION, WHICH WE COULD CONSIDER A DIFFERENT KIND OF PHASE SHIFT: TURNING ENERGY INTO MATTER.
ANYWAY, SO THE NAZIS BOMB THE FOREST--TRYING TO DIG UP SOME RUSSIANS.
A HERD OF SOVIET ARTILLERY HORSES PANICS. RUNS THROUGH THE FLAMES AND THE SNOW. THEY WANT TO FIND A ***SAFE PLACE.***
THE WATER IN THE NEARBY LAKE IS TECHNICALLY SUPPOSED TO FREEZE, BUT IT'S NOT YET FROZEN. IT'S JUST SUPERCOOLED. THERE'S TENSION. ALL IT NEEDS IS ONE MORE PUSH, ONE MORE PUSH THAT WILL SET OFF A ***CHAIN REACTION...***
PHASE SHIFT.

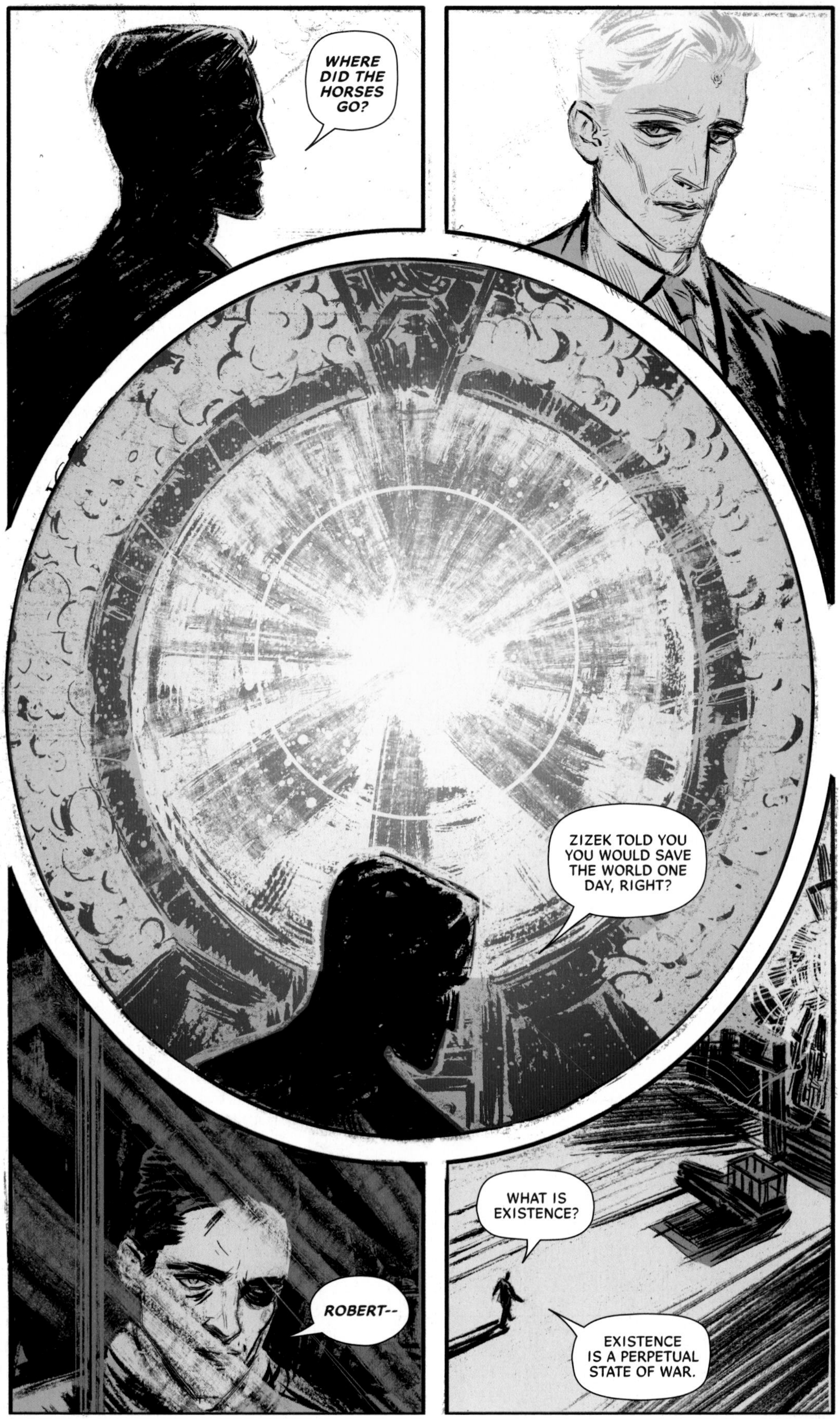
WHERE DID THE HORSES GO?
ZIZEK TOLD YOU YOU WOULD SAVE THE WORLD ONE DAY, RIGHT?
ROBERT--
WHAT IS EXISTENCE?
EXISTENCE IS A PERPETUAL STATE OF WAR.

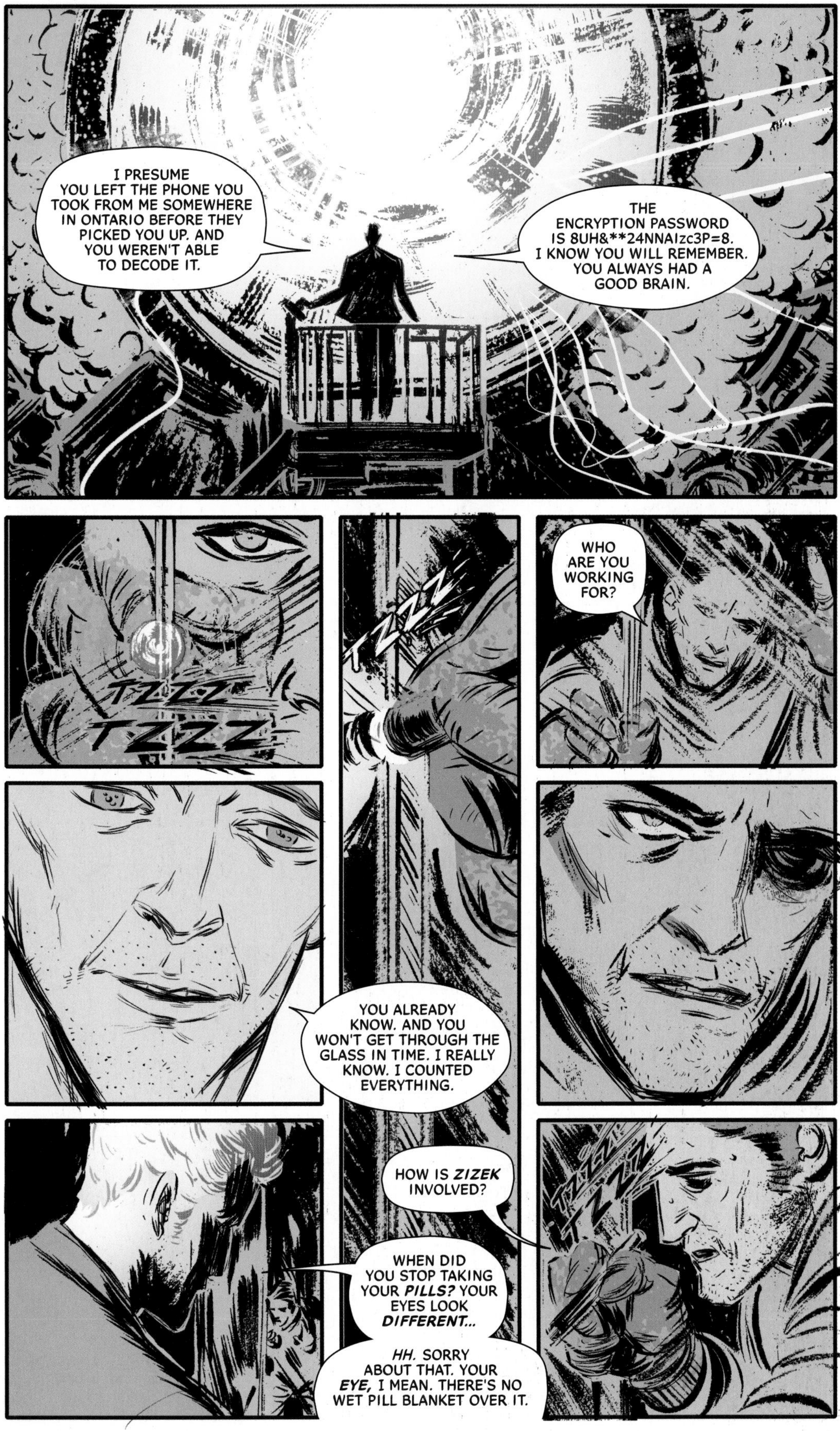
I PRESUME YOU LEFT THE PHONE YOU TOOK FROM ME SOMEWHERE IN ONTARIO BEFORE THEY PICKED YOU UP. AND YOU WEREN'T ABLE TO DECODE IT.
THE ENCRYPTION PASSWORD IS 8UH&**24NNAIzc3P=8. I KNOW YOU WILL REMEMBER. YOU ALWAYS HAD A GOOD BRAIN.
TZZZ TZZZ
TZZZZ
WHO ARE YOU WORKING FOR?
YOU ALREADY KNOW. AND YOU WON'T GET THROUGH THE GLASS IN TIME. I REALLY KNOW. I COUNTED EVERYTHING.
HOW IS *ZIZEK* INVOLVED?
WHEN DID YOU STOP TAKING YOUR ***PILLS?*** YOUR EYES LOOK ***DIFFERENT...***
HH. SORRY ABOUT THAT. YOUR ***EYE,*** I MEAN. THERE'S NO WET PILL BLANKET OVER IT.

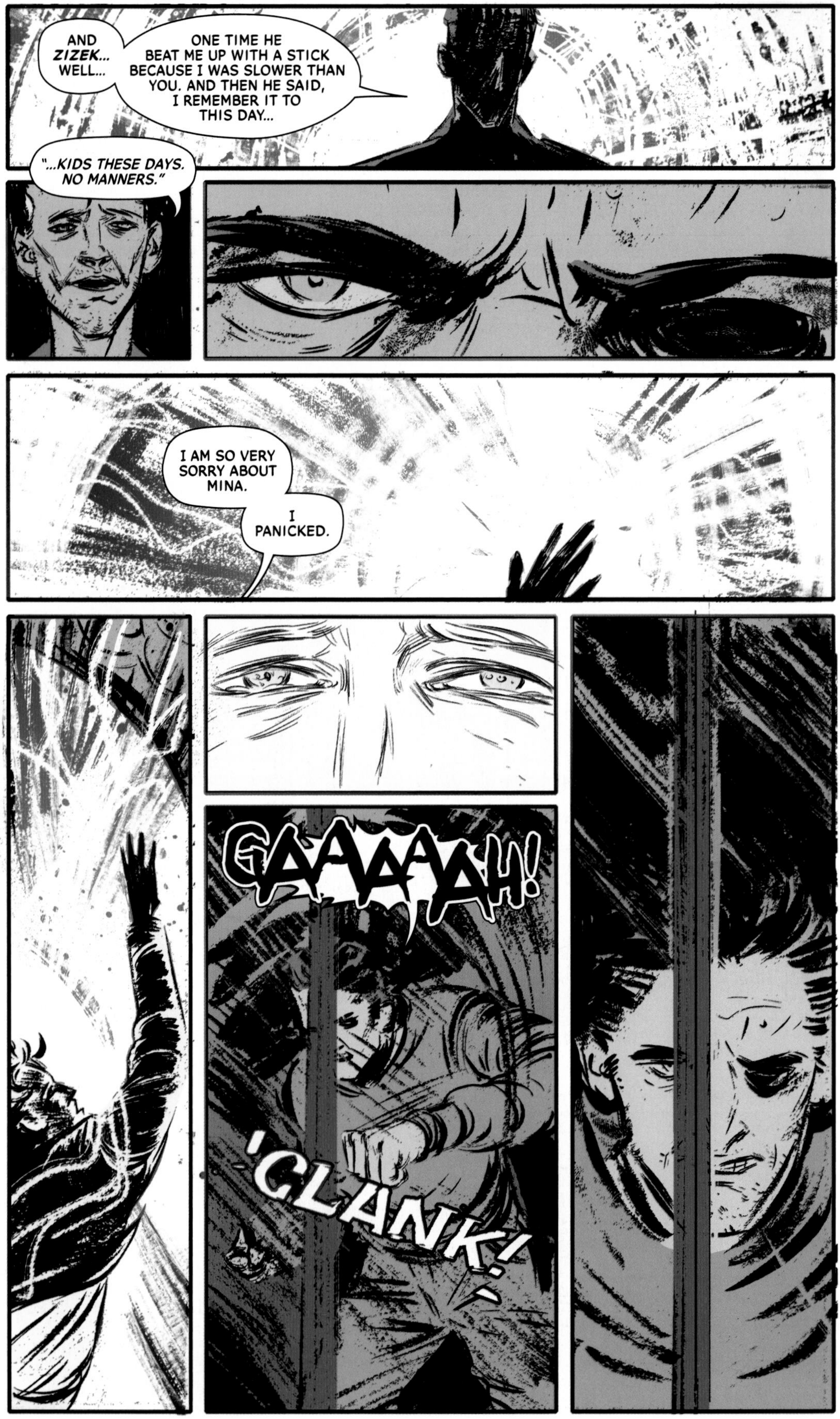
AND ZIZEK... WELL...
ONE TIME HE BEAT ME UP WITH A STICK BECAUSE I WAS SLOWER THAN YOU. AND THEN HE SAID, I REMEMBER IT TO THIS DAY...
"...KIDS THESE DAYS. NO MANNERS."
I AM SO VERY SORRY ABOUT MINA.
I PANICKED.
GAAAAAH!
CLANK!

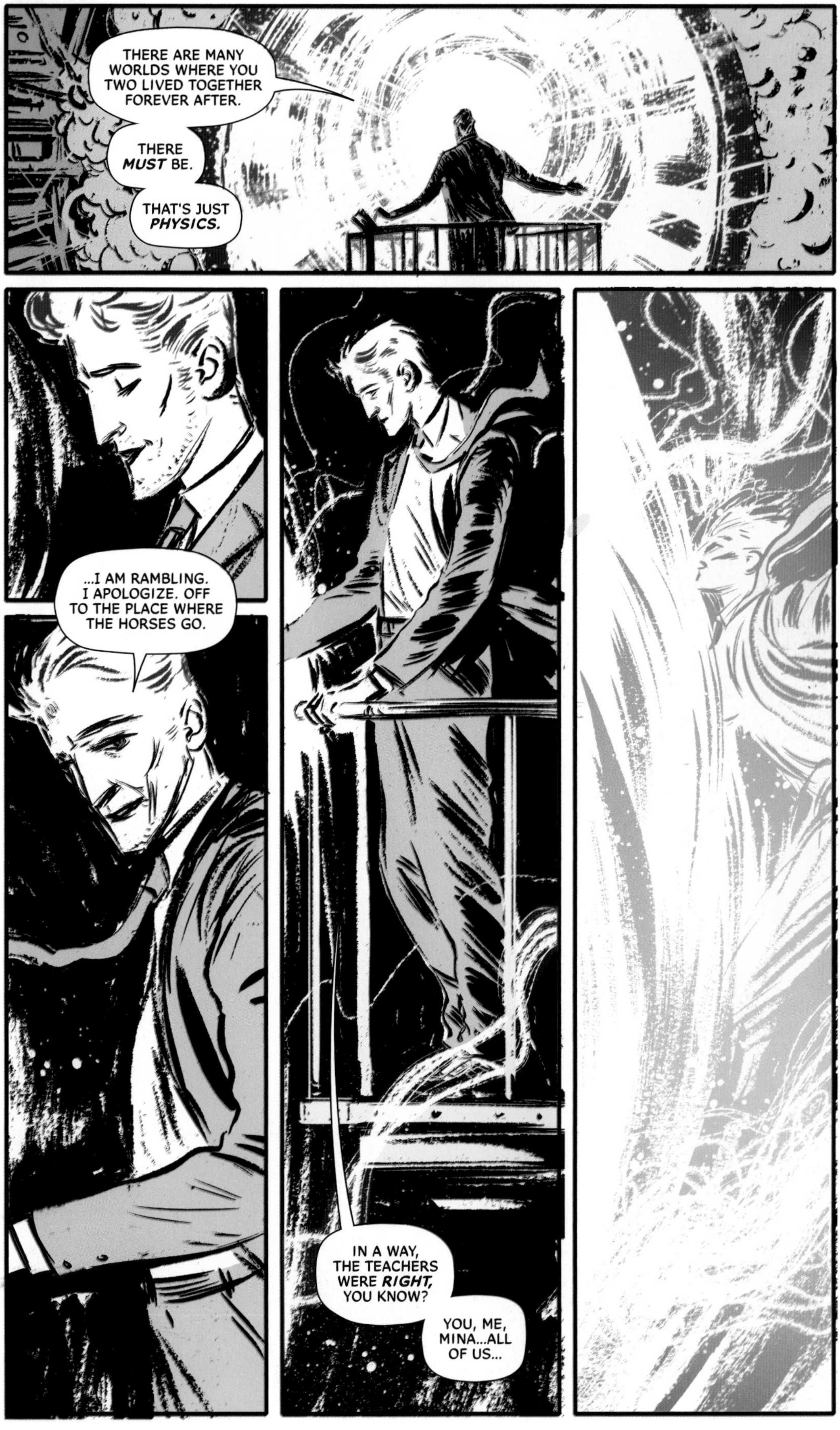
THERE ARE MANY WORLDS WHERE YOU TWO LIVED TOGETHER FOREVER AFTER.
THERE *MUST* BE.
THAT'S JUST *PHYSICS.*
...I AM RAMBLING. I APOLOGIZE. OFF TO THE PLACE WHERE THE HORSES GO.
IN A WAY, THE TEACHERS WERE *RIGHT,* YOU KNOW?
YOU, ME, MINA...ALL OF US...

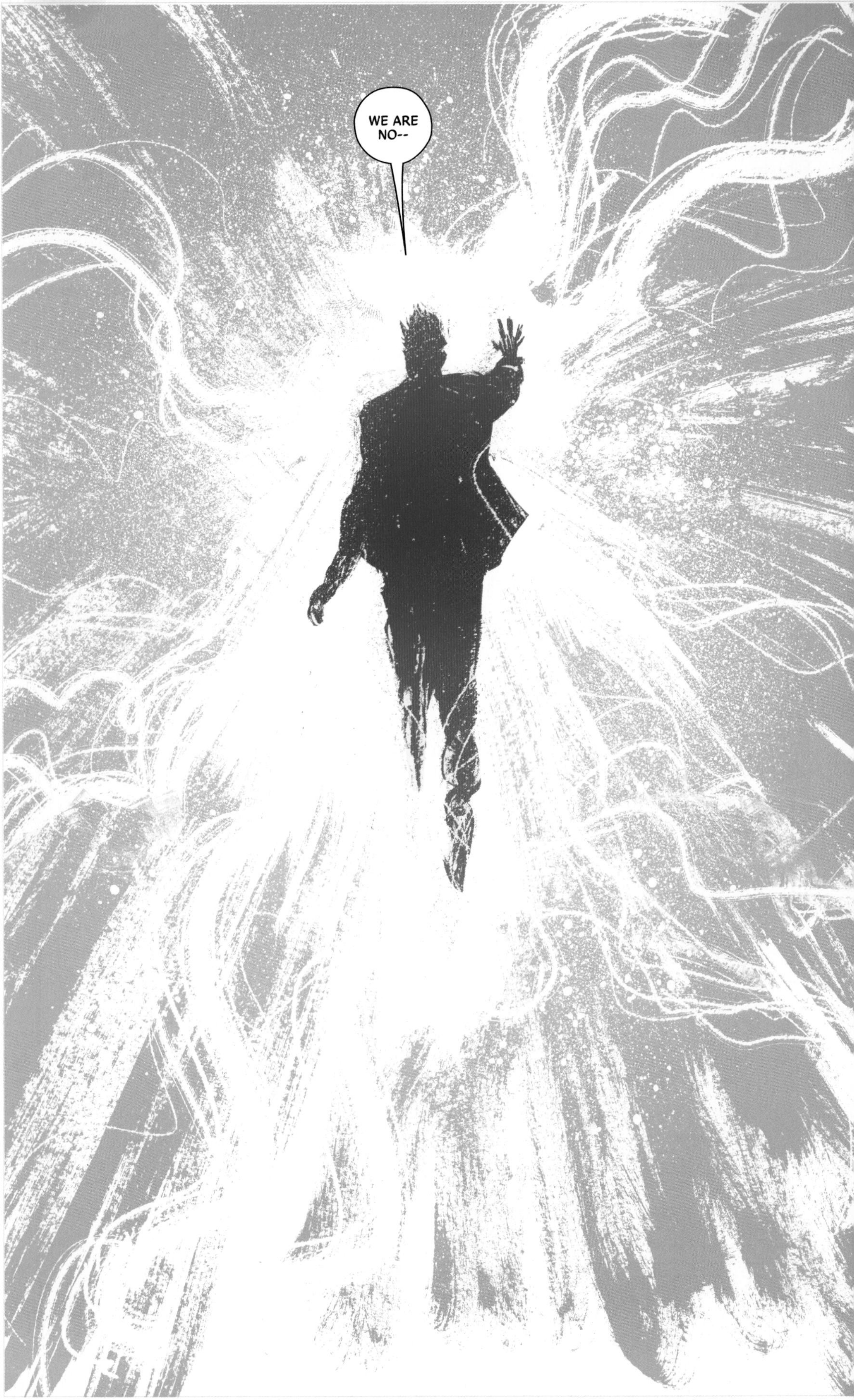
WE ARE NO--

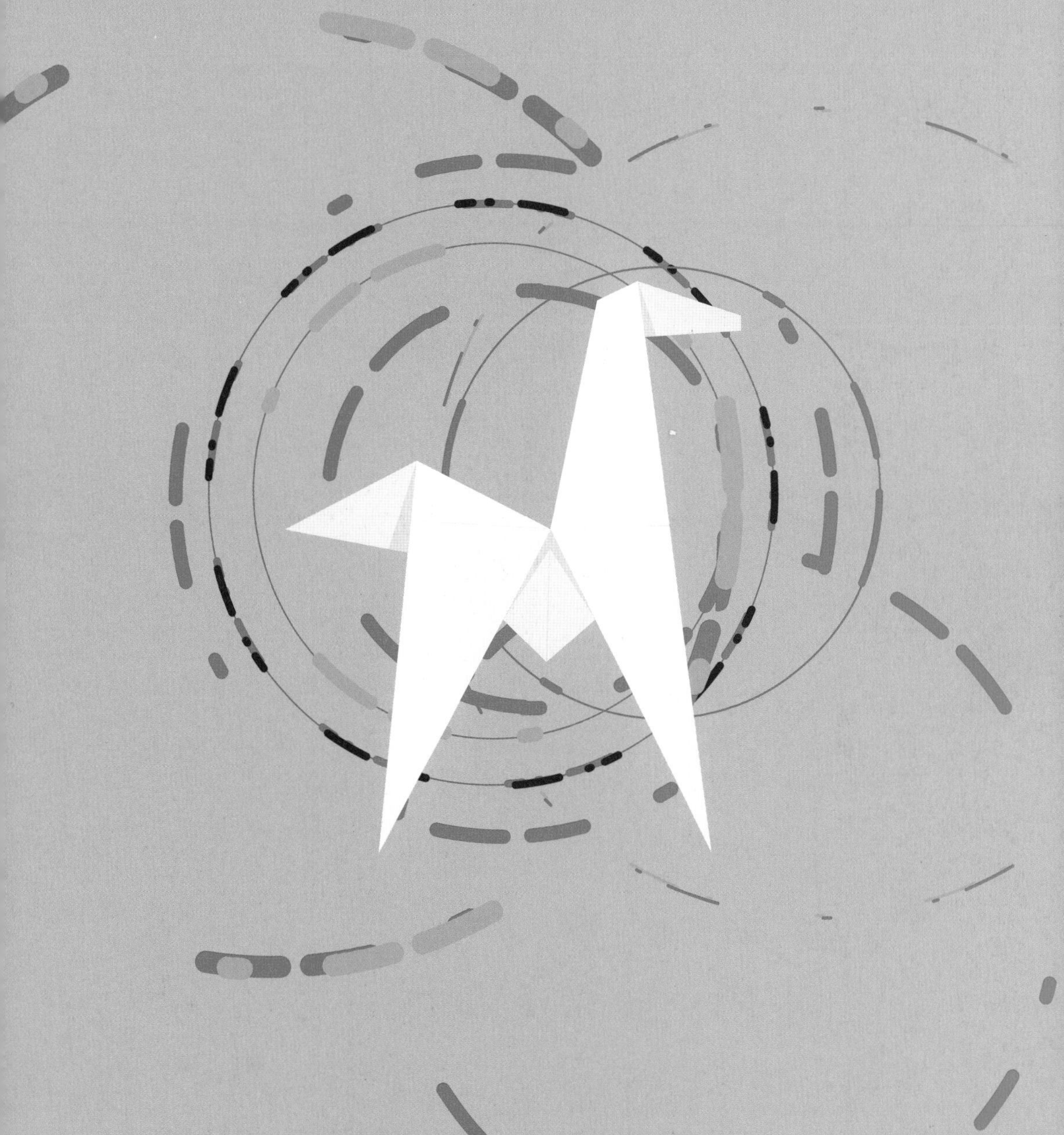

CHAPTER 6:
HORSE COLLECTORS

INTERROGATION OF ZERO, POST-MISSION.

1 ZIZEK: ALL THE CAMERAS WERE WIPED OUT.

2 ZERO: THAT MUST HAVE HAPPENED BEFORE I GOT THERE.

3 ZIZEK: NO WAY WE CAN TELL.

4 ZIZEK: SO WHAT YOU'RE SAYING IS THERE WAS A SURGE OF ENERGY. AND THEN AN EXPLOSION -- WHICH DID NOT SEEM TO DAMAGE A THING.

5 ZERO: YES.

6 ZIZEK: AND THE PERSON WHO SEEMED TO BE LEADING THE OPERATION WAS...

7 ZERO: MALE, IN HIS FIFTIES, WHITE HAIR, MEDIUM BUILD, ABOUT 170 CM. BOXER NOSE. WELL-GROOMED. FACIAL SCARRING.

8 ZIZEK: EYE COLOR?

9 ZERO: I COULDN'T QUITE TELL. BROWN, I THINK.

10 ZIZEK: AND HE DIDN'T SAY A WORD BEFORE...

11 ZERO: YES. HE JUST WALKED IN.

12 ZIZEK: STRANGE.

13 ZIZEK: WHEN DID YOU DISCOVER THE BODIES?

14 ZERO: I DISCOVERED THE BODIES OF THE HOSTAGES APPROXIMATELY SEVEN MINUTES AFTER THE INCIDENT.

15 ZIZEK: NO-ONE SURVIVED THIS.

16 ZERO: THAT SEEMS TO BE THE CASE.

CHAPTER 7

KALI YUGA
Illustrated by Matt Taylor

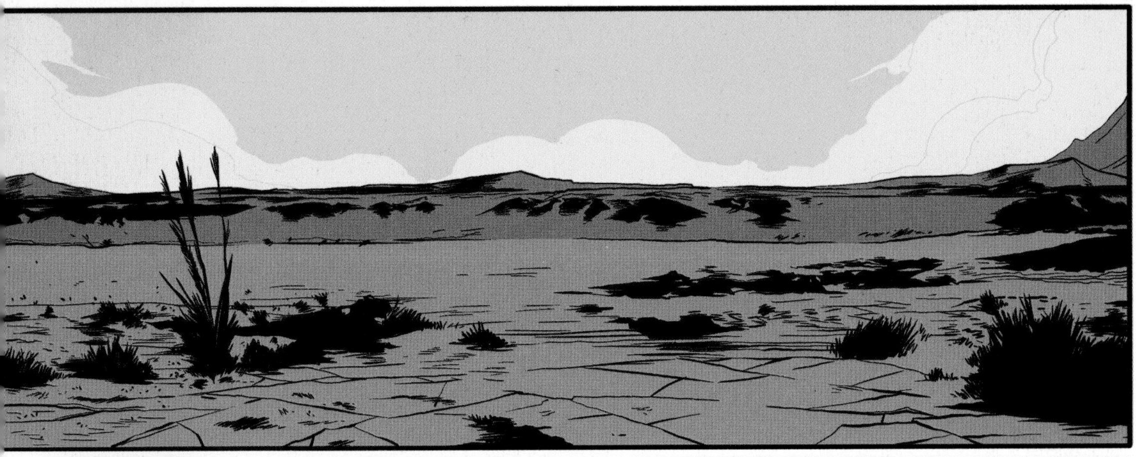
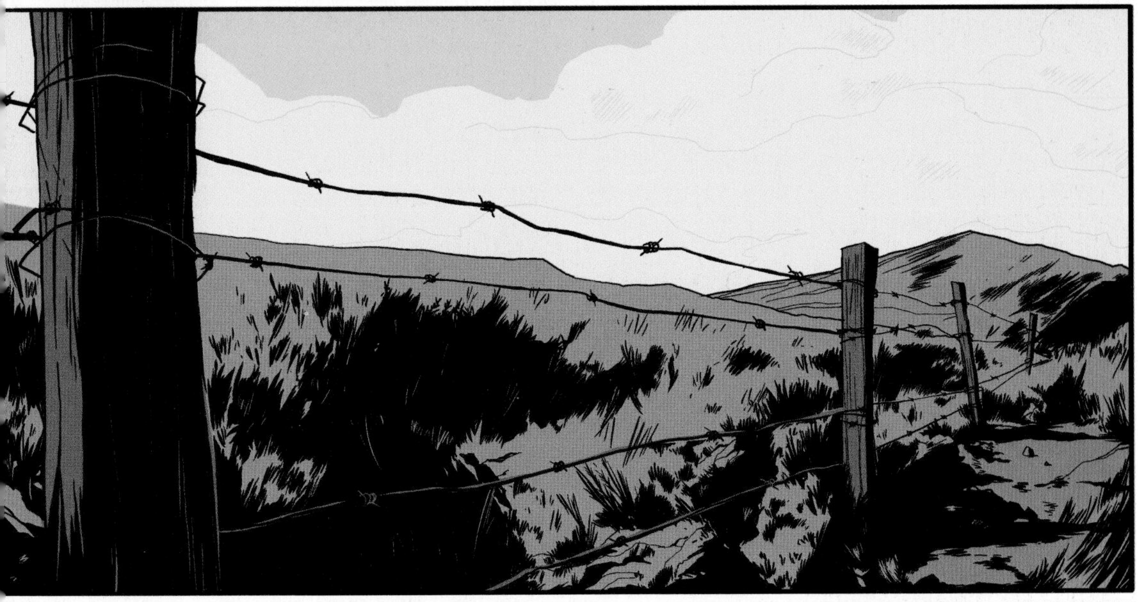
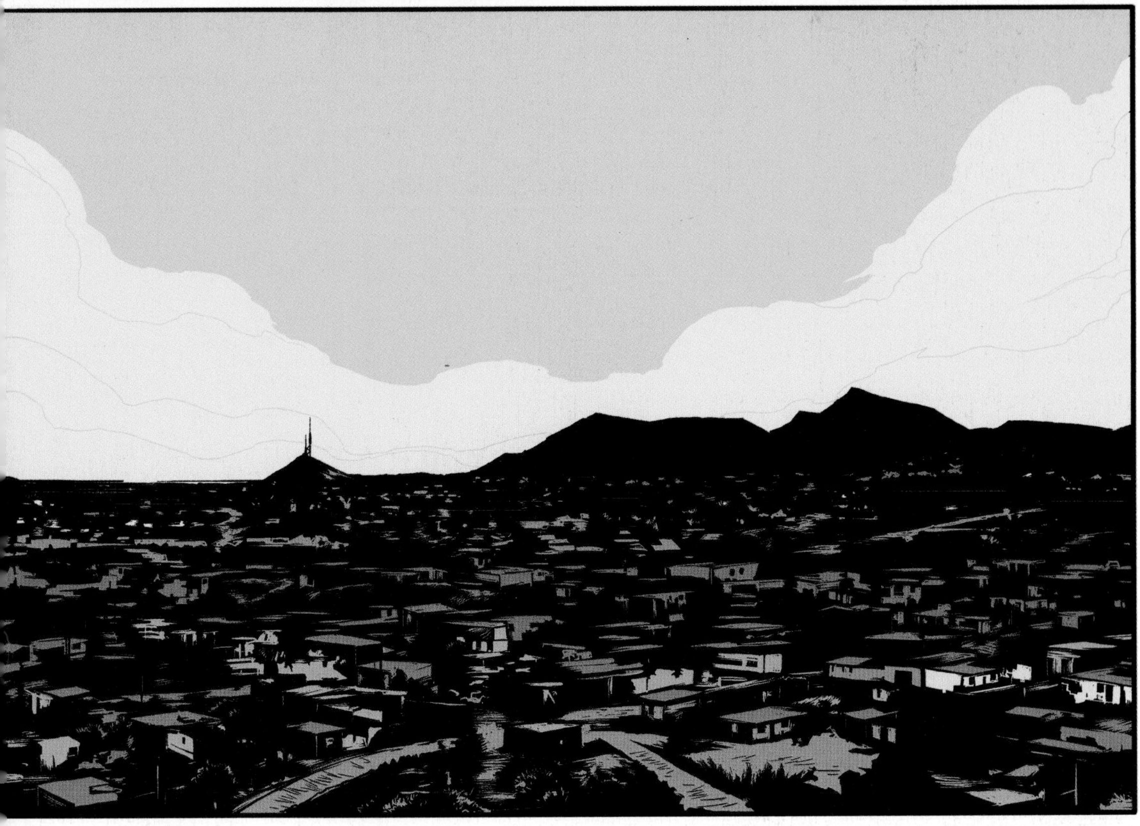

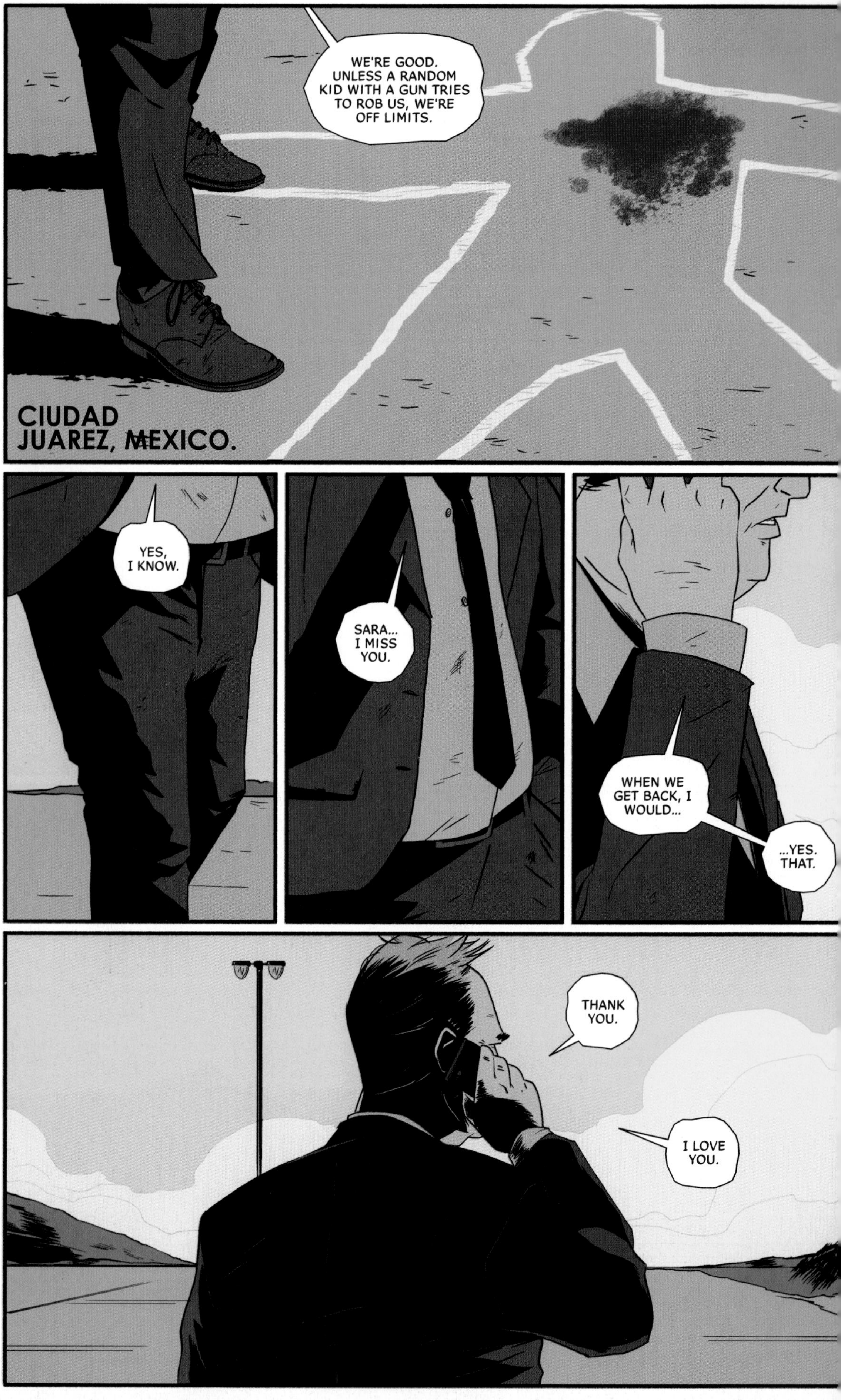
WE'RE GOOD. UNLESS A RANDOM KID WITH A GUN TRIES TO ROB US, WE'RE OFF LIMITS.
CIUDAD JUAREZ, MEXICO.
YES, I KNOW.
SARA... I MISS YOU.
WHEN WE GET BACK, I WOULD...
...YES. THAT.
THANK YOU.
I LOVE YOU.

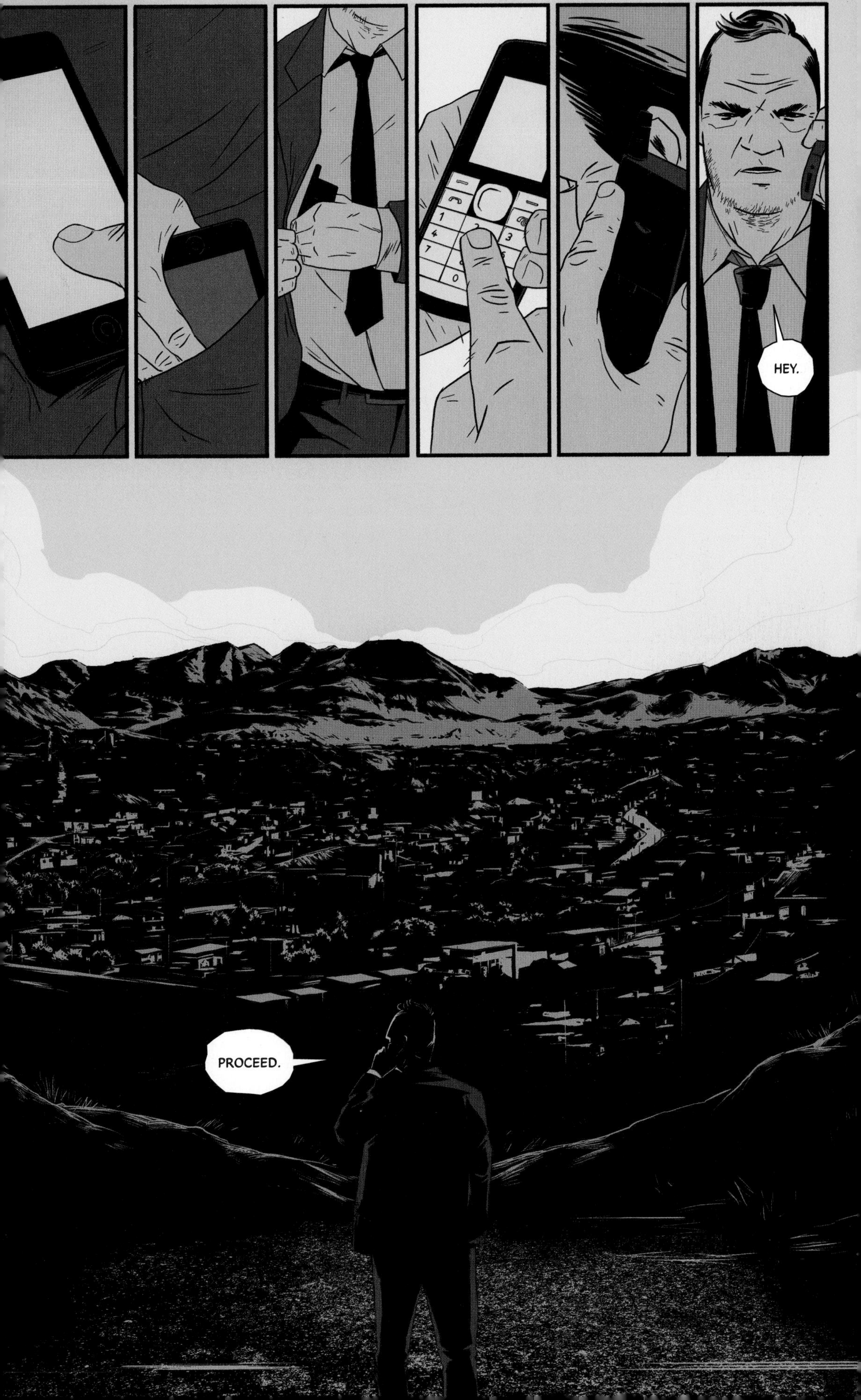
HEY.
PROCEED.

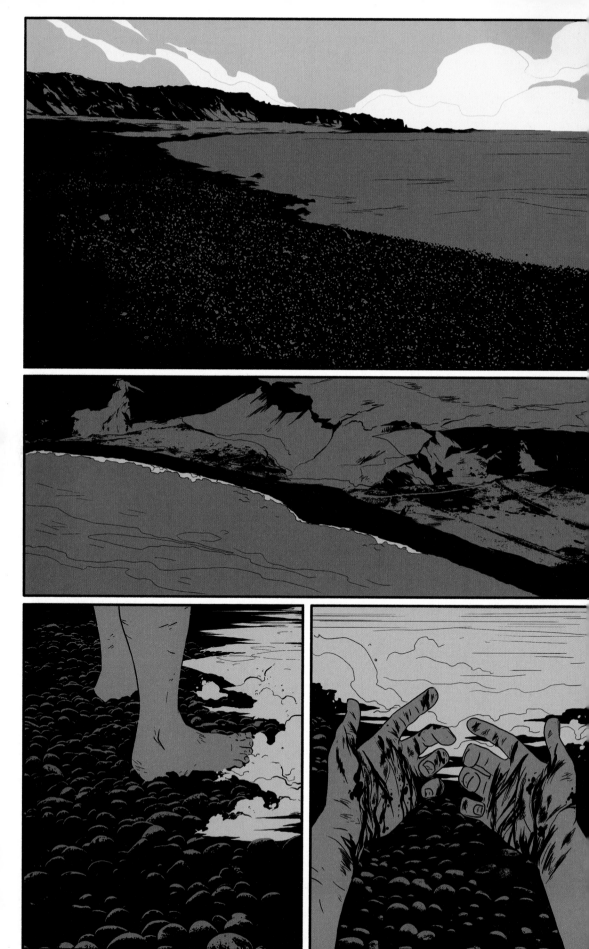

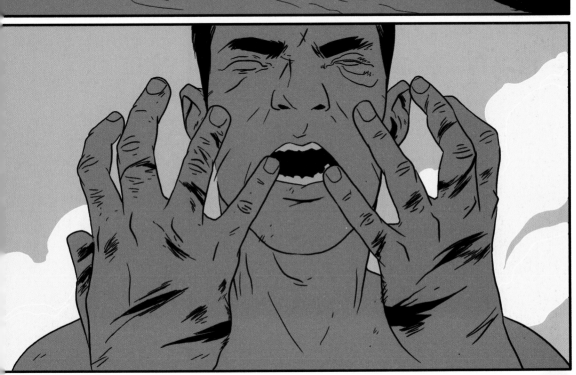

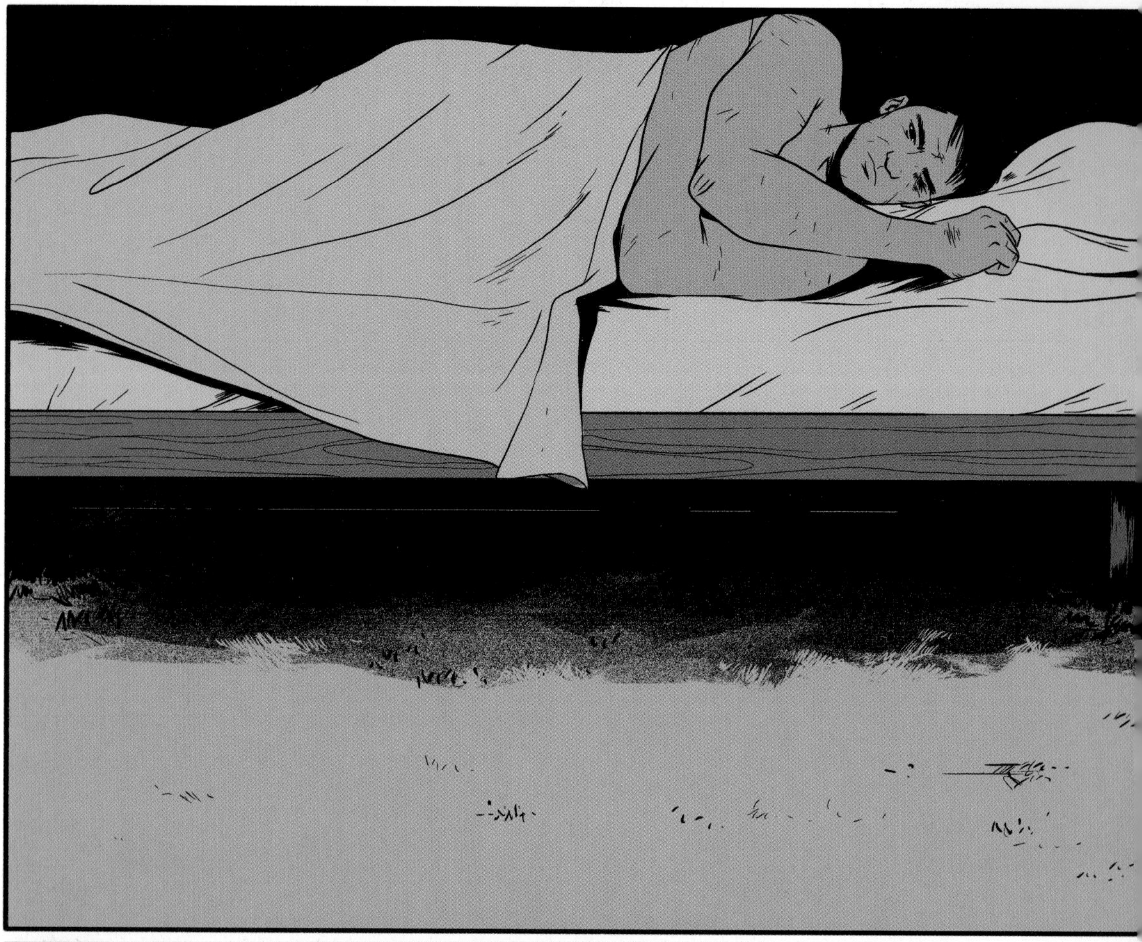

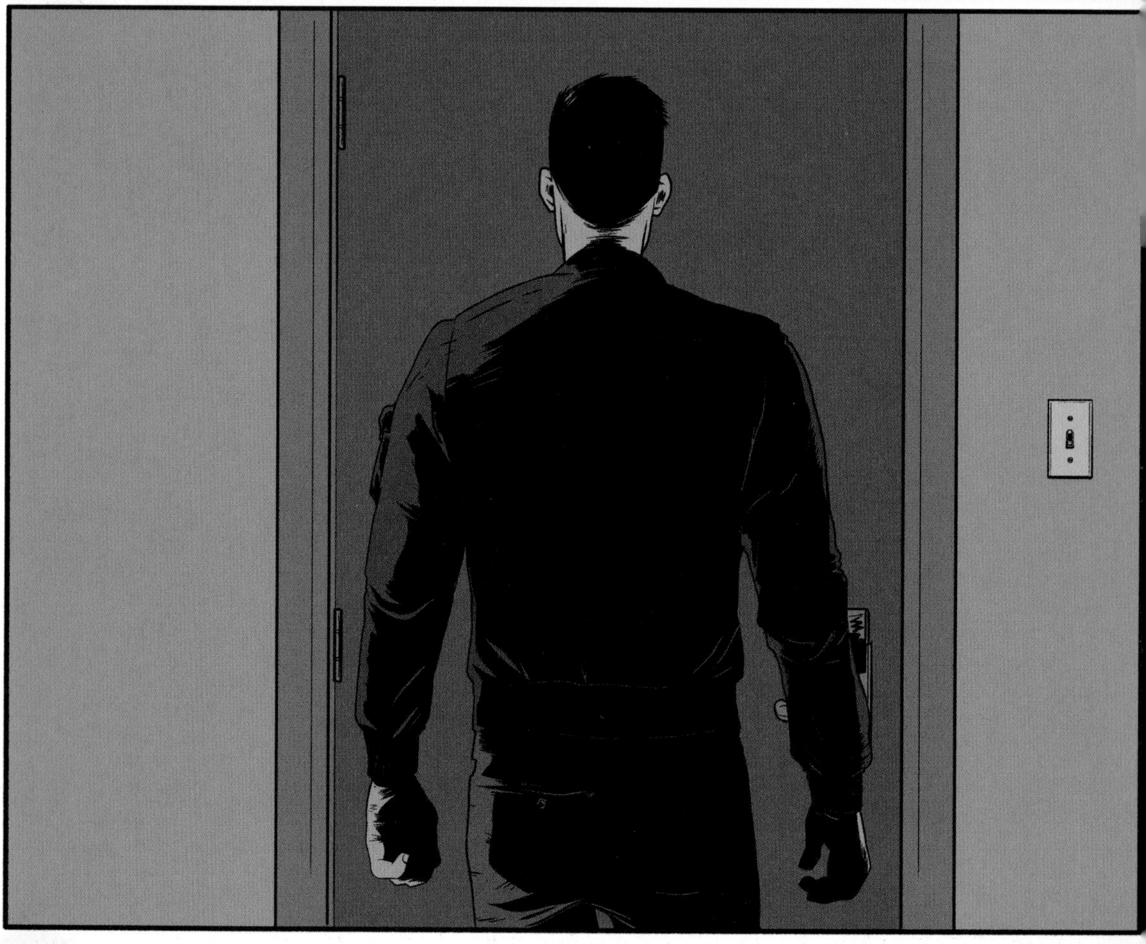

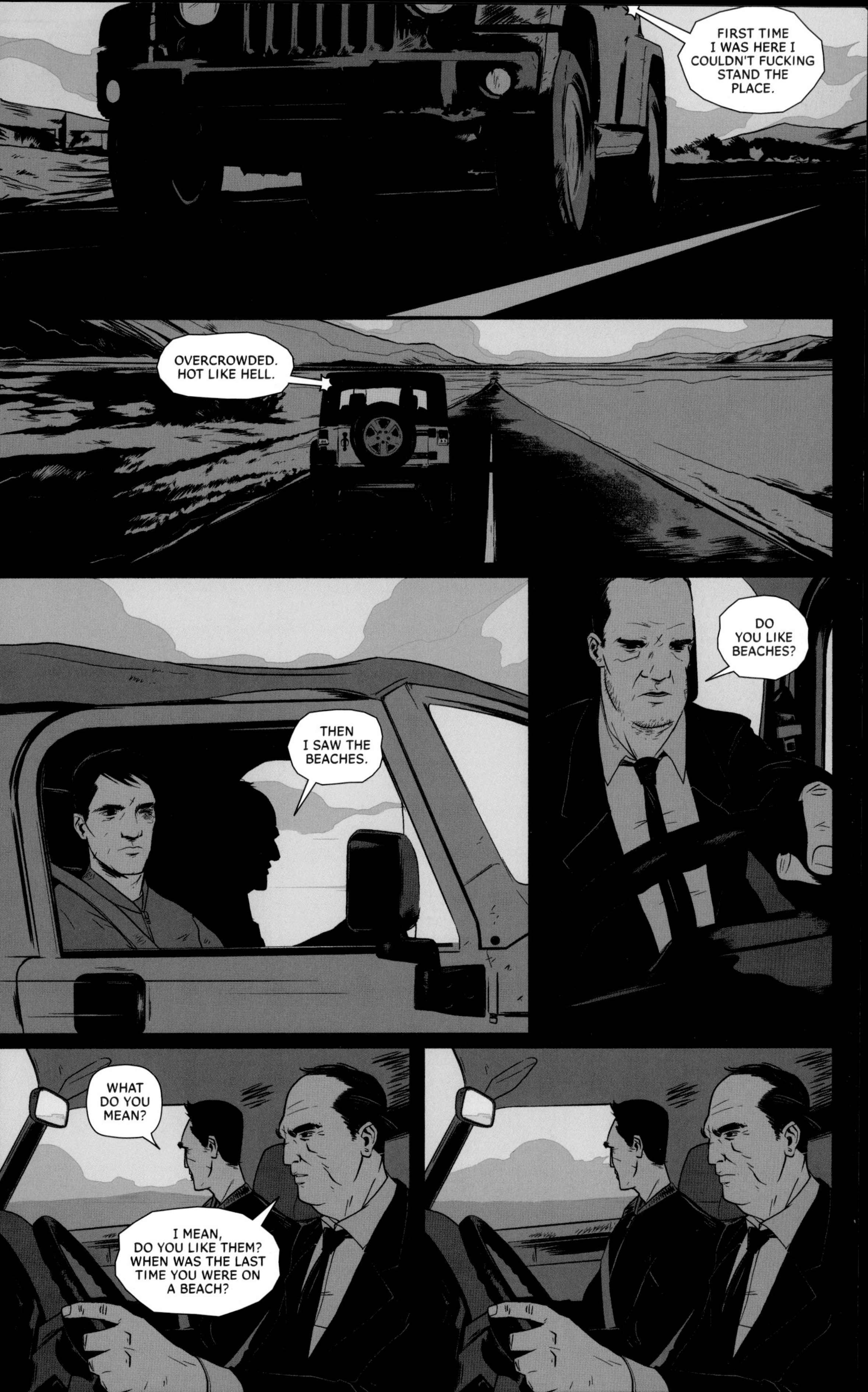
FIRST TIME I WAS HERE I COULDN'T FUCKING STAND THE PLACE.
OVERCROWDED. HOT LIKE HELL.
THEN I SAW THE BEACHES.
DO YOU LIKE BEACHES?
WHAT DO YOU MEAN?
I MEAN, DO YOU LIKE THEM? WHEN WAS THE LAST TIME YOU WERE ON A BEACH?

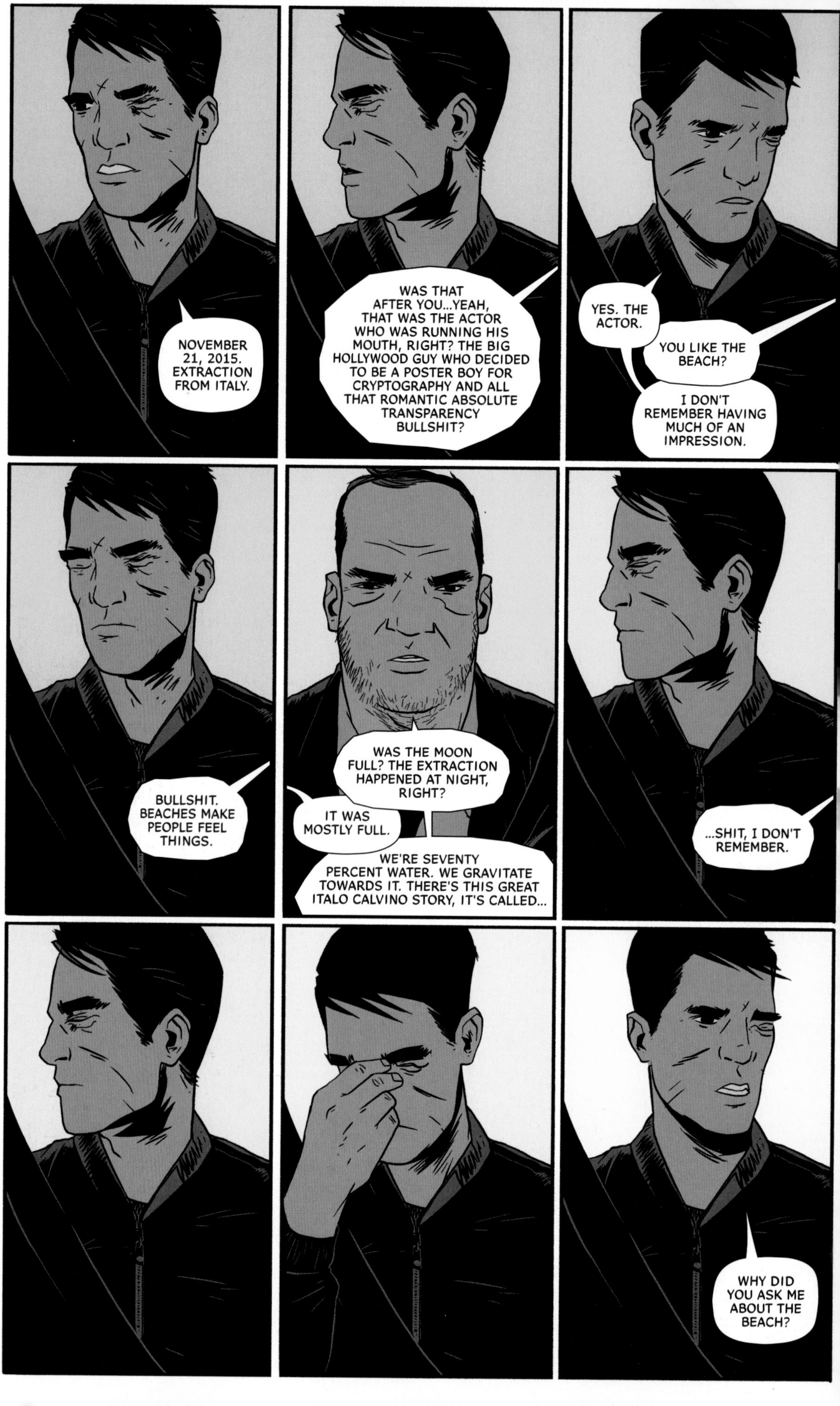
NOVEMBER 21, 2015. EXTRACTION FROM ITALY.
WAS THAT AFTER YOU...YEAH, THAT WAS THE ACTOR WHO WAS RUNNING HIS MOUTH, RIGHT? THE BIG HOLLYWOOD GUY WHO DECIDED TO BE A POSTER BOY FOR CRYPTOGRAPHY AND ALL THAT ROMANTIC ABSOLUTE TRANSPARENCY BULLSHIT?
YES. THE ACTOR.
YOU LIKE THE BEACH?
I DON'T REMEMBER HAVING MUCH OF AN IMPRESSION.
BULLSHIT. BEACHES MAKE PEOPLE FEEL THINGS.
WAS THE MOON FULL? THE EXTRACTION HAPPENED AT NIGHT, RIGHT?
IT WAS MOSTLY FULL.
WE'RE SEVENTY PERCENT WATER. WE GRAVITATE TOWARDS IT. THERE'S THIS GREAT ITALO CALVINO STORY, IT'S CALLED...
...SHIT, I DON'T REMEMBER.
WHY DID YOU ASK ME ABOUT THE BEACH?

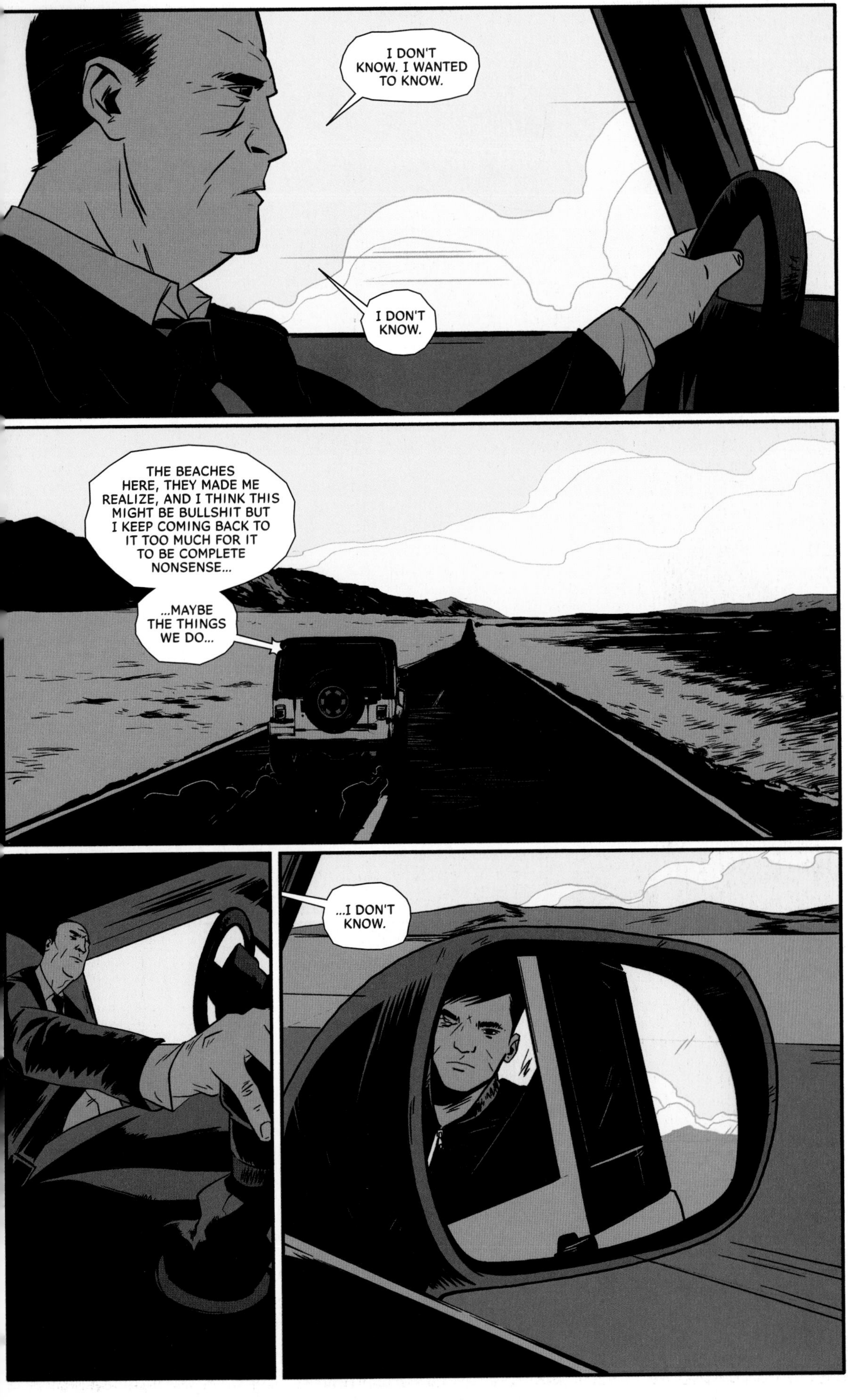
I DON'T KNOW. I WANTED TO KNOW.
I DON'T KNOW.
THE BEACHES HERE, THEY MADE ME REALIZE, AND I THINK THIS MIGHT BE BULLSHIT BUT I KEEP COMING BACK TO IT TOO MUCH FOR IT TO BE COMPLETE NONSENSE...
...MAYBE THE THINGS WE DO...
...I DON'T KNOW.

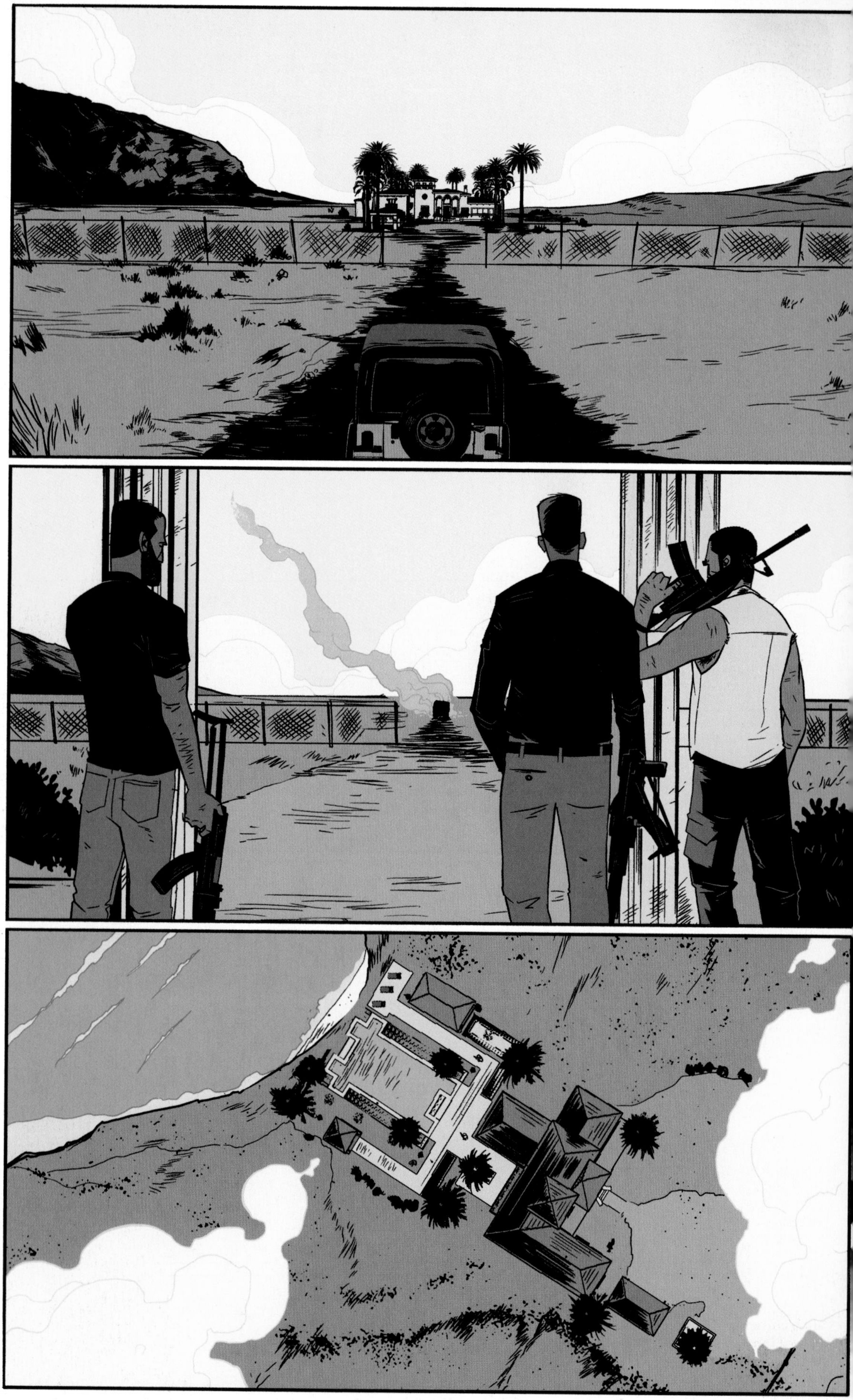

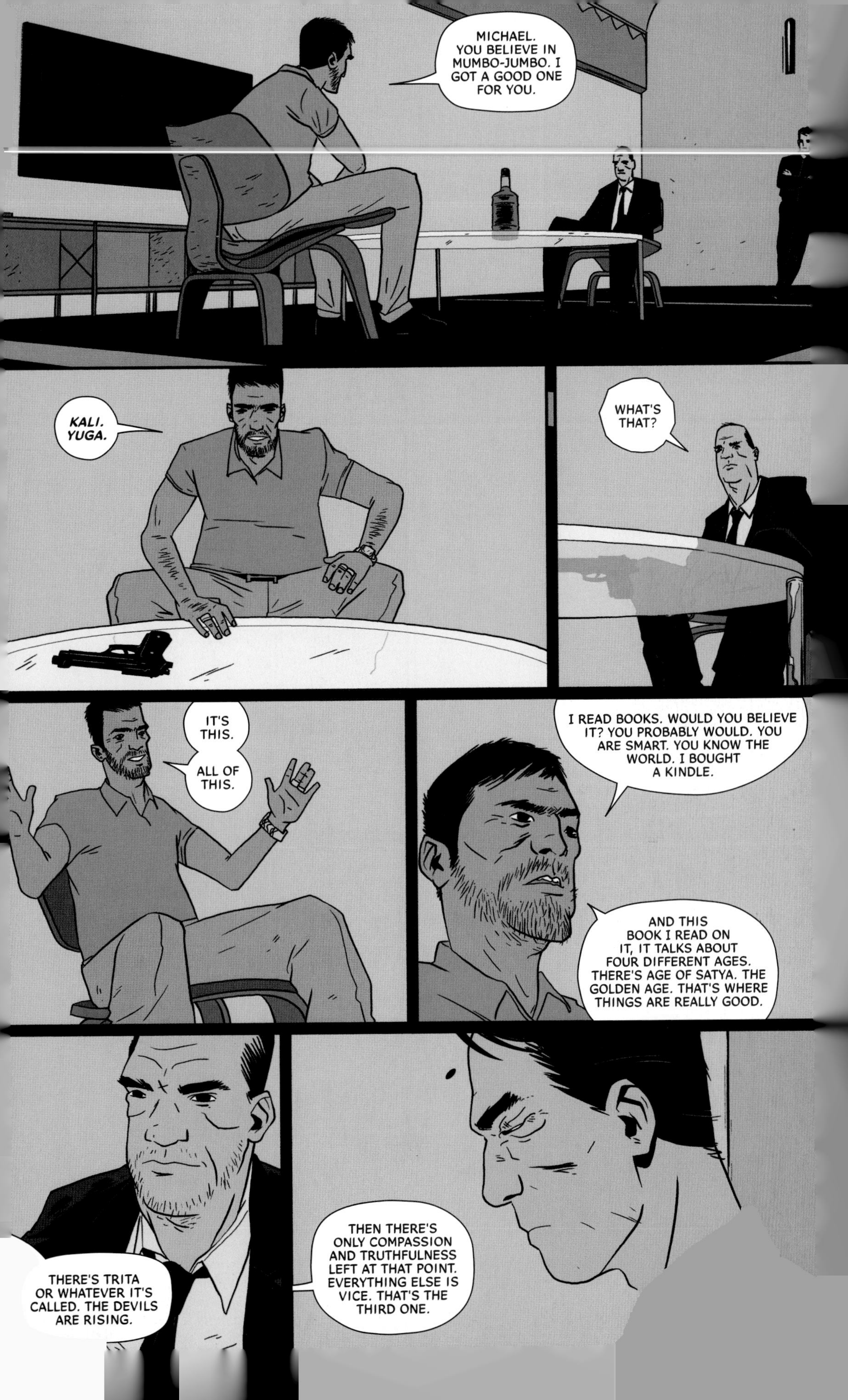
MICHAEL. YOU BELIEVE IN MUMBO-JUMBO. I GOT A GOOD ONE FOR YOU.
KALI. YUGA.
WHAT'S THAT?
IT'S THIS.
ALL OF THIS.
I READ BOOKS. WOULD YOU BELIEVE IT? YOU PROBABLY WOULD. YOU ARE SMART. YOU KNOW THE WORLD. I BOUGHT A KINDLE.
AND THIS BOOK I READ ON IT, IT TALKS ABOUT FOUR DIFFERENT AGES. THERE'S AGE OF SATYA. THE GOLDEN AGE. THAT'S WHERE THINGS ARE REALLY GOOD.
THERE'S TRITA OR WHATEVER IT'S CALLED. THE DEVILS ARE RISING.
THEN THERE'S ONLY COMPASSION AND TRUTHFULNESS LEFT AT THAT POINT. EVERYTHING ELSE IS VICE. THAT'S THE THIRD ONE.

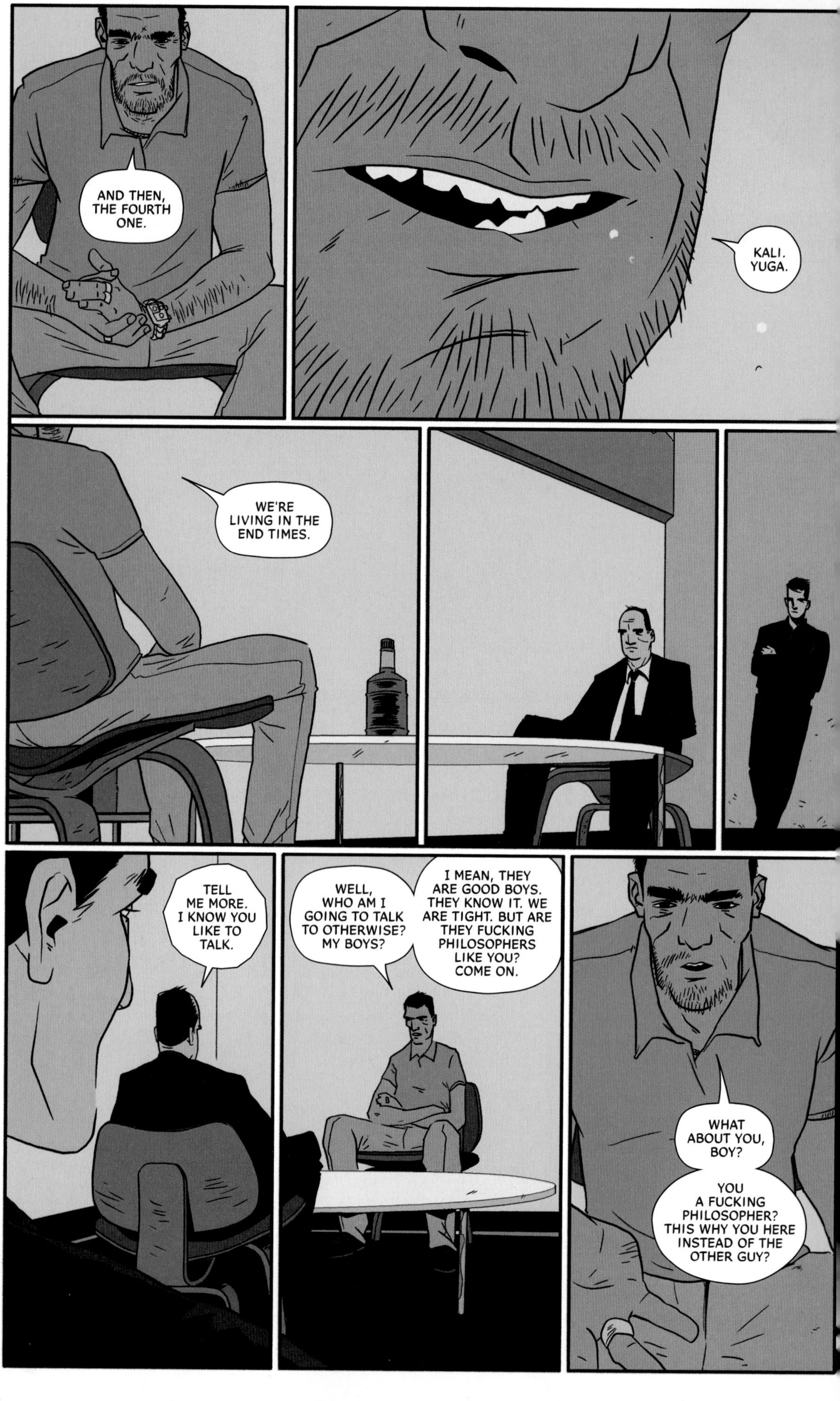
AND THEN, THE FOURTH ONE.
KALI. YUGA.
WE'RE LIVING IN THE END TIMES.
TELL ME MORE. I KNOW YOU LIKE TO TALK.
WELL, WHO AM I GOING TO TALK TO OTHERWISE? MY BOYS?
I MEAN, THEY ARE GOOD BOYS. THEY KNOW IT. WE ARE TIGHT. BUT ARE THEY FUCKING PHILOSOPHERS LIKE YOU? COME ON.
WHAT ABOUT YOU, BOY?
YOU A FUCKING PHILOSOPHER? THIS WHY YOU HERE INSTEAD OF THE OTHER GUY?

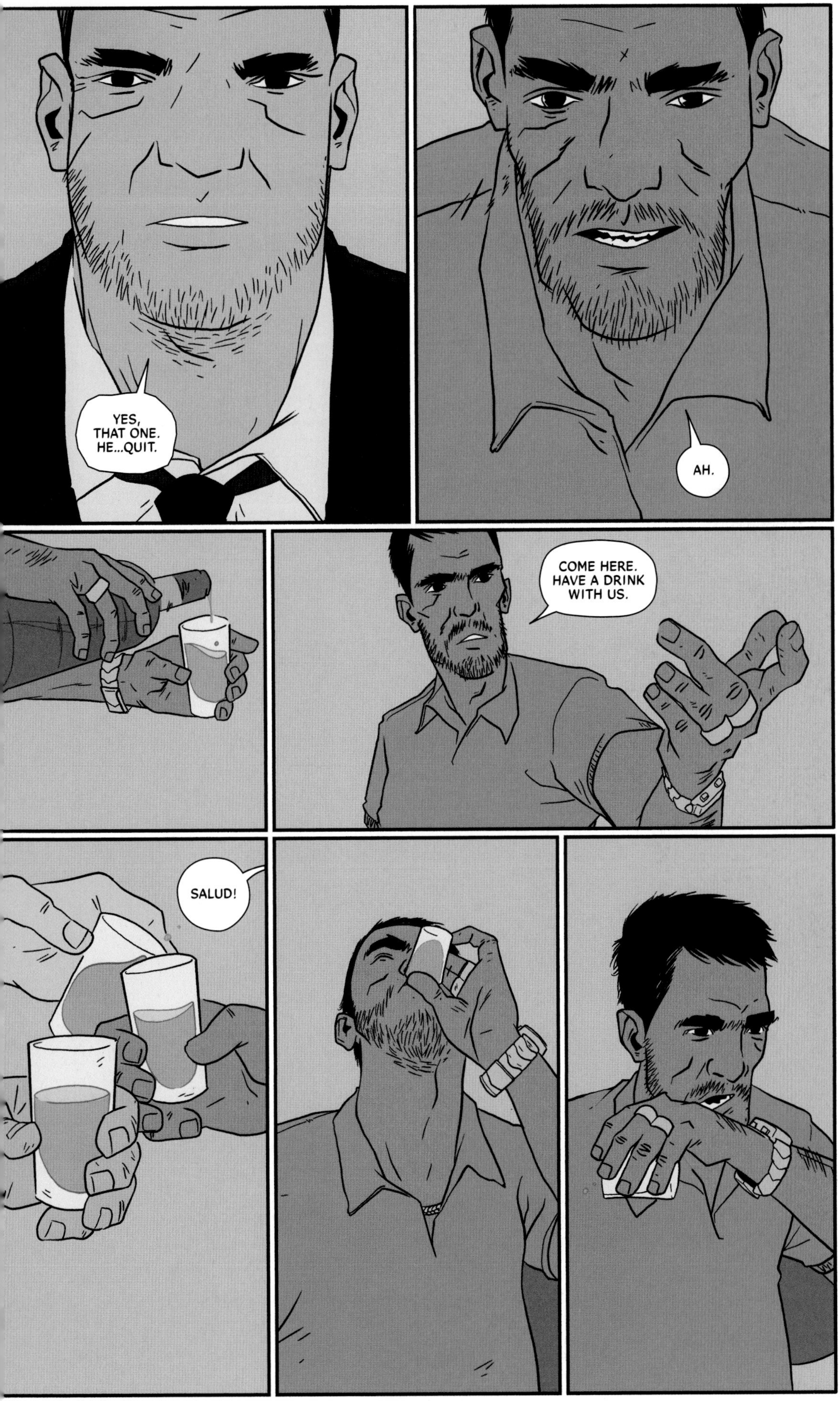
YES, THAT ONE. HE...QUIT.
AH.
COME HERE. HAVE A DRINK WITH US.
SALUD!

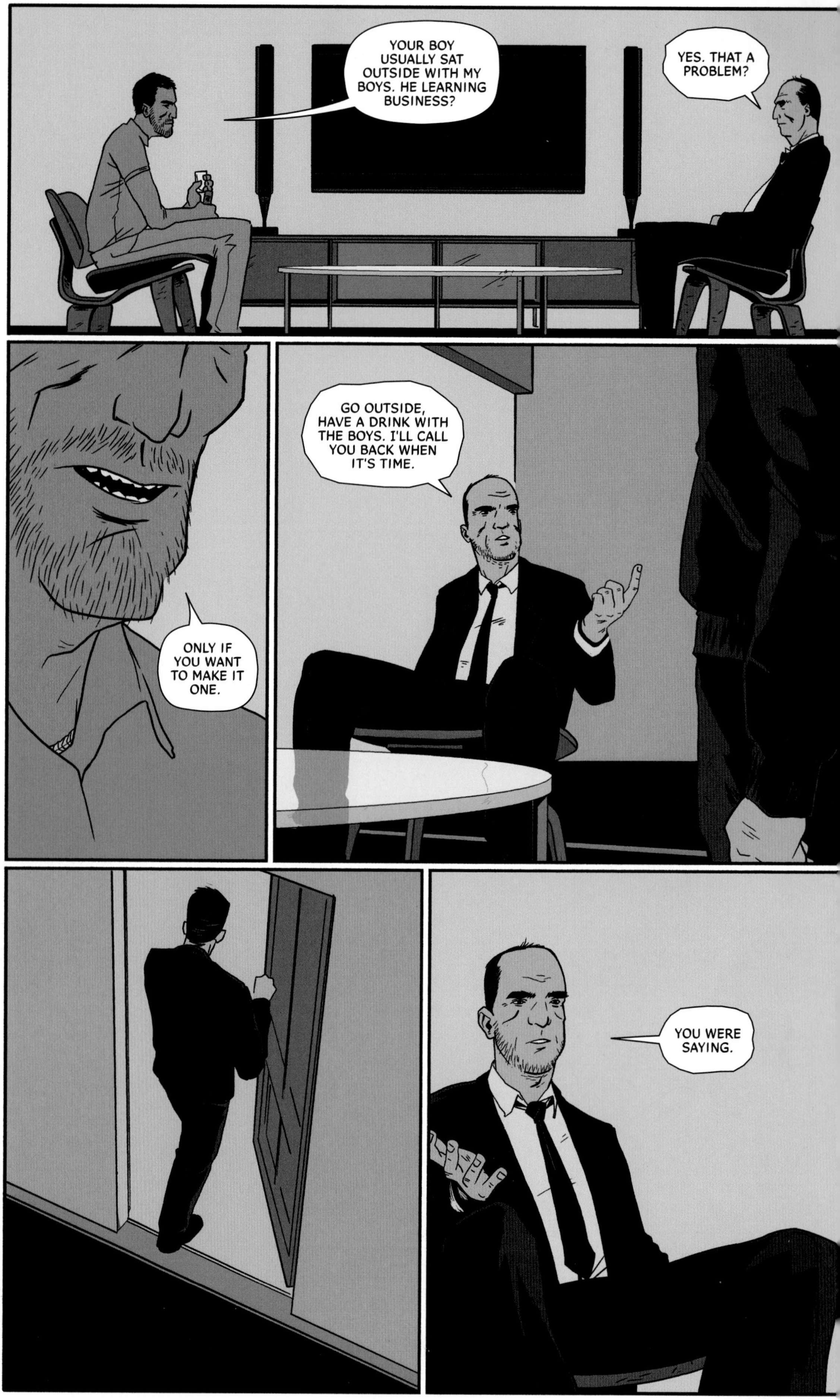
YOUR BOY USUALLY SAT OUTSIDE WITH MY BOYS. HE LEARNING BUSINESS?
YES. THAT A PROBLEM?
ONLY IF YOU WANT TO MAKE IT ONE.
GO OUTSIDE, HAVE A DRINK WITH THE BOYS. I'LL CALL YOU BACK WHEN IT'S TIME.
YOU WERE SAYING.

"IT MAKES SENSE, DOESN'T IT?"

THE BOSSES TOLD ME TO GO HAVE A DRINK.

"KALI YUGA.

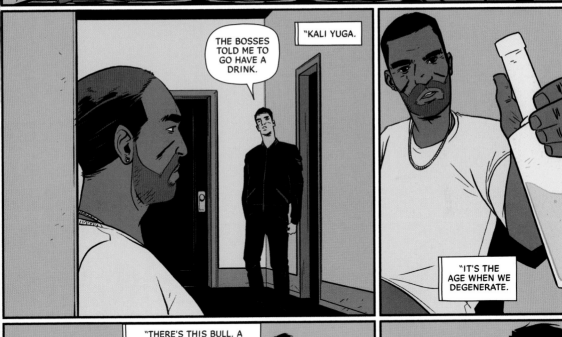

"IT'S THE AGE WHEN WE DEGENERATE.

"THERE'S THIS BULL. A SYMBOL. AND IN THE FIRST YUGA IT HAS FOUR LEGS, BUT BY THE LAST ONE, THERE'S JUST ONE. BECAUSE IT'S-- IT'S SYMBOLIC OF THE TIMES.

"LIKE, THE RULERS WILL BE SHIT.

"PEOPLE WILL BREAK PROMISES.

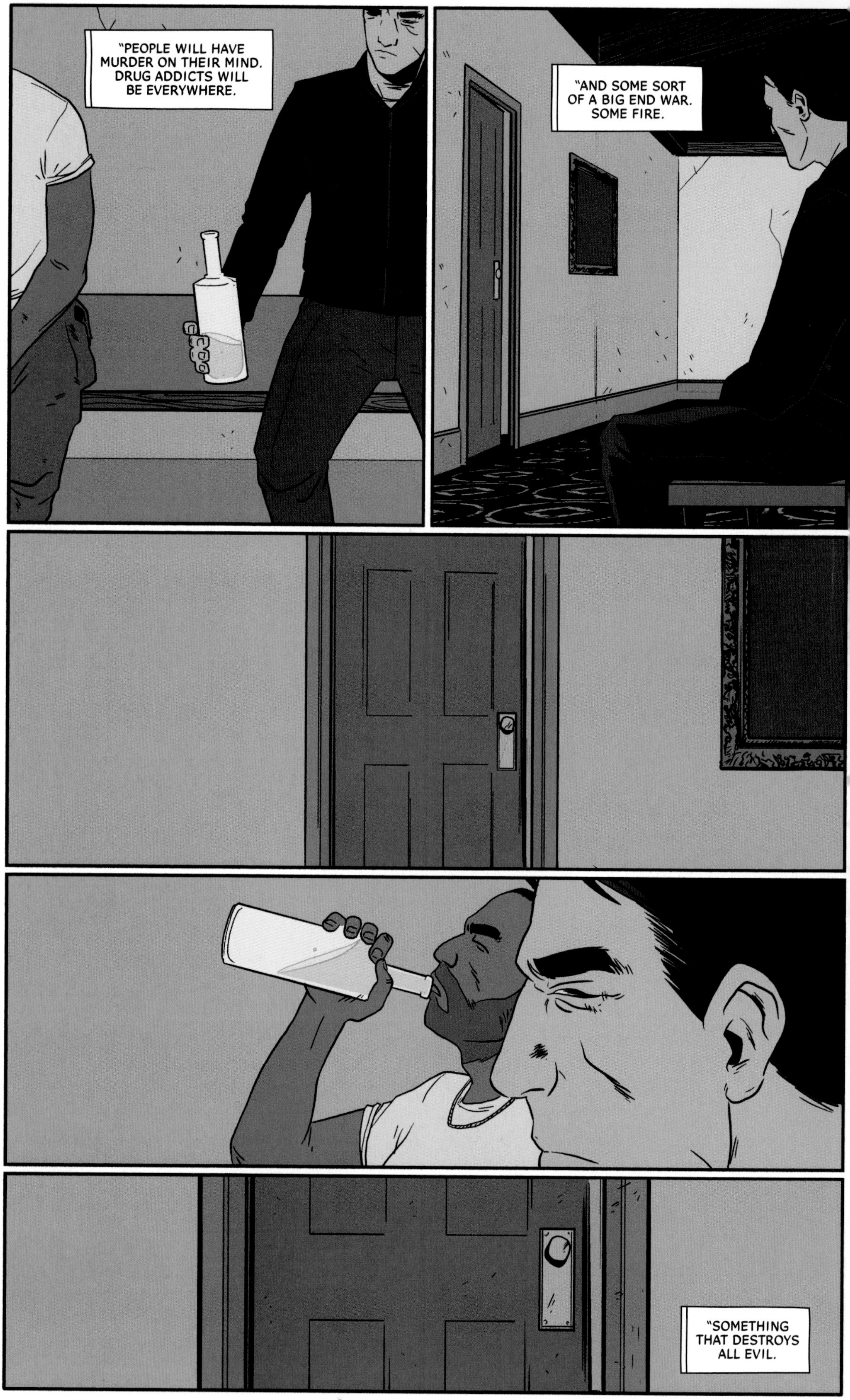
"PEOPLE WILL HAVE MURDER ON THEIR MIND. DRUG ADDICTS WILL BE EVERYWHERE.
"AND SOME SORT OF A BIG END WAR. SOME FIRE.
"SOMETHING THAT DESTROYS ALL EVIL.

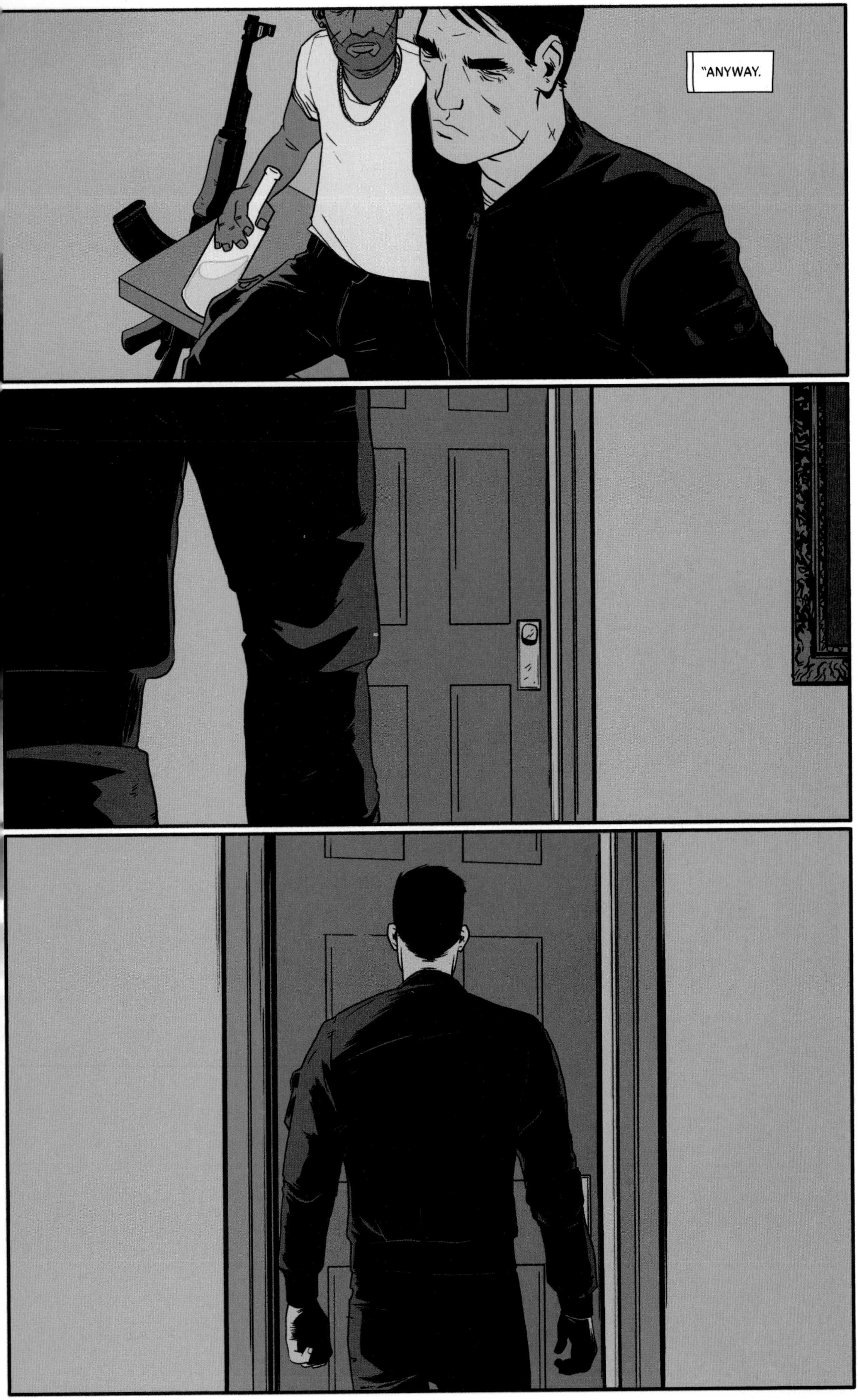
"ANYWAY.

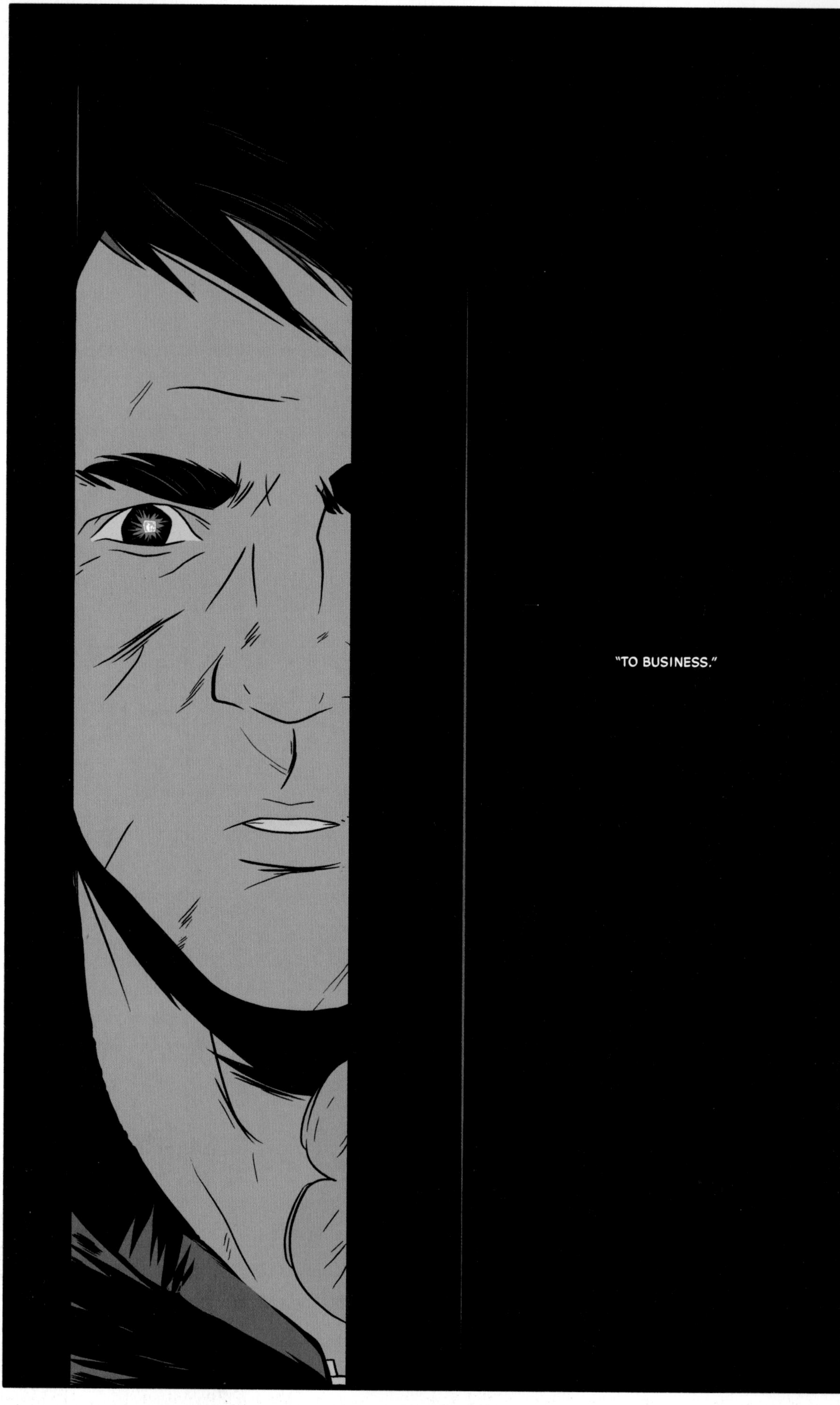
"TO BUSINESS."

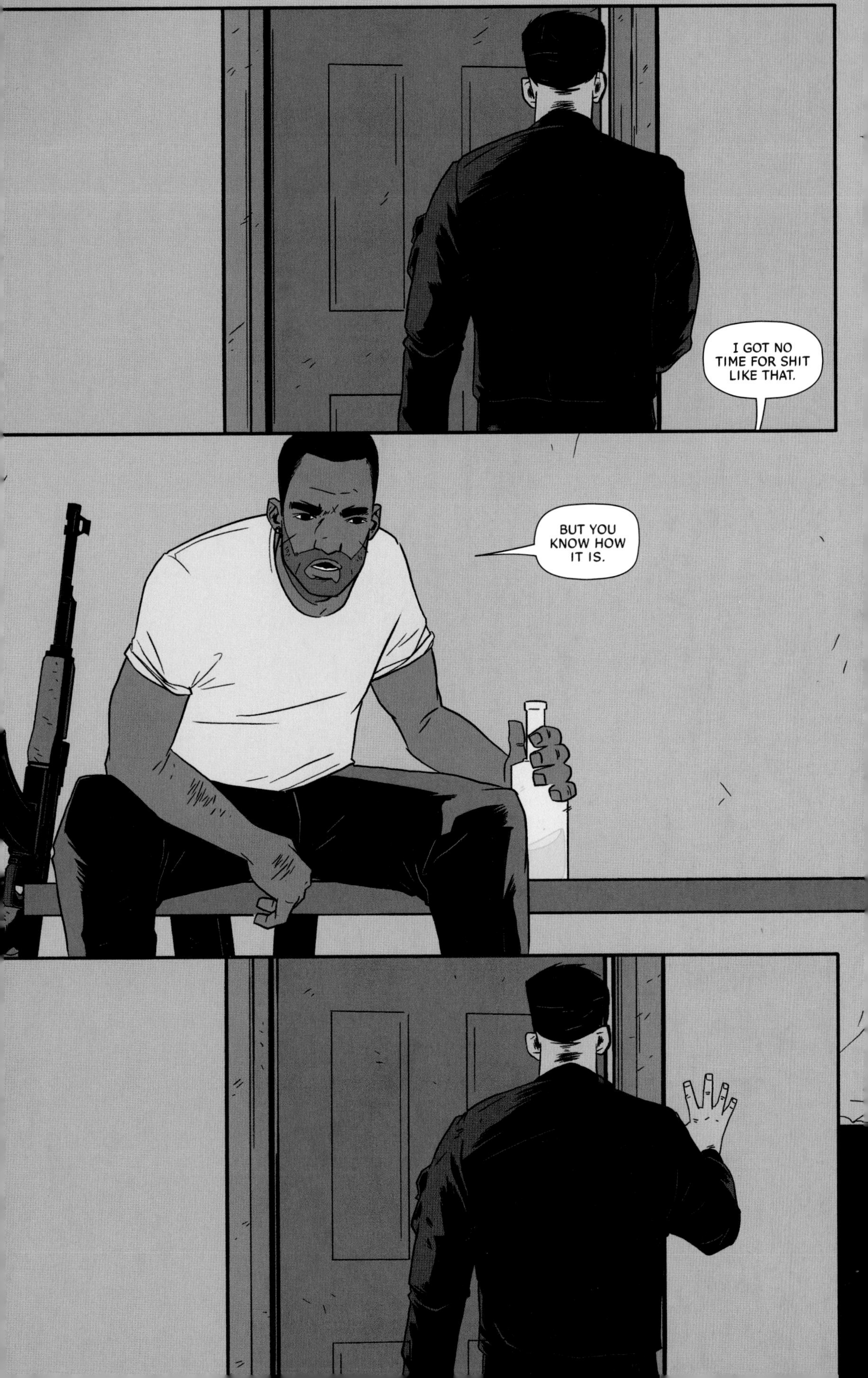
I GOT NO TIME FOR SHIT LIKE THAT.
BUT YOU KNOW HOW IT IS.

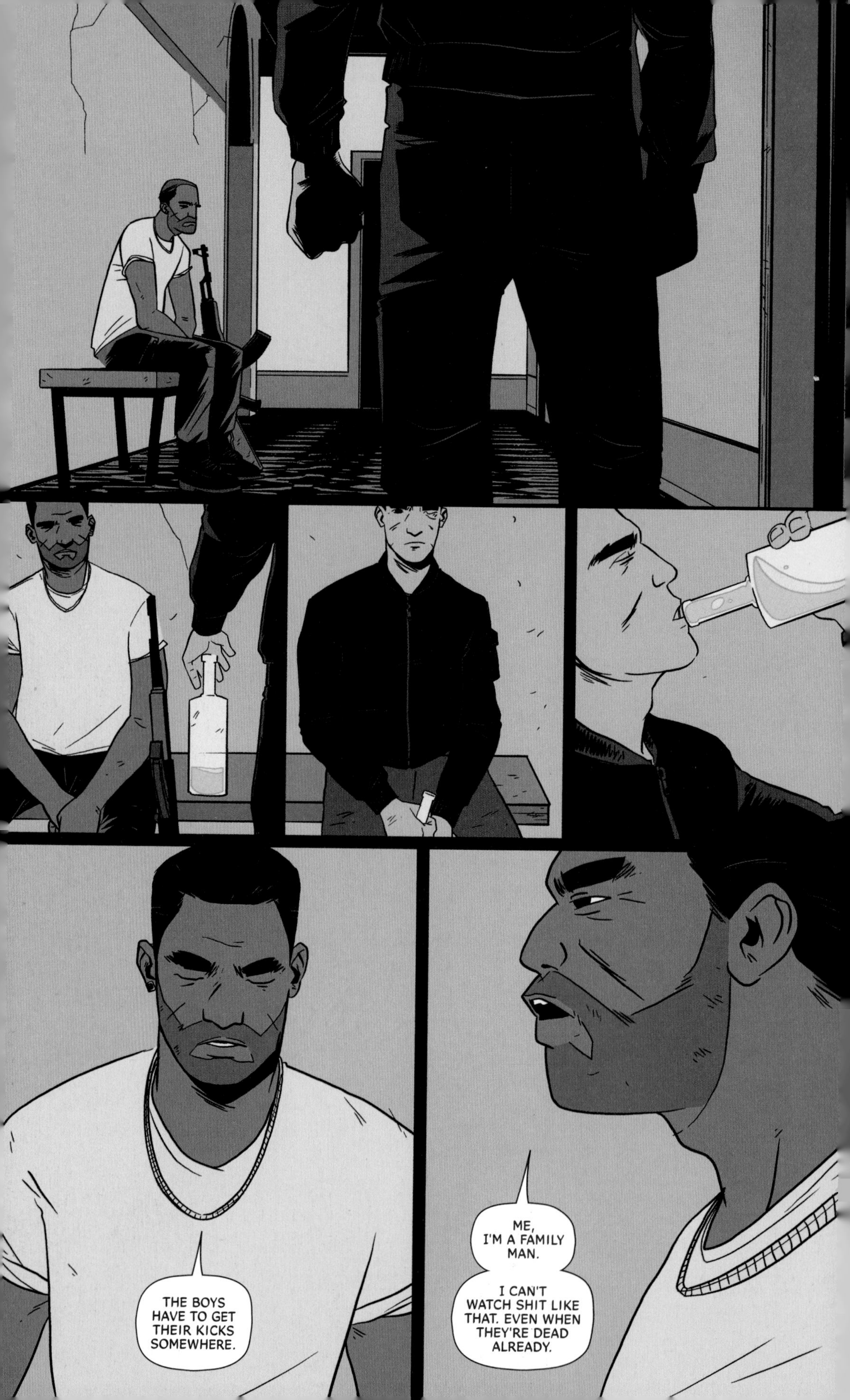
THE BOYS HAVE TO GET THEIR KICKS SOMEWHERE.
ME, I'M A FAMILY MAN.
I CAN'T WATCH SHIT LIKE THAT. EVEN WHEN THEY'RE DEAD ALREADY.

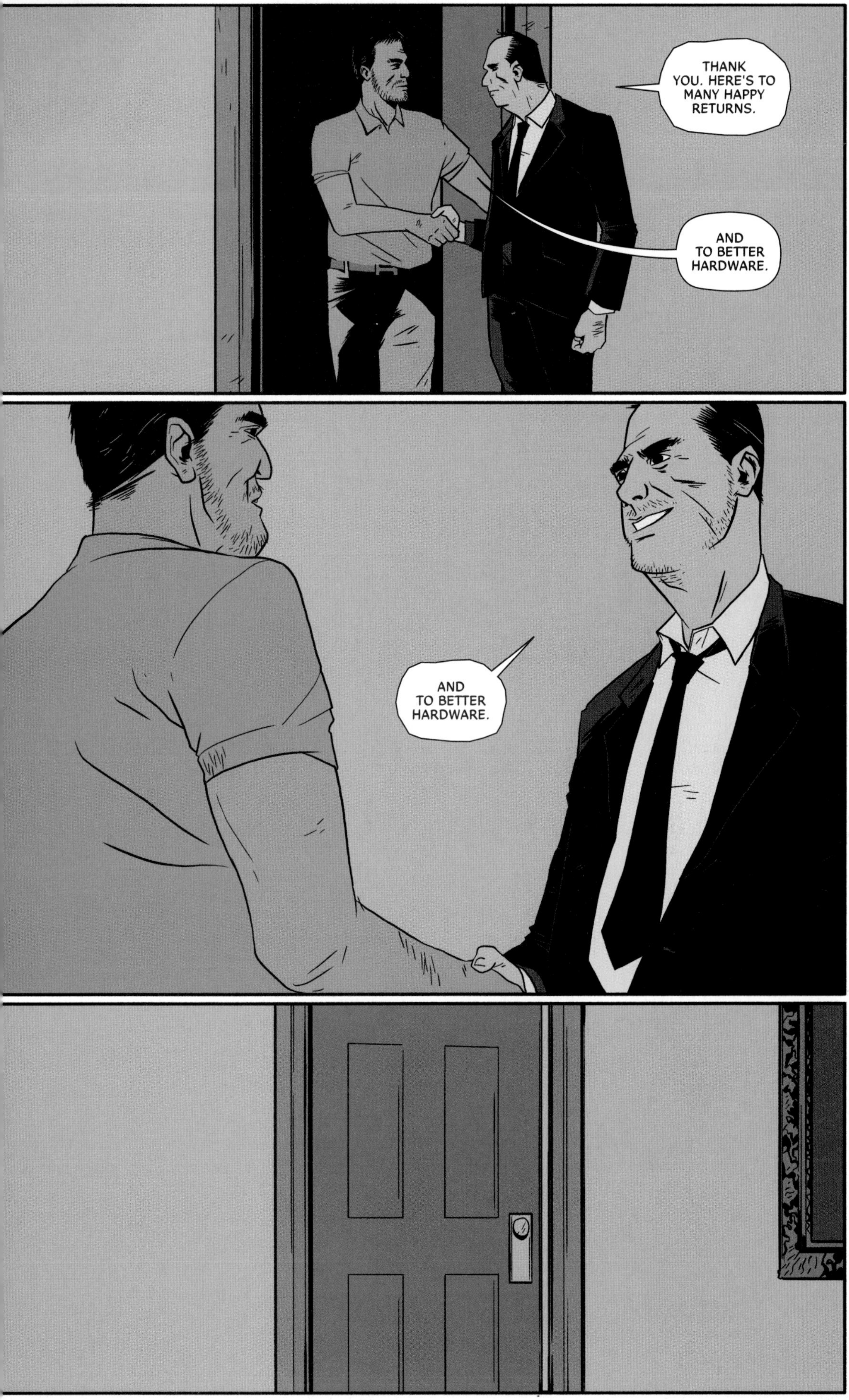
THANK YOU. HERE'S TO MANY HAPPY RETURNS.
AND TO BETTER HARDWARE.
AND TO BETTER HARDWARE.

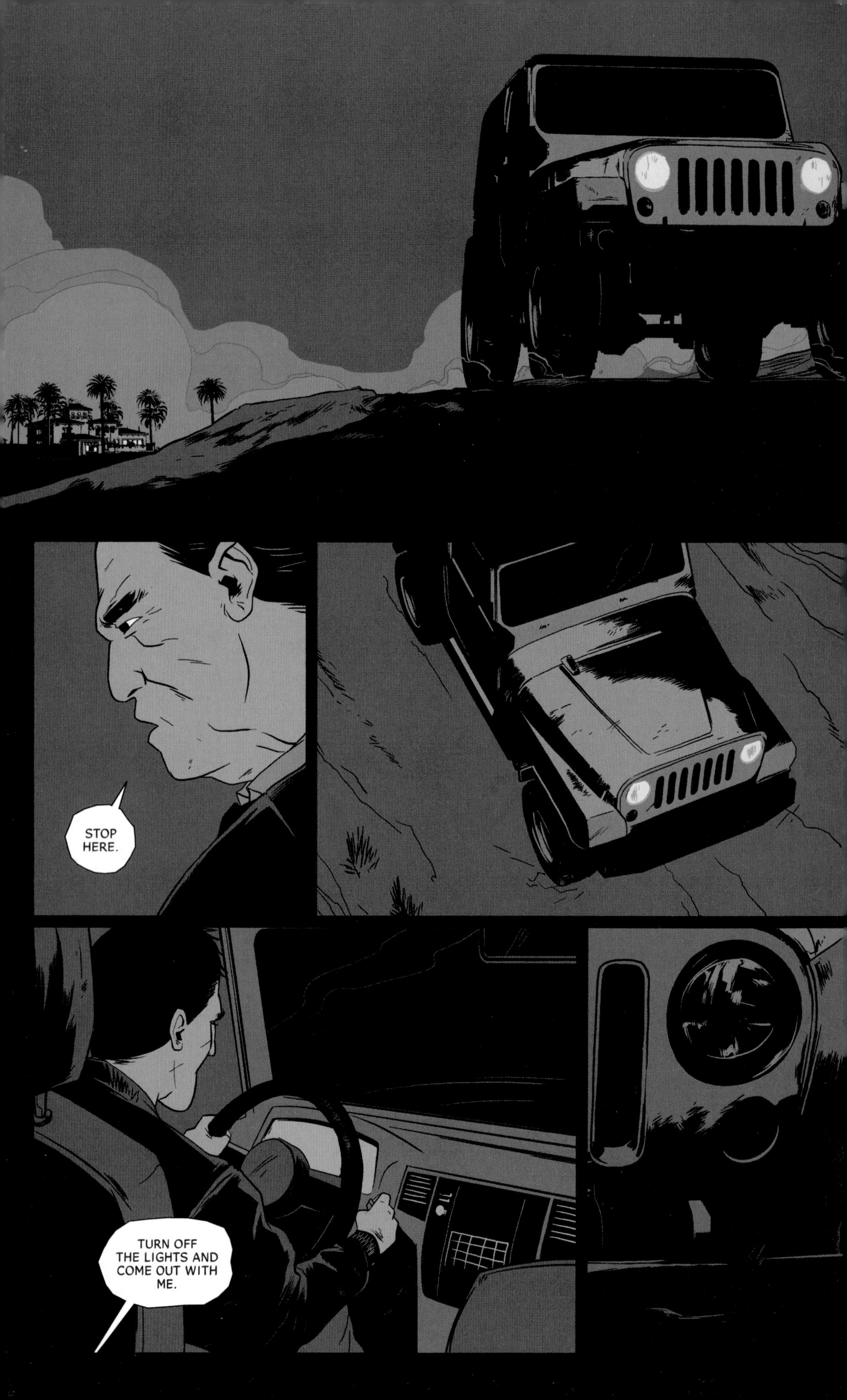
STOP HERE.
TURN OFF THE LIGHTS AND COME OUT WITH ME.

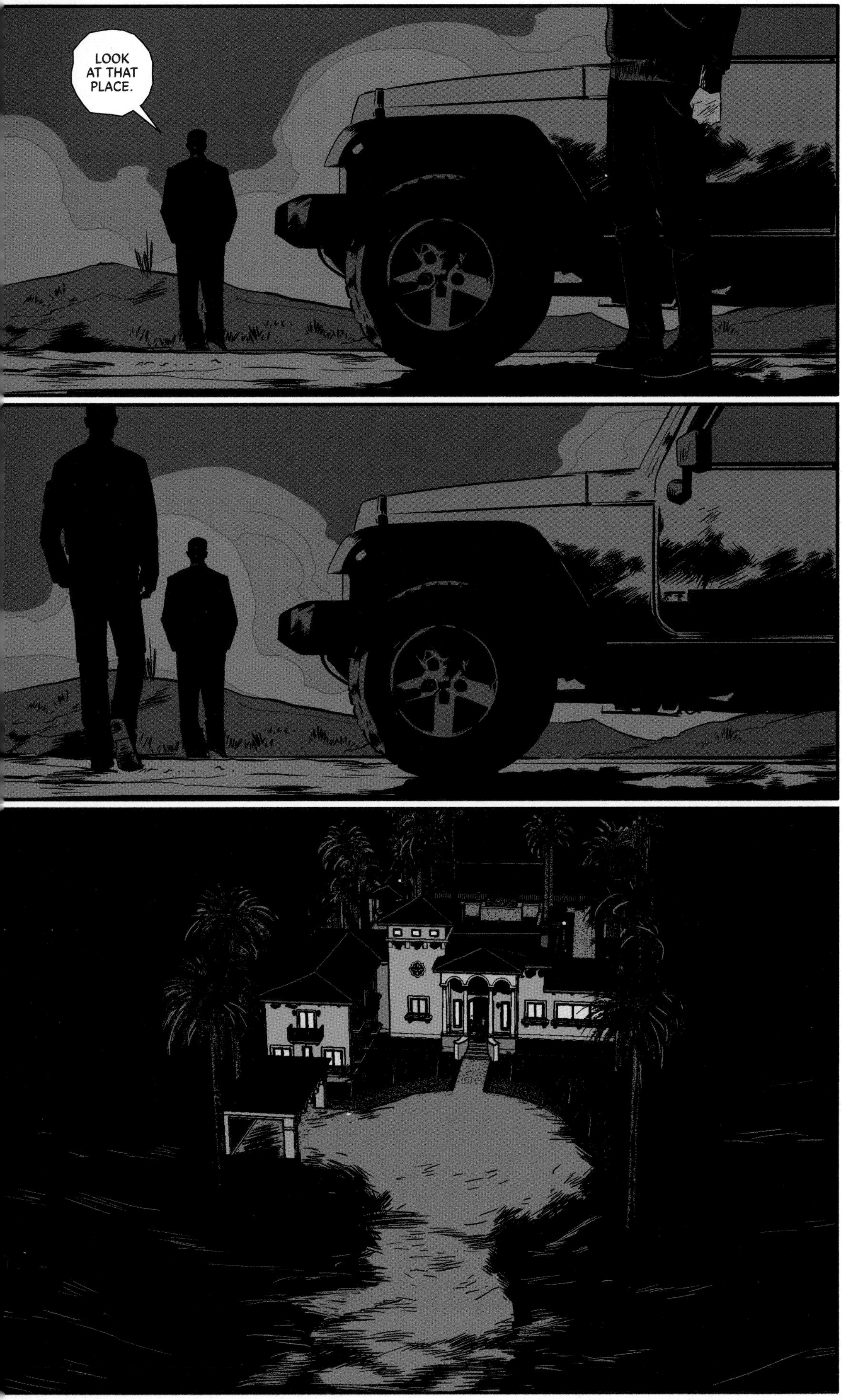
LOOK AT THAT PLACE.

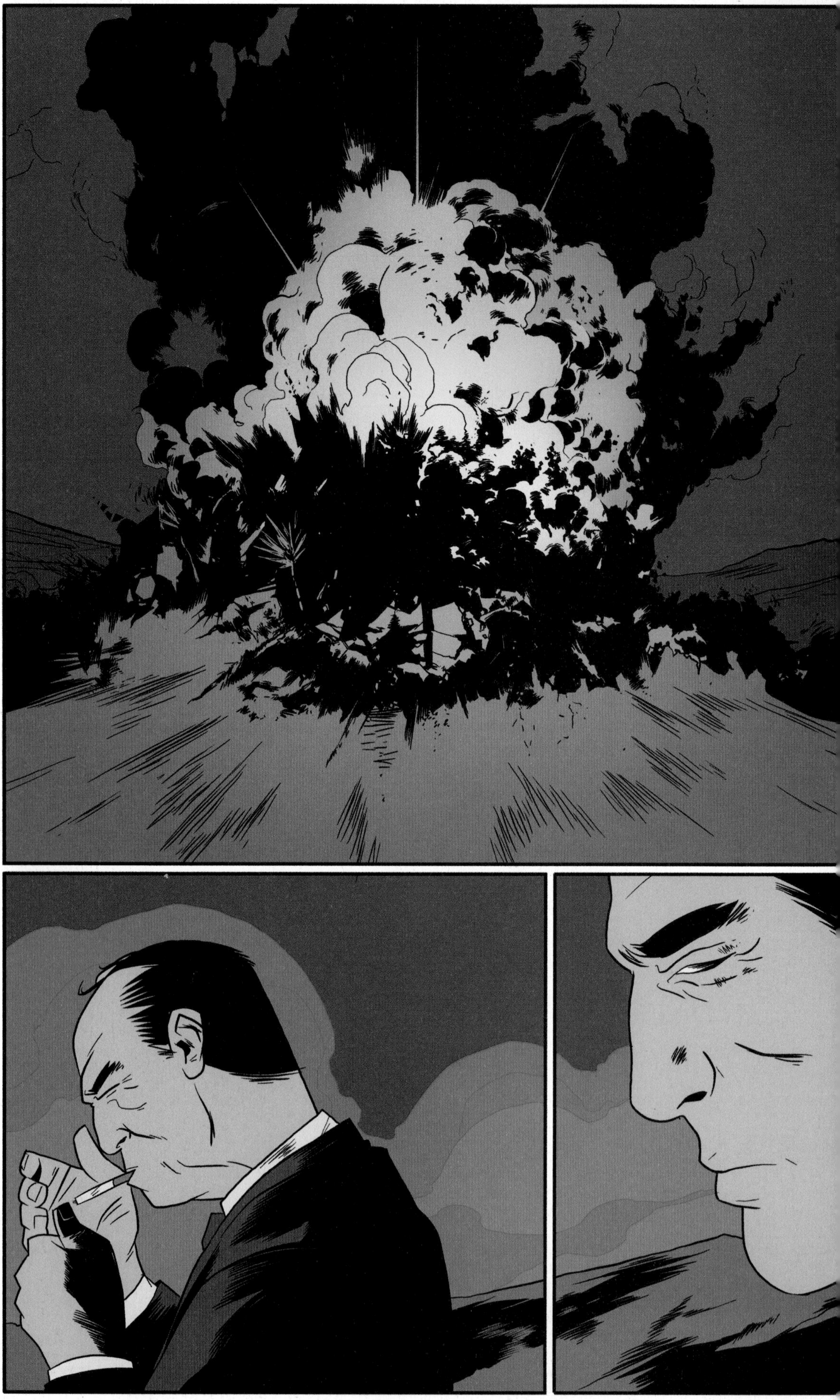

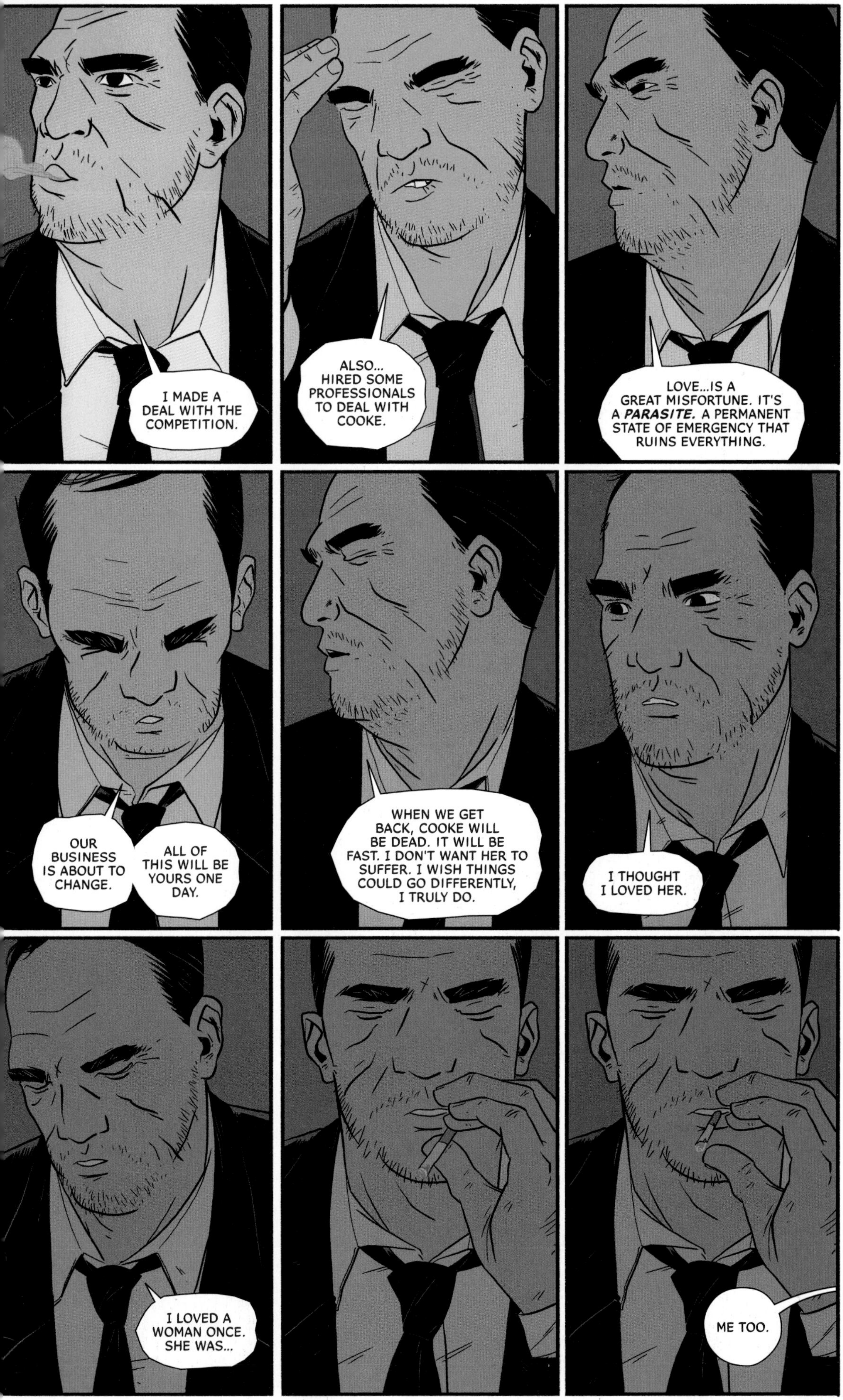
I MADE A DEAL WITH THE COMPETITION.
ALSO... HIRED SOME PROFESSIONALS TO DEAL WITH COOKE.
LOVE...IS A GREAT MISFORTUNE. IT'S A *PARASITE.* A PERMANENT STATE OF EMERGENCY THAT RUINS EVERYTHING.
OUR BUSINESS IS ABOUT TO CHANGE.
ALL OF THIS WILL BE YOURS ONE DAY.
WHEN WE GET BACK, COOKE WILL BE DEAD. IT WILL BE FAST. I DON'T WANT HER TO SUFFER. I WISH THINGS COULD GO DIFFERENTLY, I TRULY DO.
I THOUGHT I LOVED HER.
I LOVED A WOMAN ONCE. SHE WAS...
ME TOO.

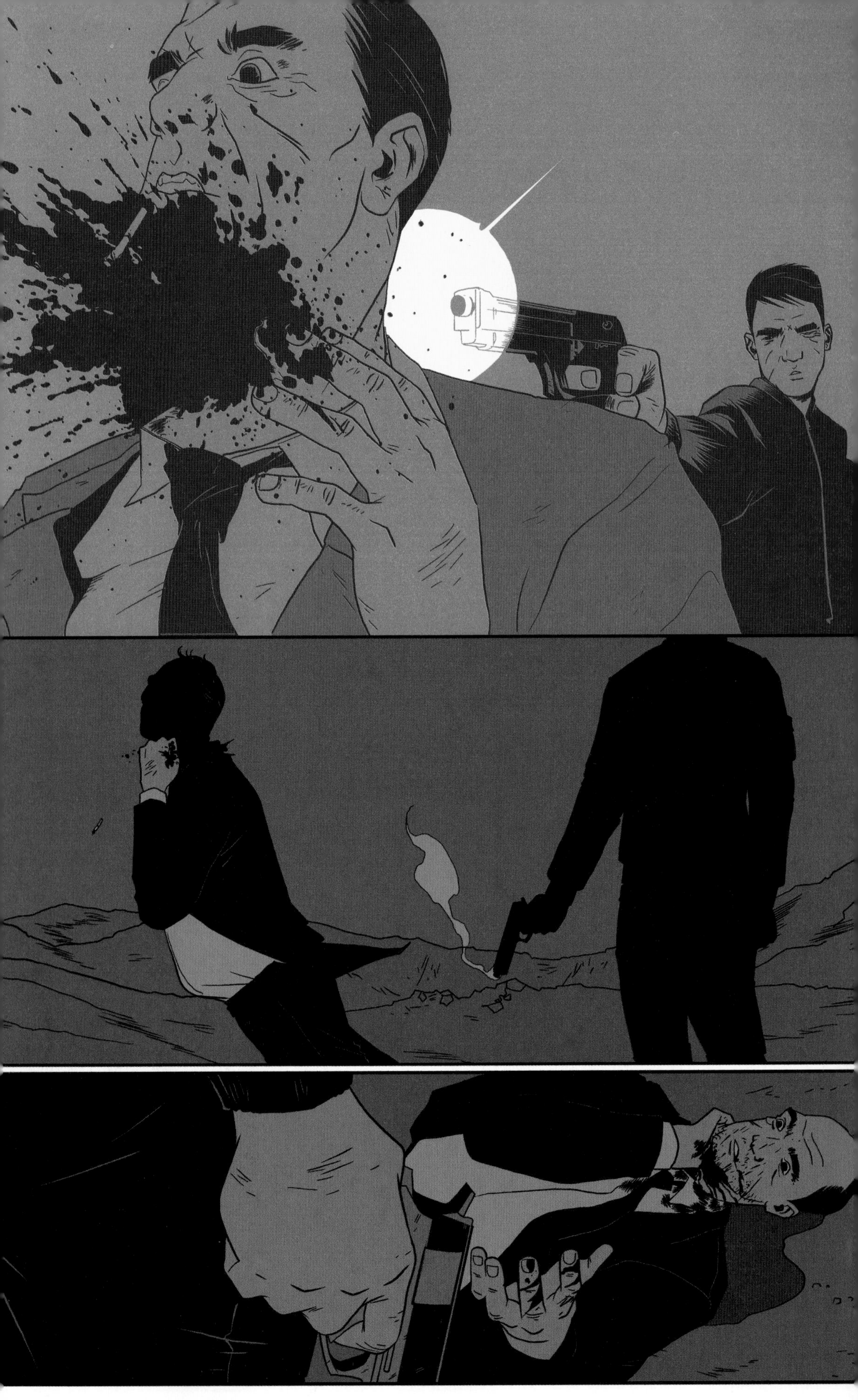

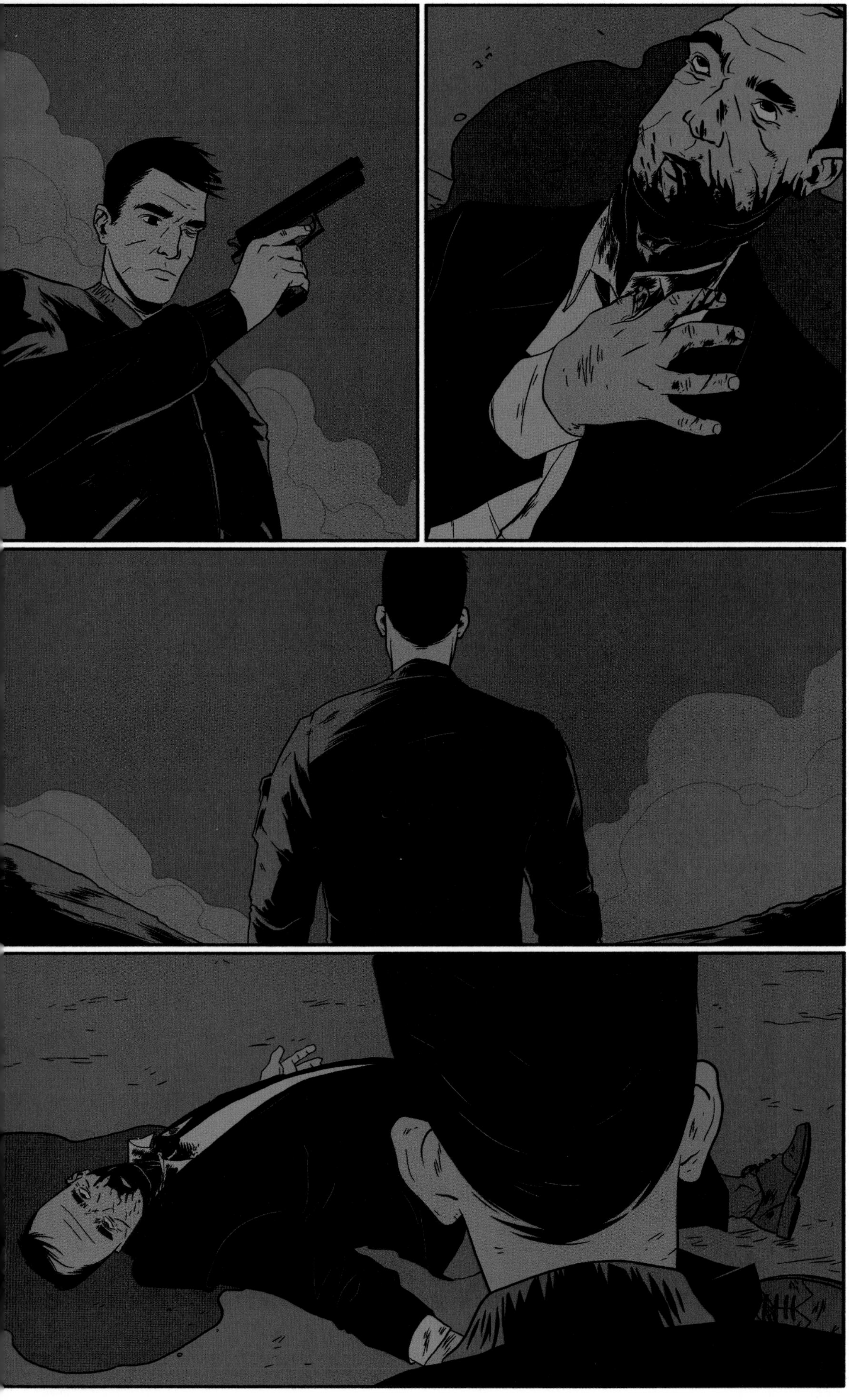

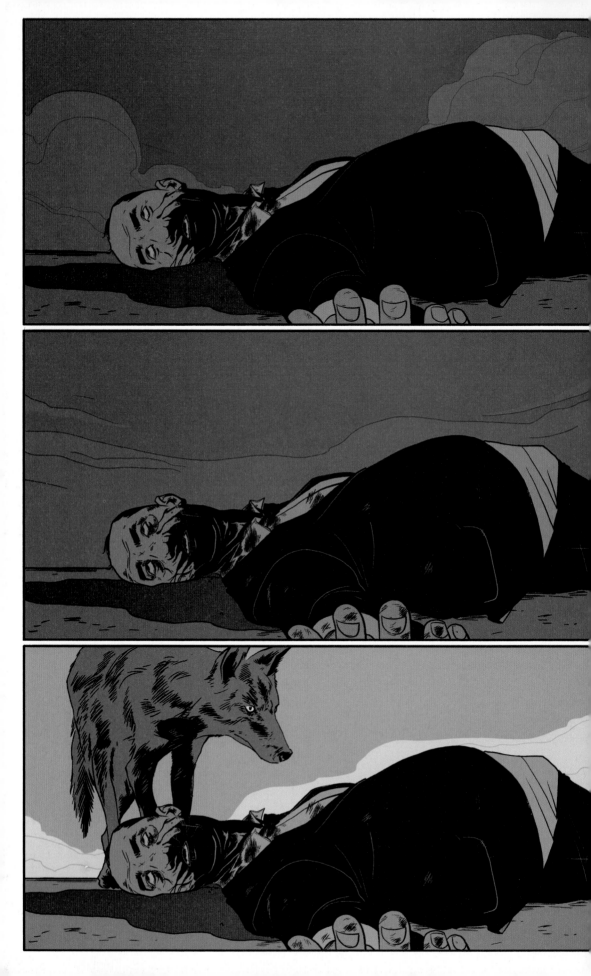

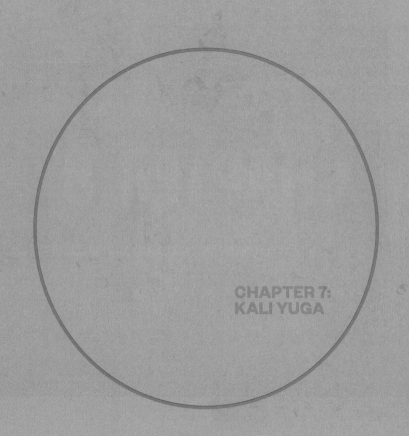

CHAPTER 7:
KALI YUGA

CHAPTER 8

SHAME AS THE INCITING FACTOR OF VIOLENCE

Illustrated by Jorge Coelho

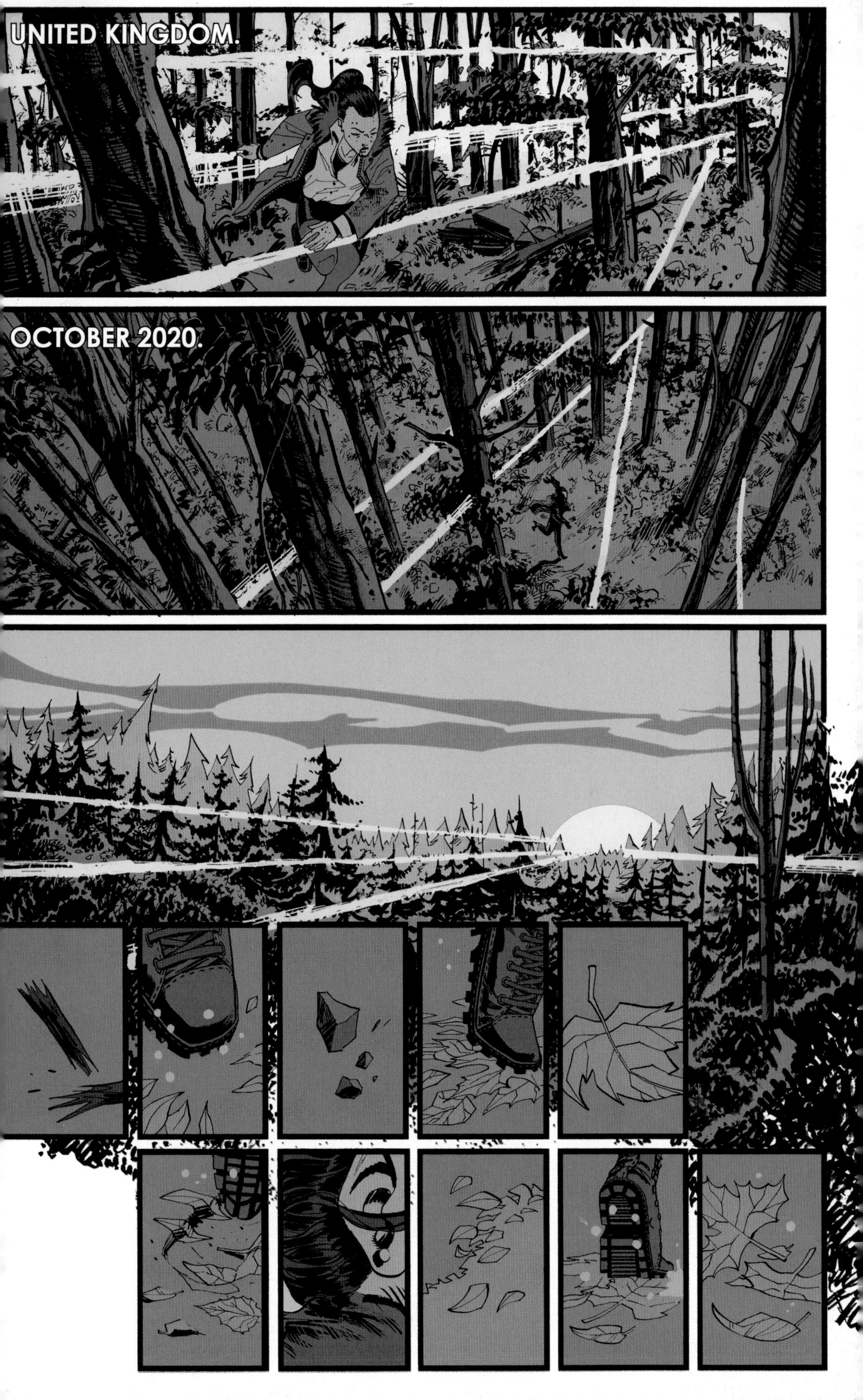
UNITED KINGDOM.
OCTOBER 2020.

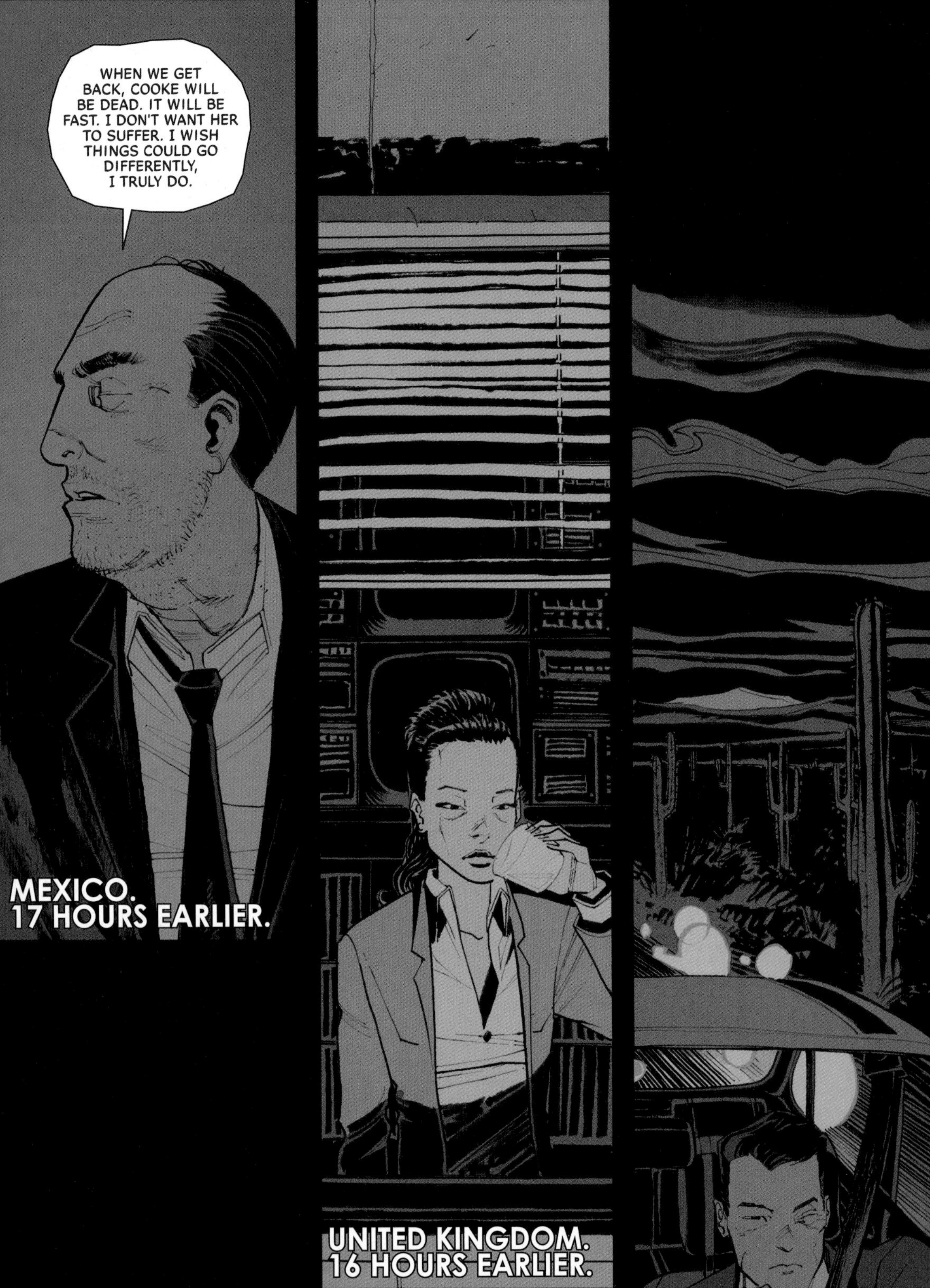
WHEN WE GET BACK, COOKE WILL BE DEAD. IT WILL BE FAST. I DON'T WANT HER TO SUFFER. I WISH THINGS COULD GO DIFFERENTLY, I TRULY DO.
MEXICO. 17 HOURS EARLIER.
UNITED KINGDOM. 16 HOURS EARLIER.

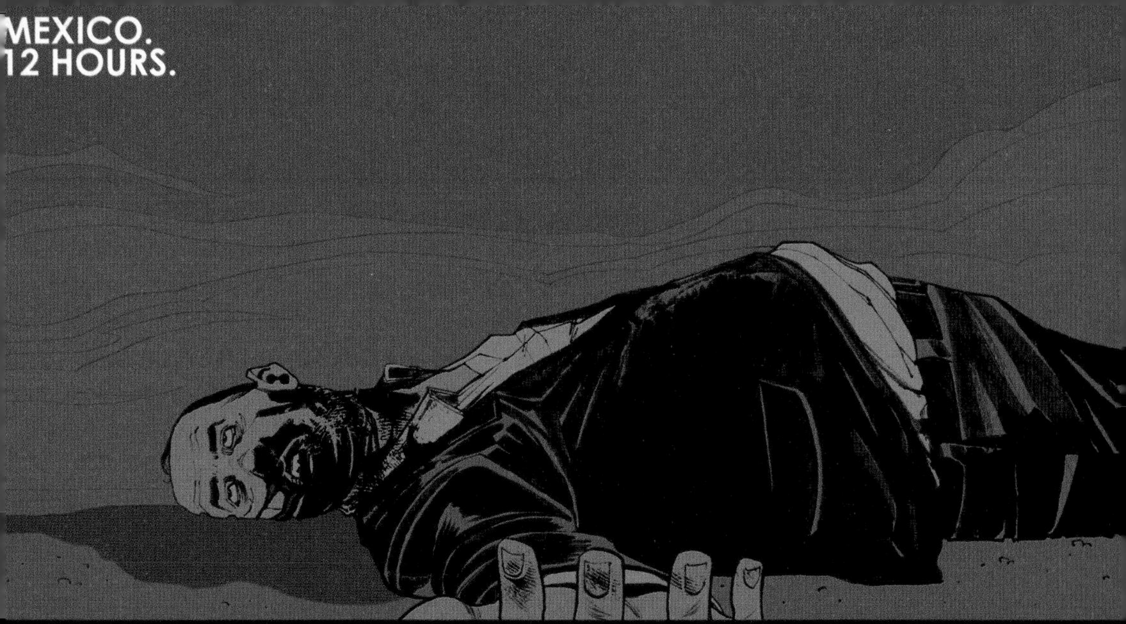
MEXICO.
12 HOURS.

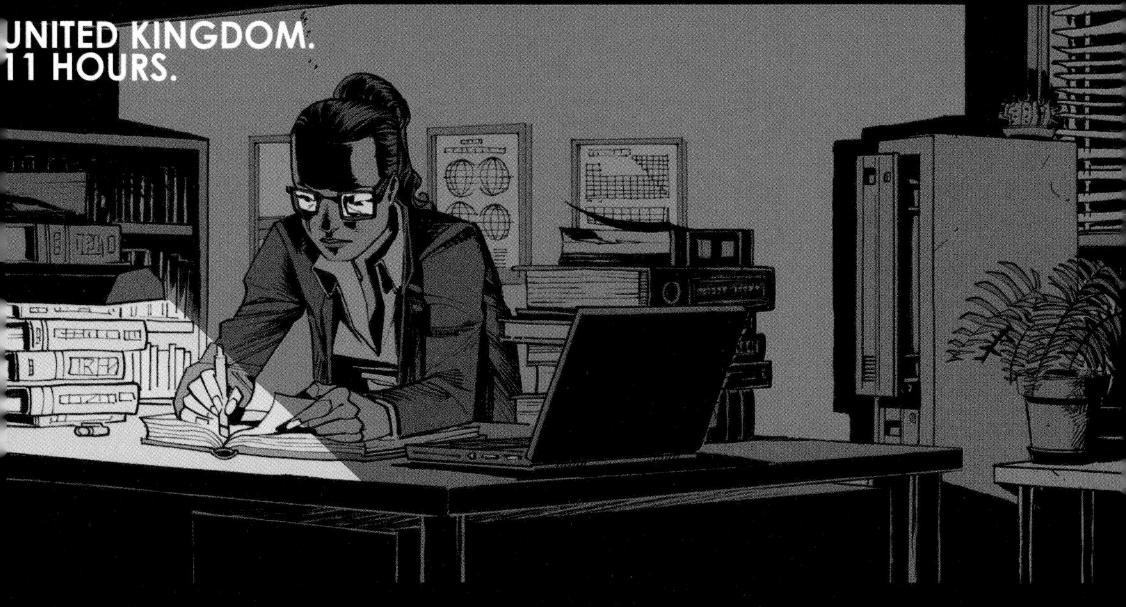
UNITED KINGDOM.
11 HOURS.

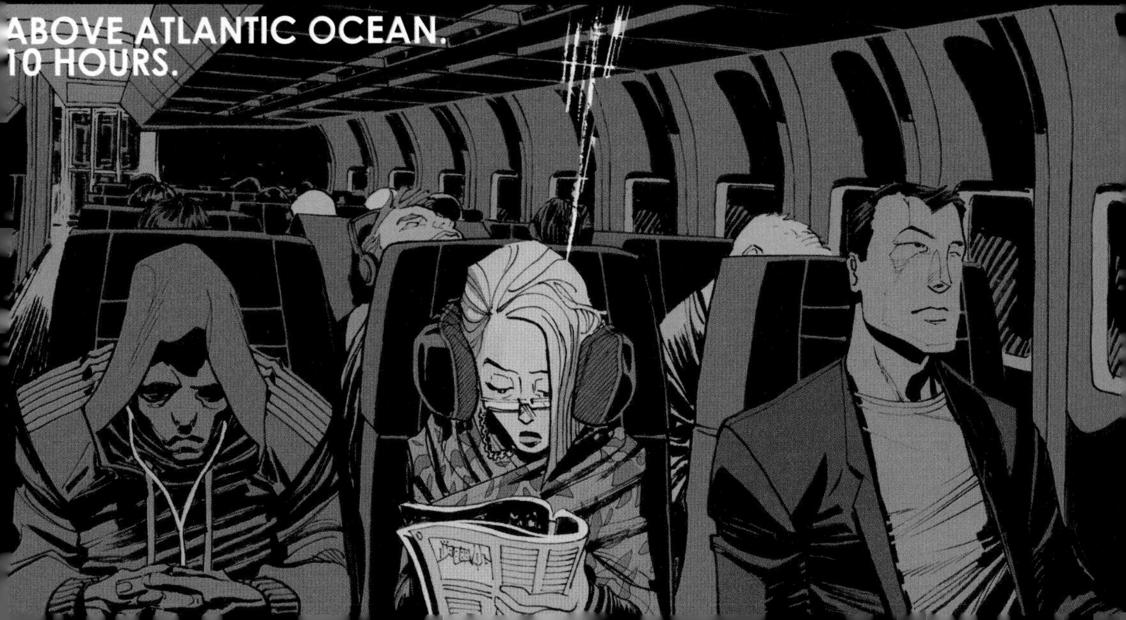
ABOVE ATLANTIC OCEAN.
10 HOURS.

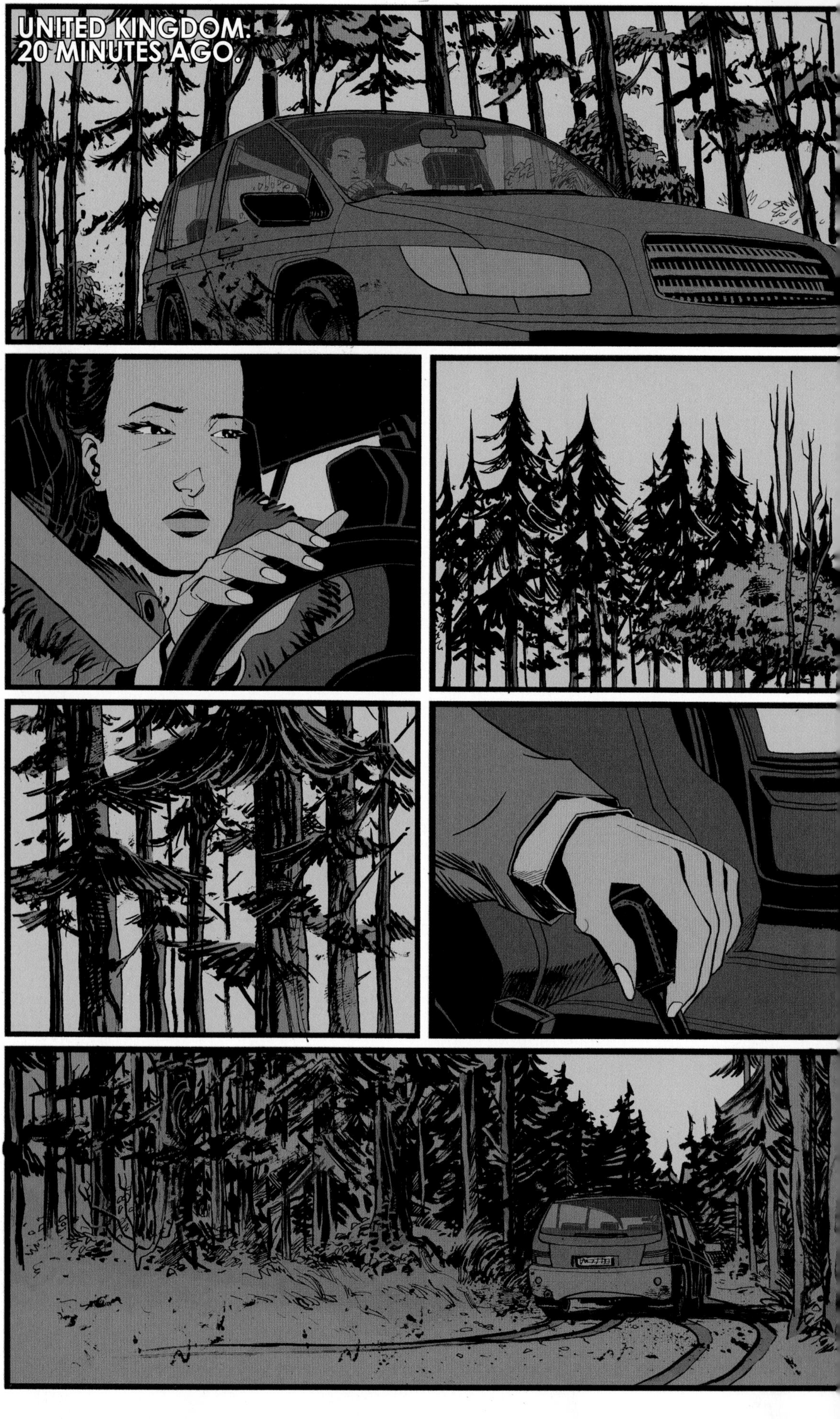
UNITED KINGDOM.
20 MINUTES AGO.

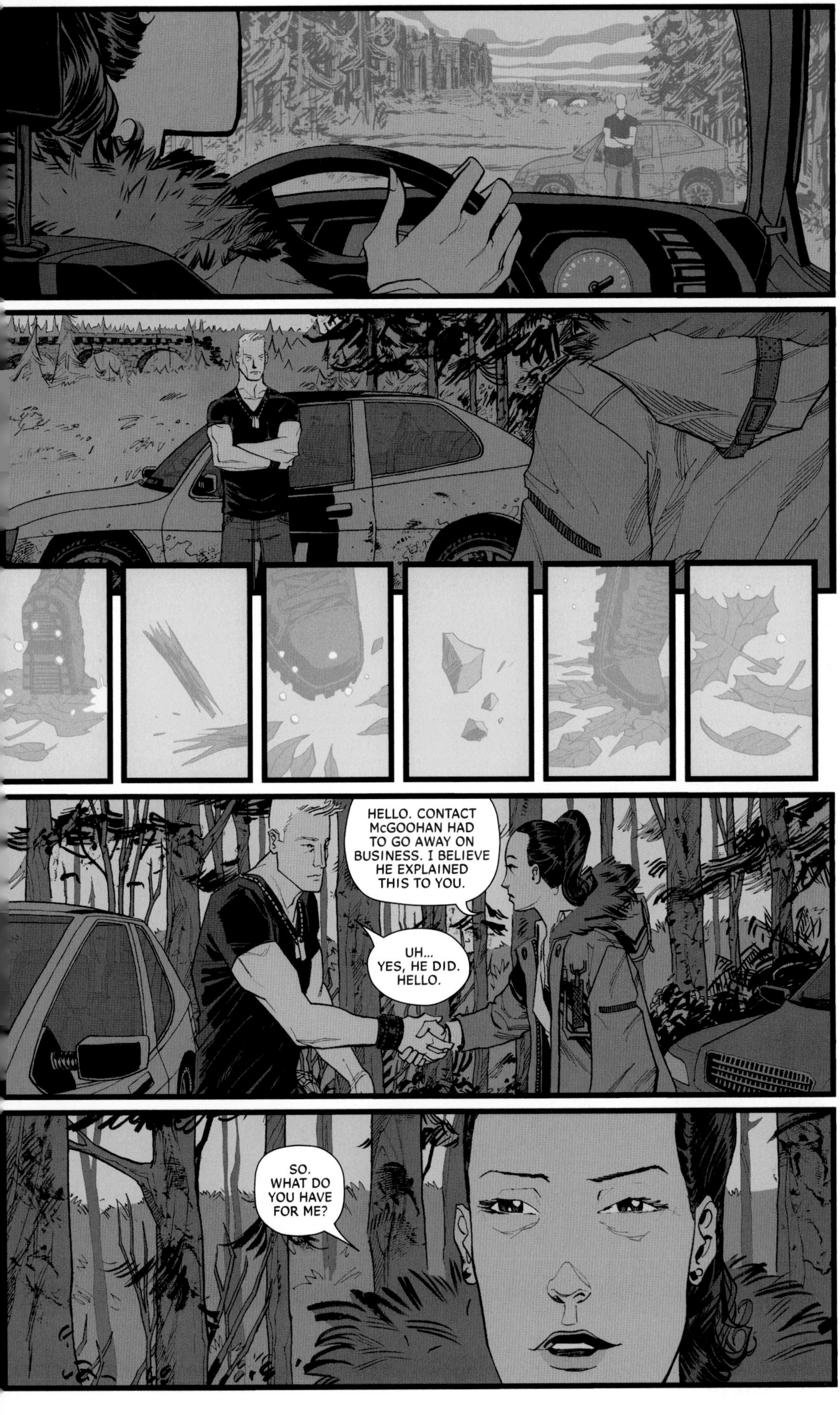
HELLO. CONTACT McGOOHAN HAD TO GO AWAY ON BUSINESS. I BELIEVE HE EXPLAINED THIS TO YOU.
UH... YES, HE DID. HELLO.
SO. WHAT DO YOU HAVE FOR ME?

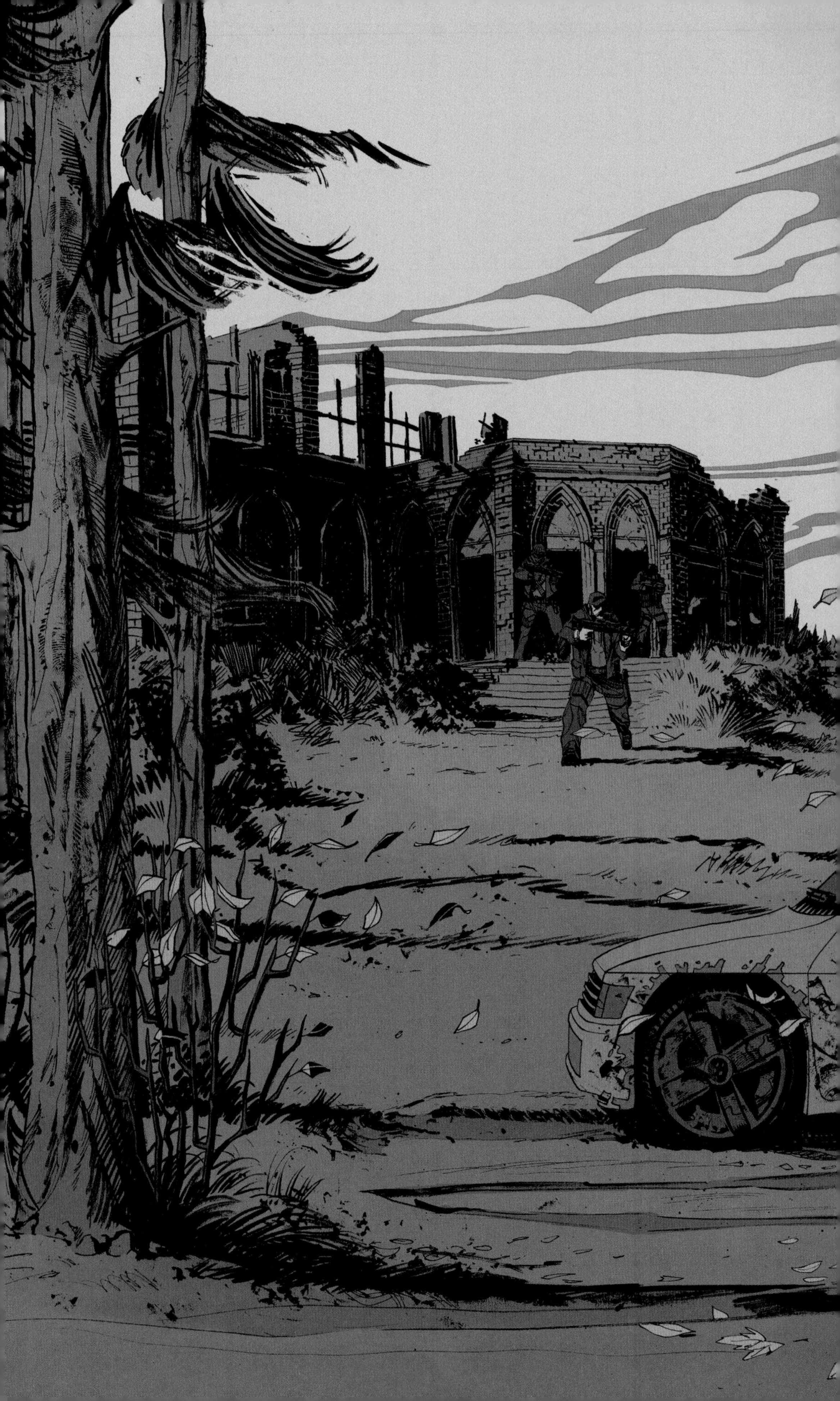

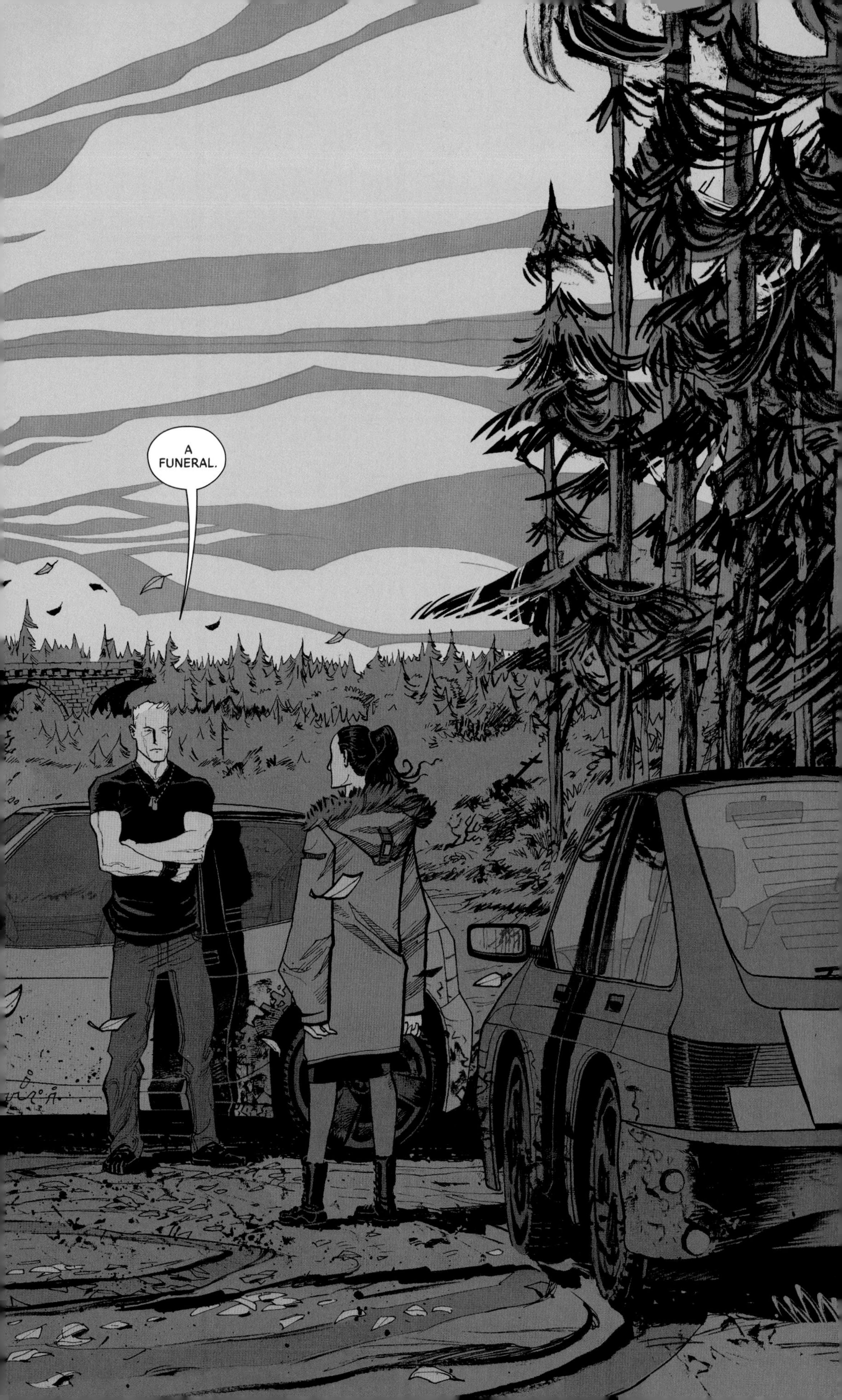
A FUNERAL.

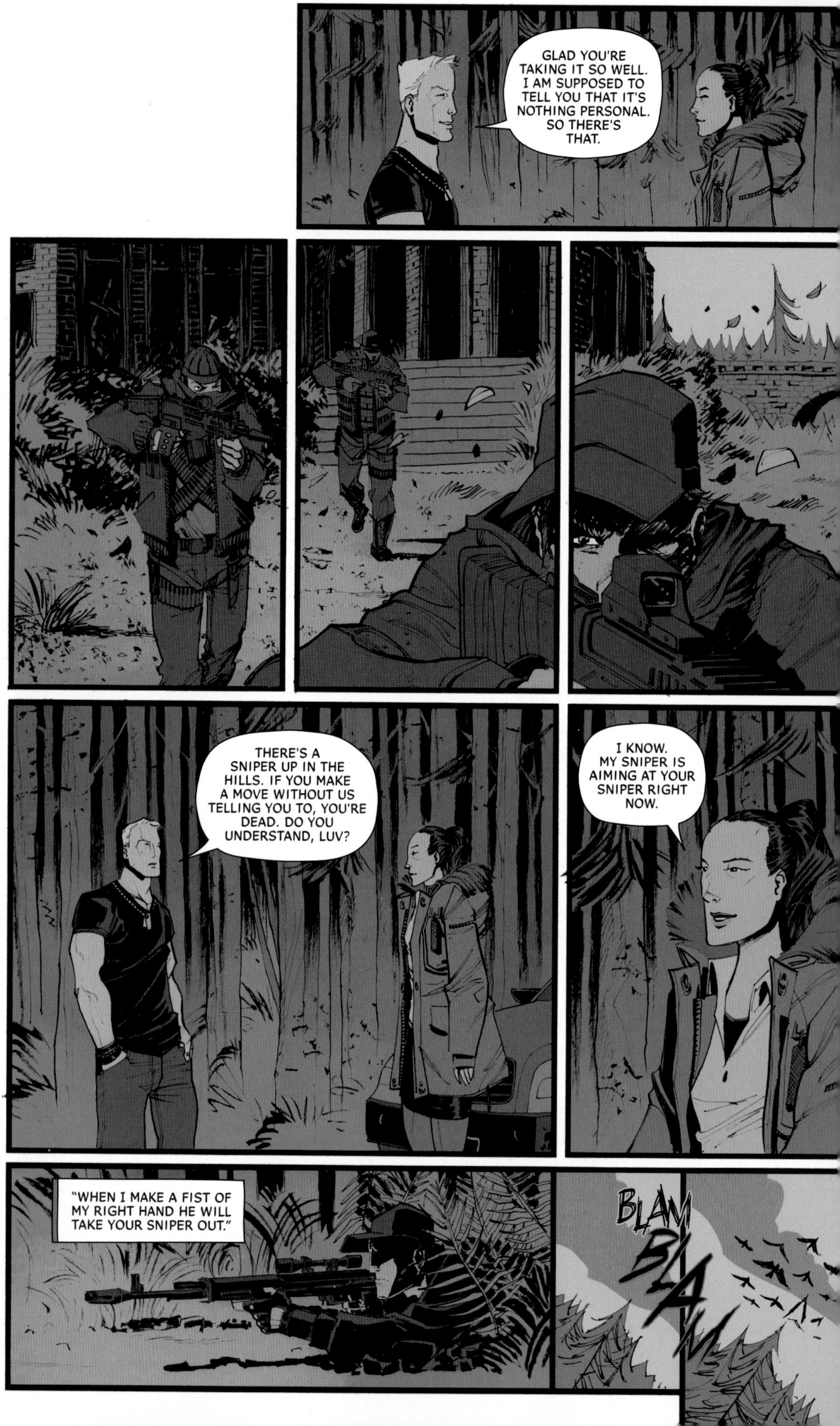
GLAD YOU'RE TAKING IT SO WELL. I AM SUPPOSED TO TELL YOU THAT IT'S NOTHING PERSONAL. SO THERE'S THAT.
THERE'S A SNIPER UP IN THE HILLS. IF YOU MAKE A MOVE WITHOUT US TELLING YOU TO, YOU'RE DEAD. DO YOU UNDERSTAND, LUV?
I KNOW. MY SNIPER IS AIMING AT YOUR SNIPER RIGHT NOW.
"WHEN I MAKE A FIST OF MY RIGHT HAND HE WILL TAKE YOUR SNIPER OUT."
BLAM
BLAM

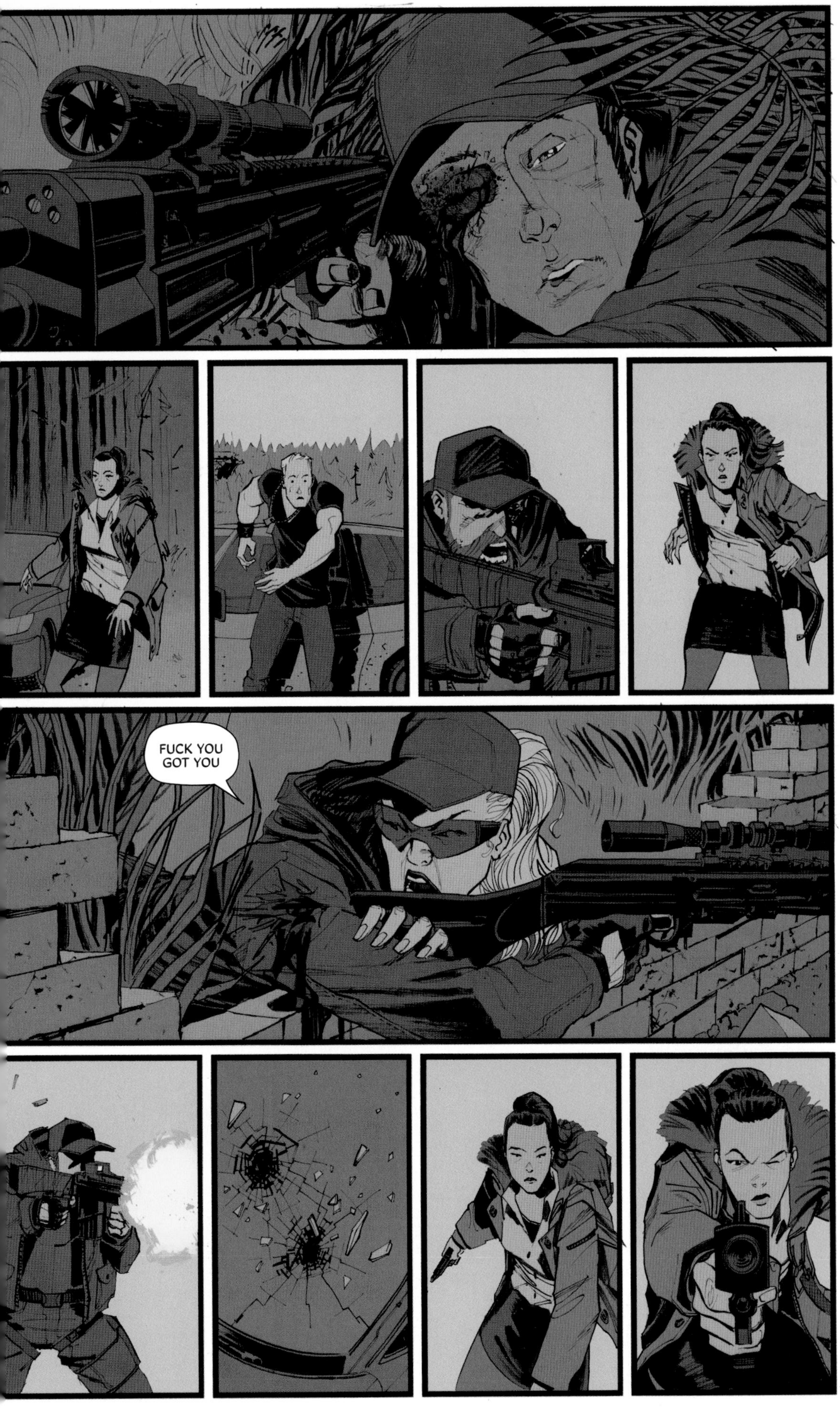
FUCK YOU
GOT YOU

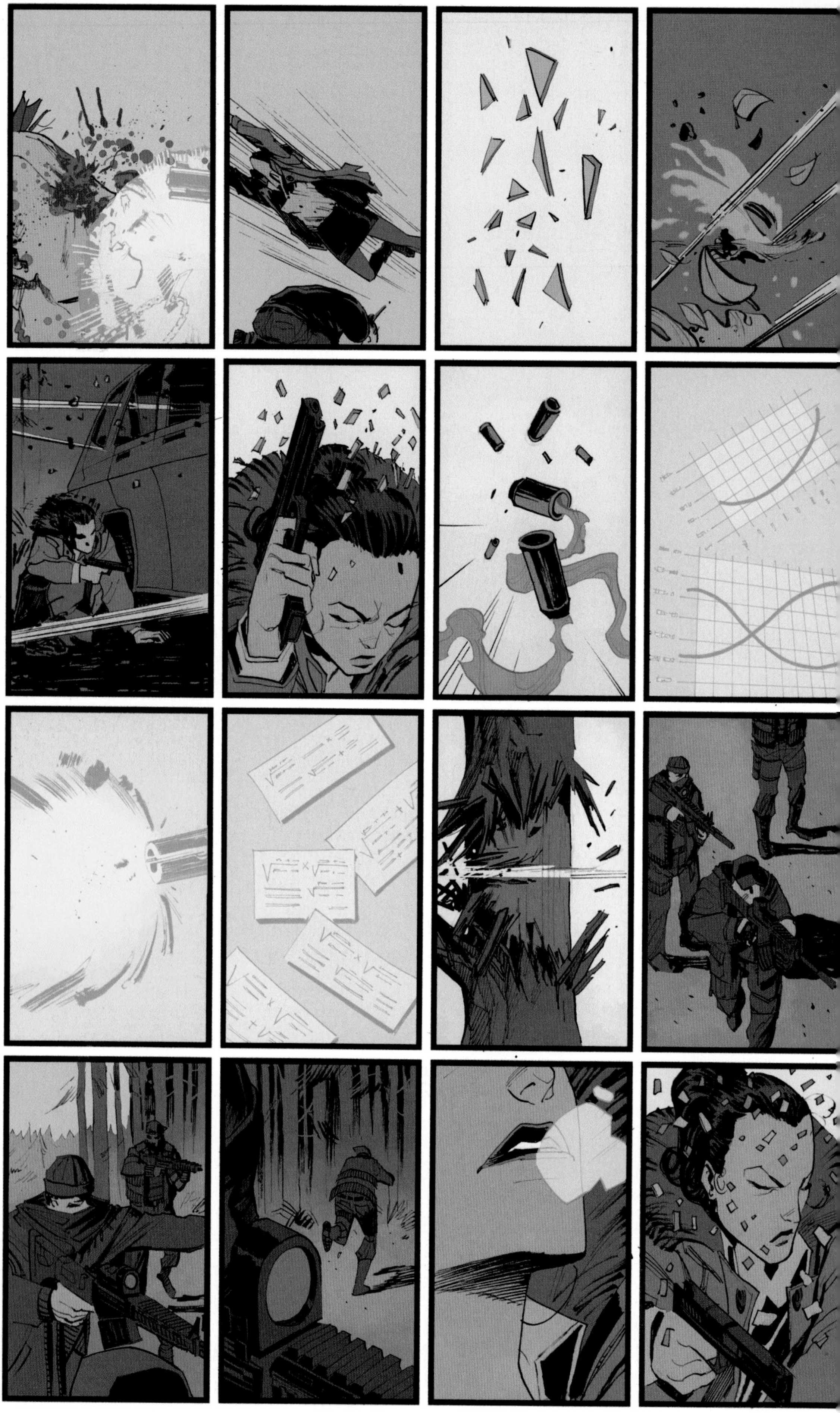

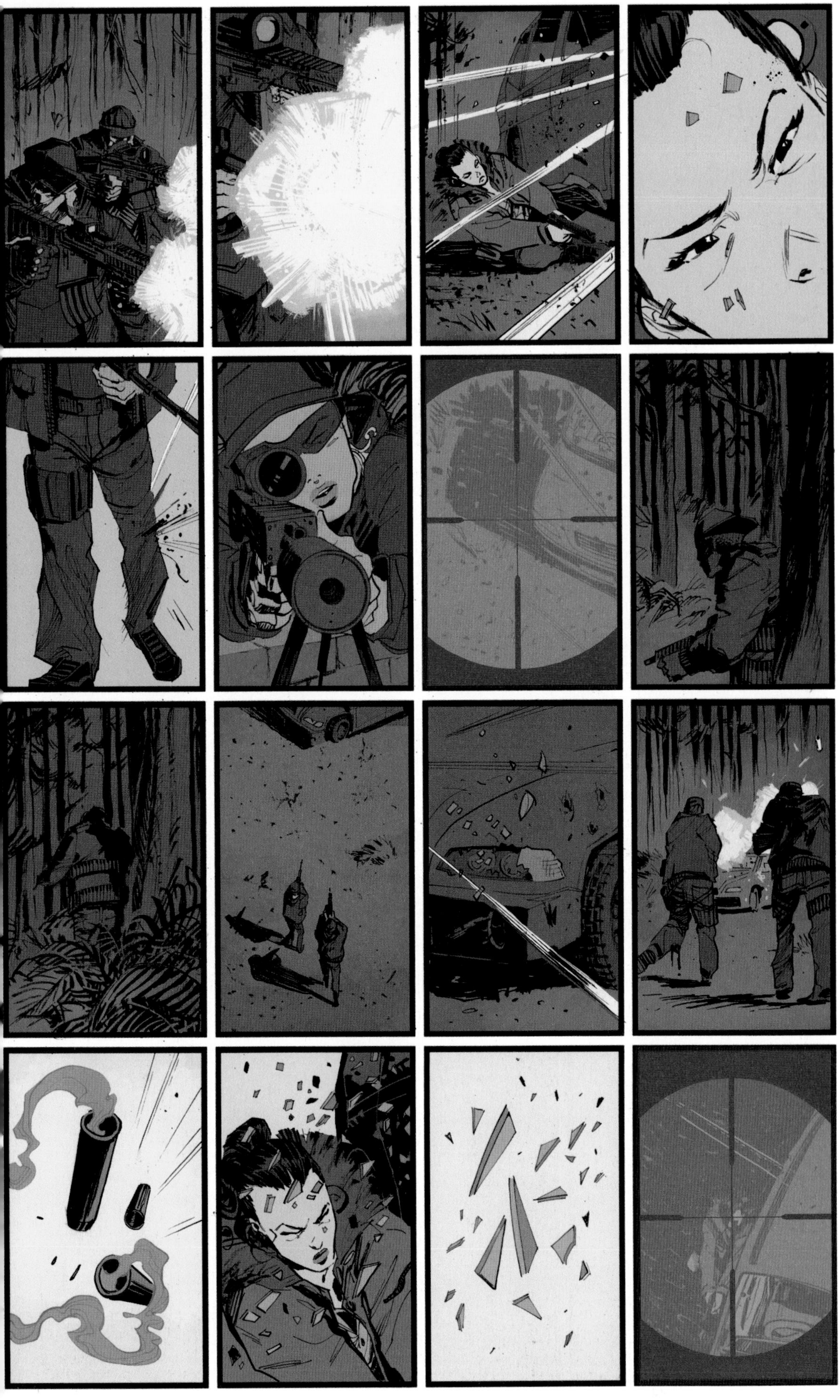

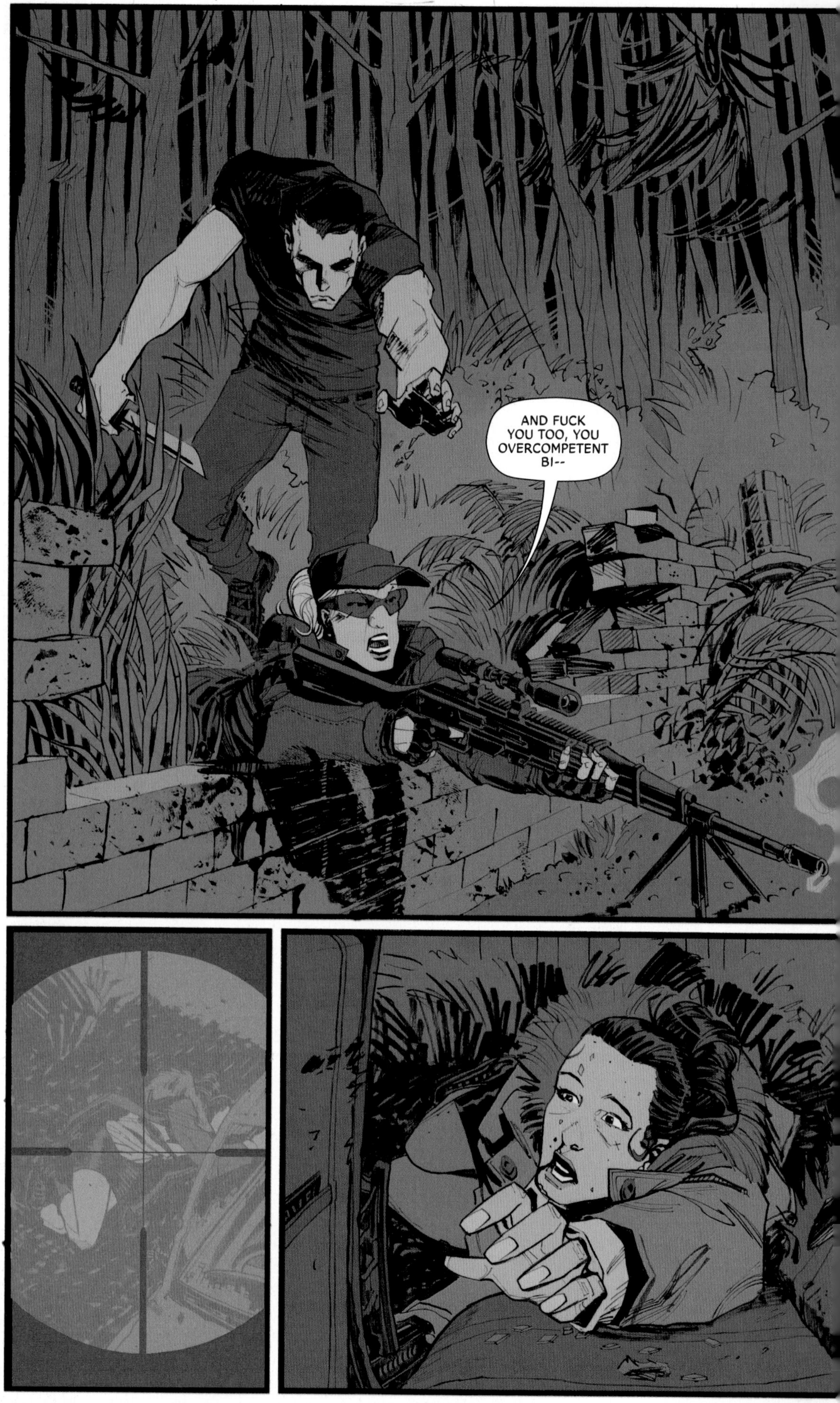
AND FUCK YOU TOO, YOU OVERCOMPETENT BI--

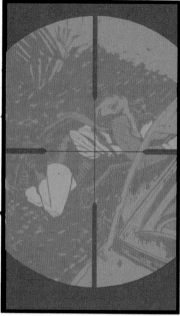

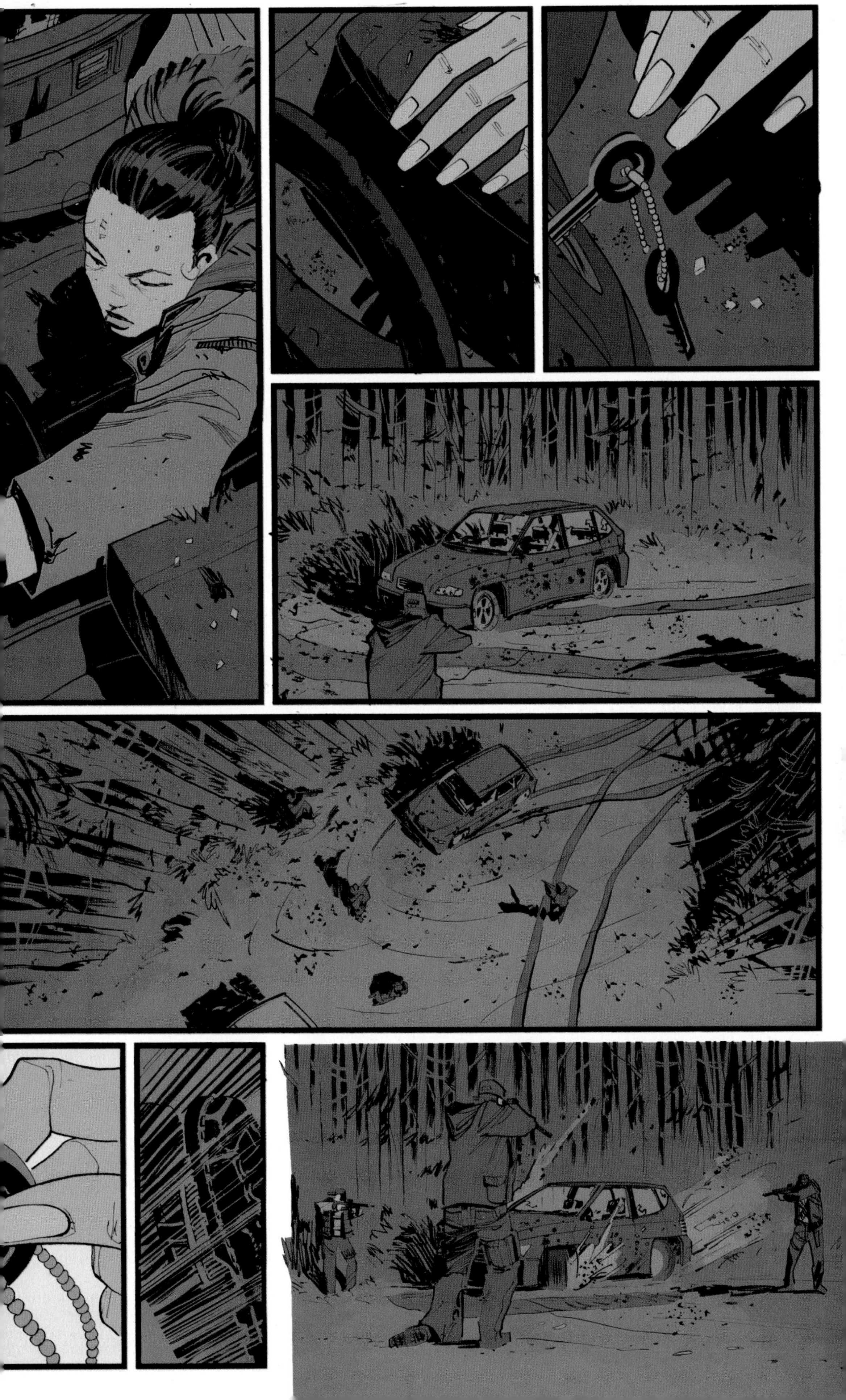

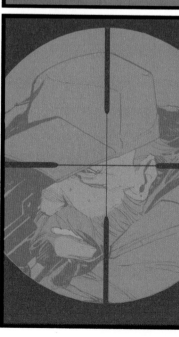

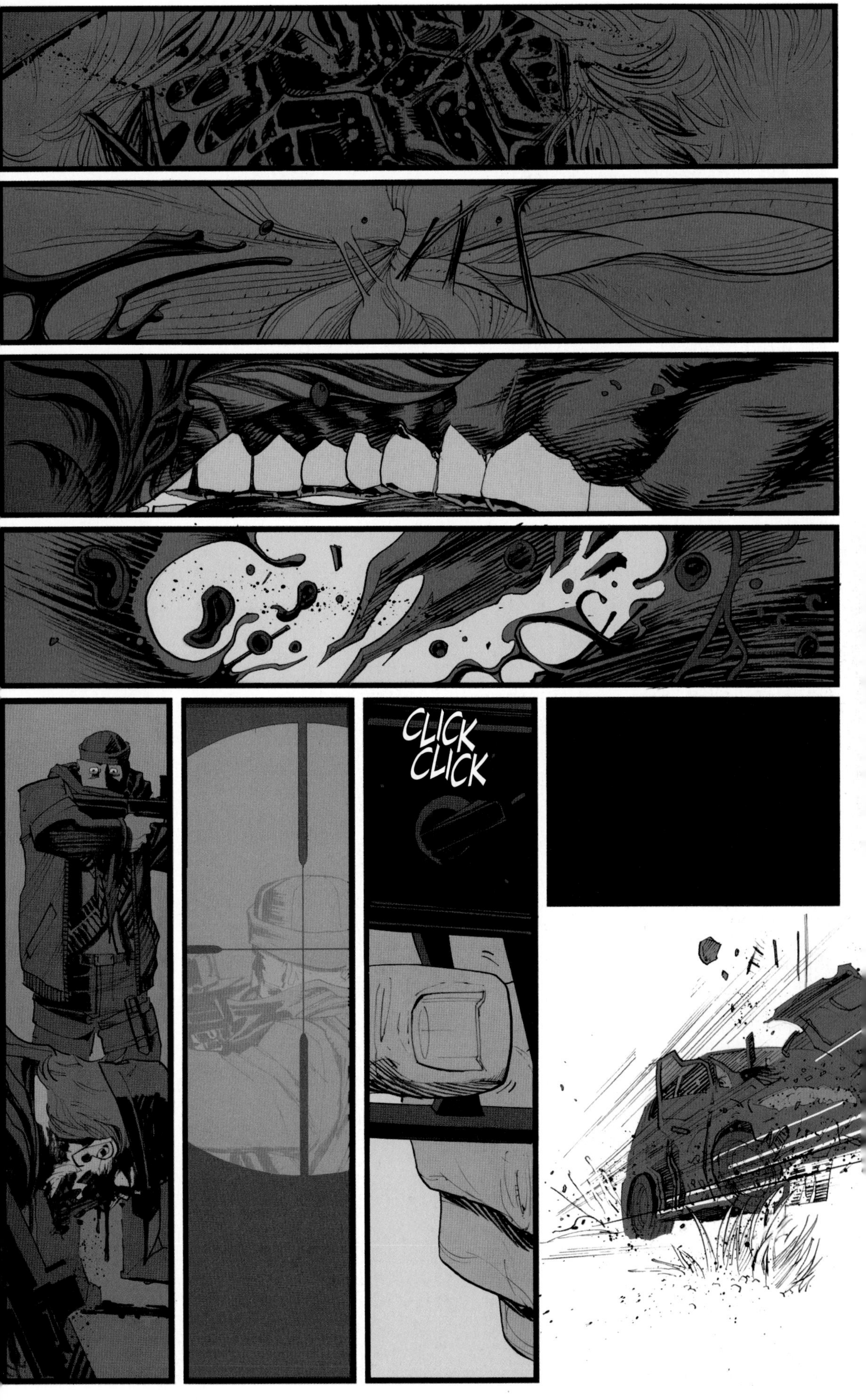
CLICK
CLICK

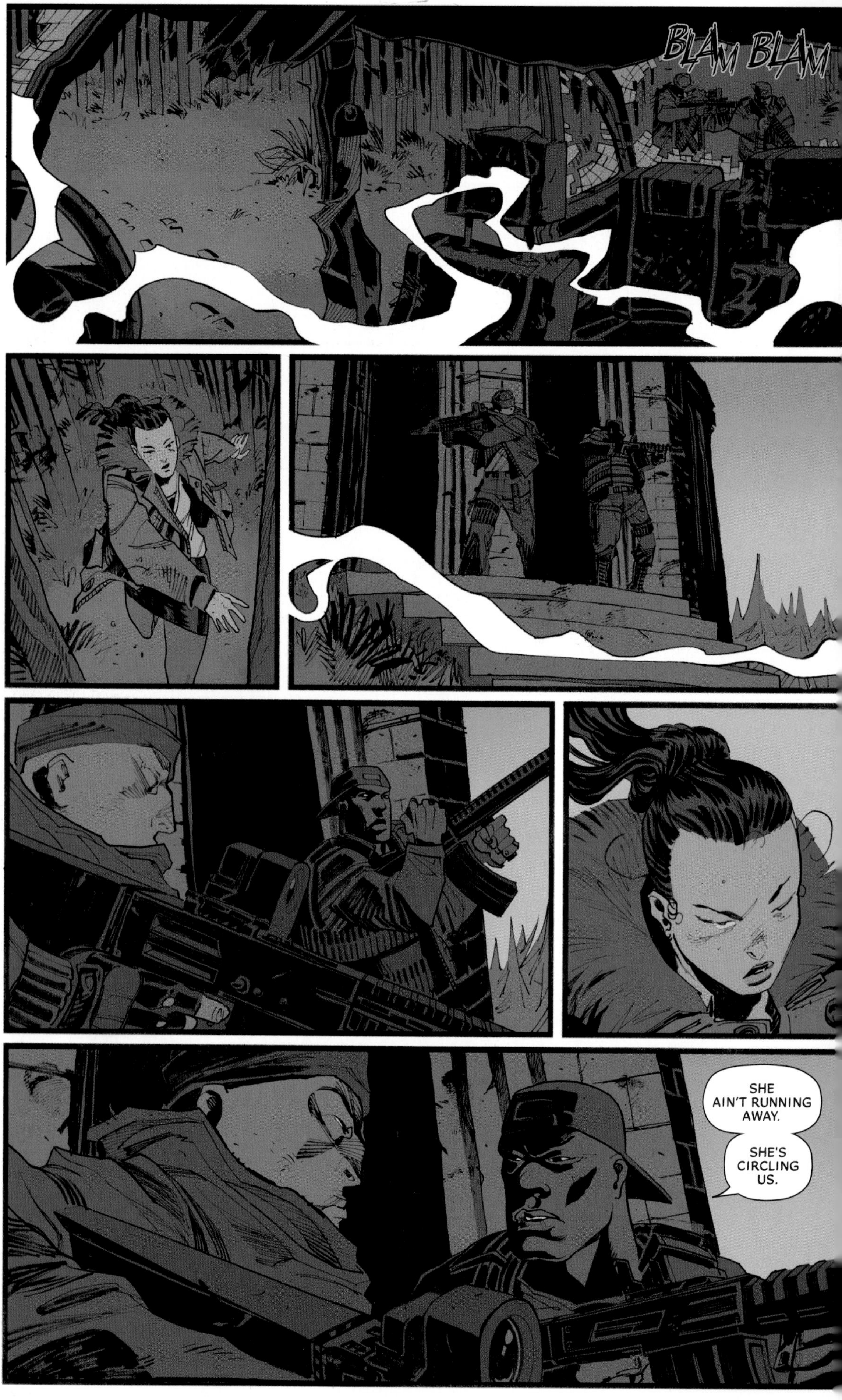
BLAM BLAM
SHE AIN'T RUNNING AWAY.
SHE'S CIRCLING US.

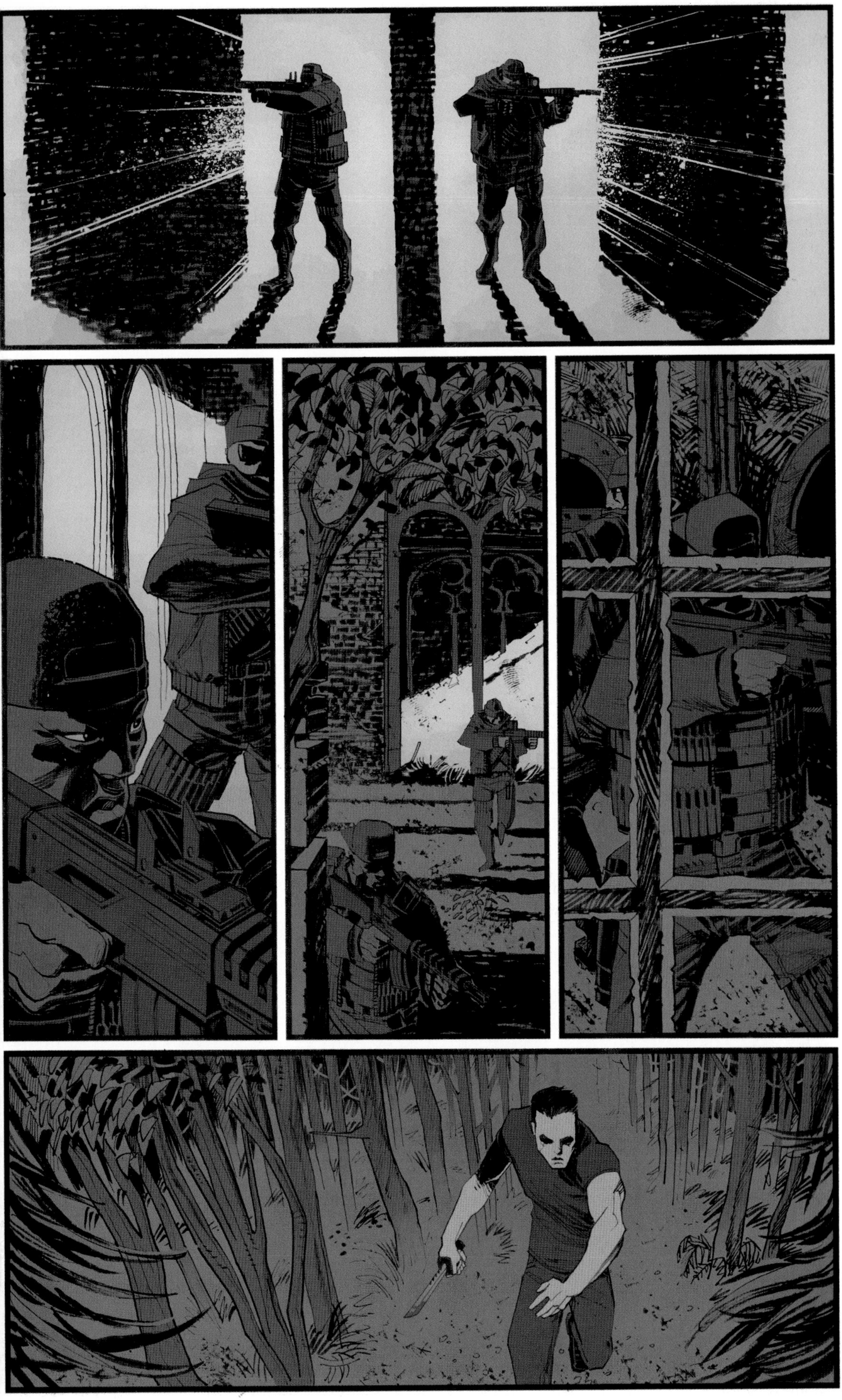

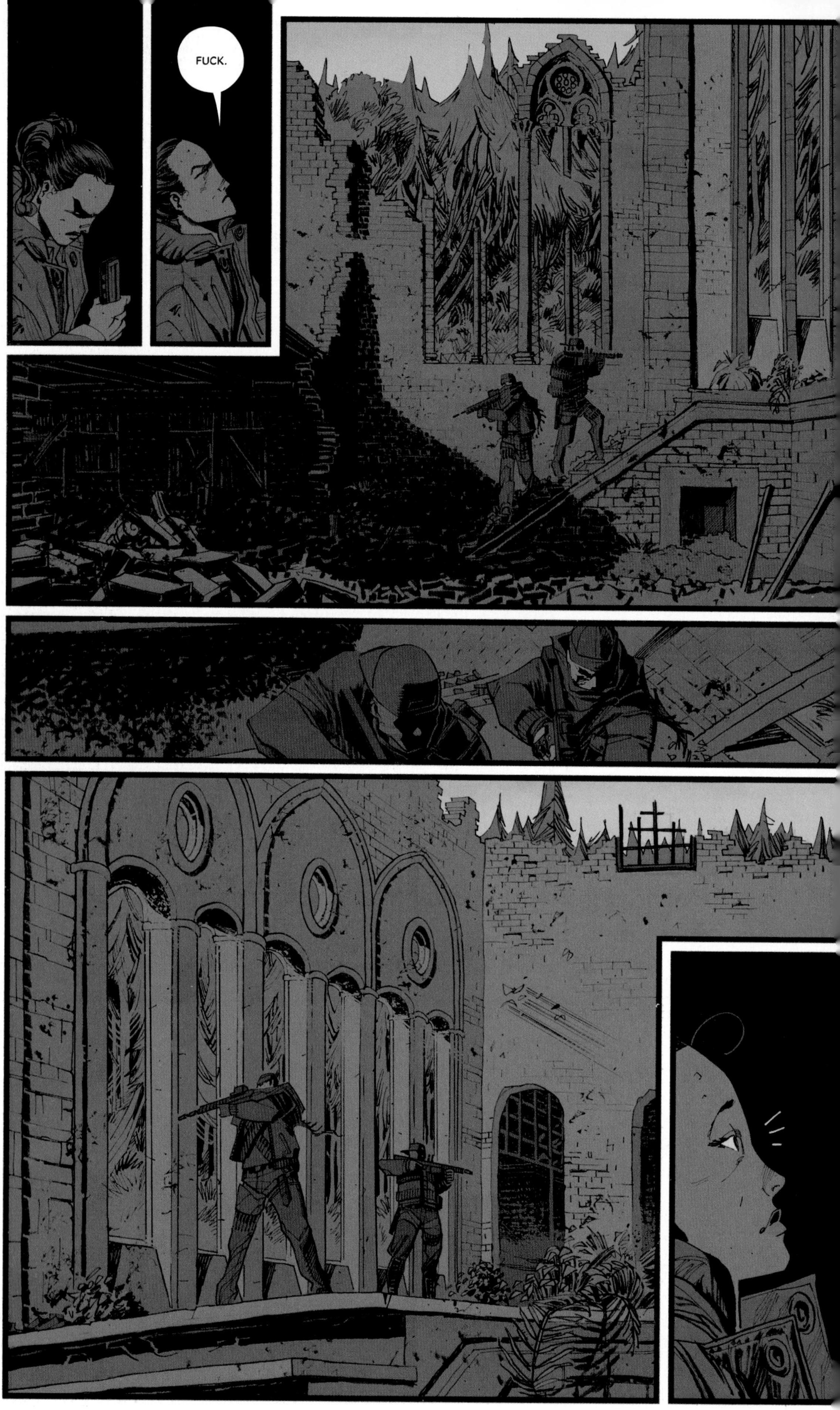
FUCK.

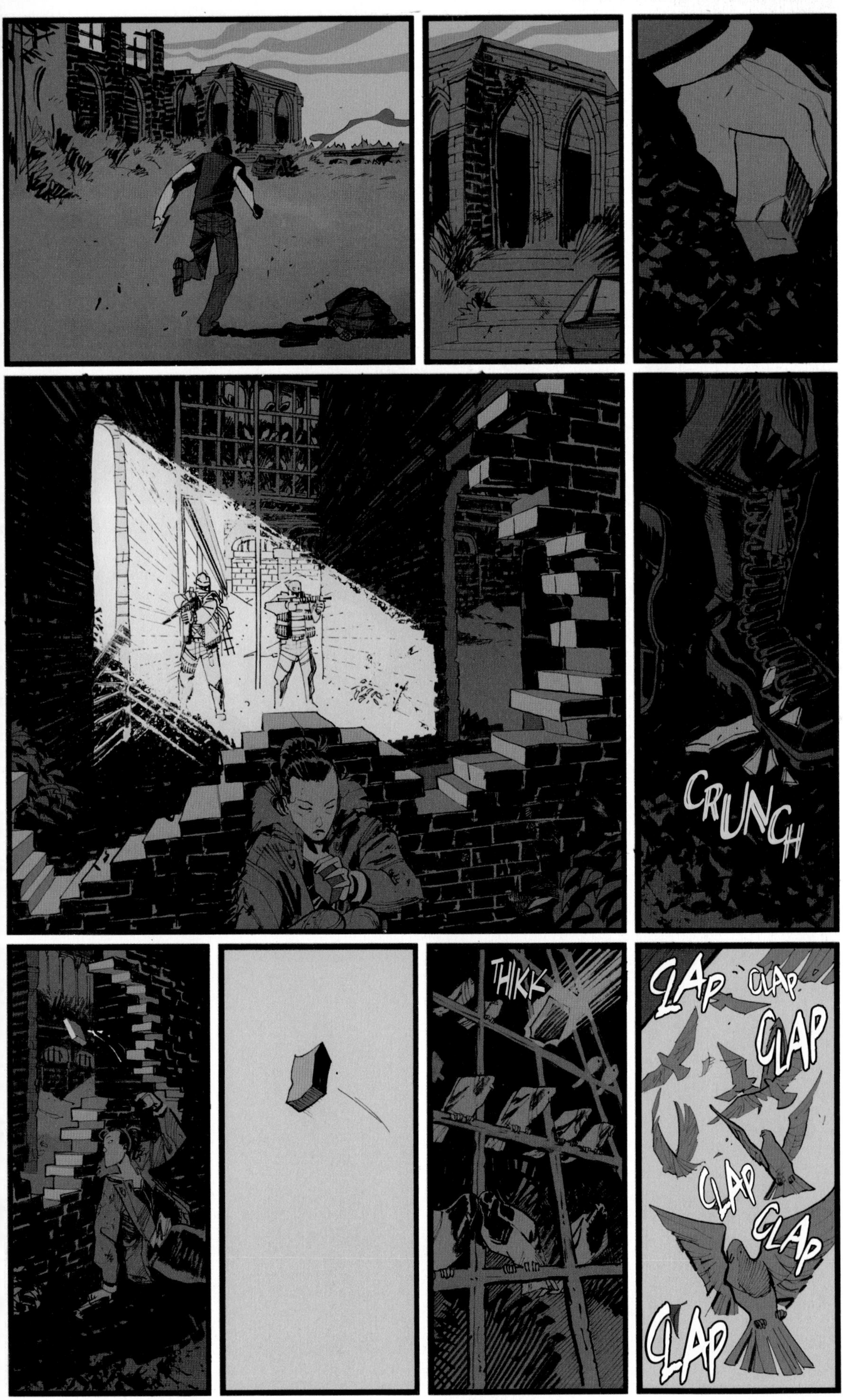
CRUNCH
THIKK
CLAP
CLAP
CLAP
CLAP
CLAP
CLAP

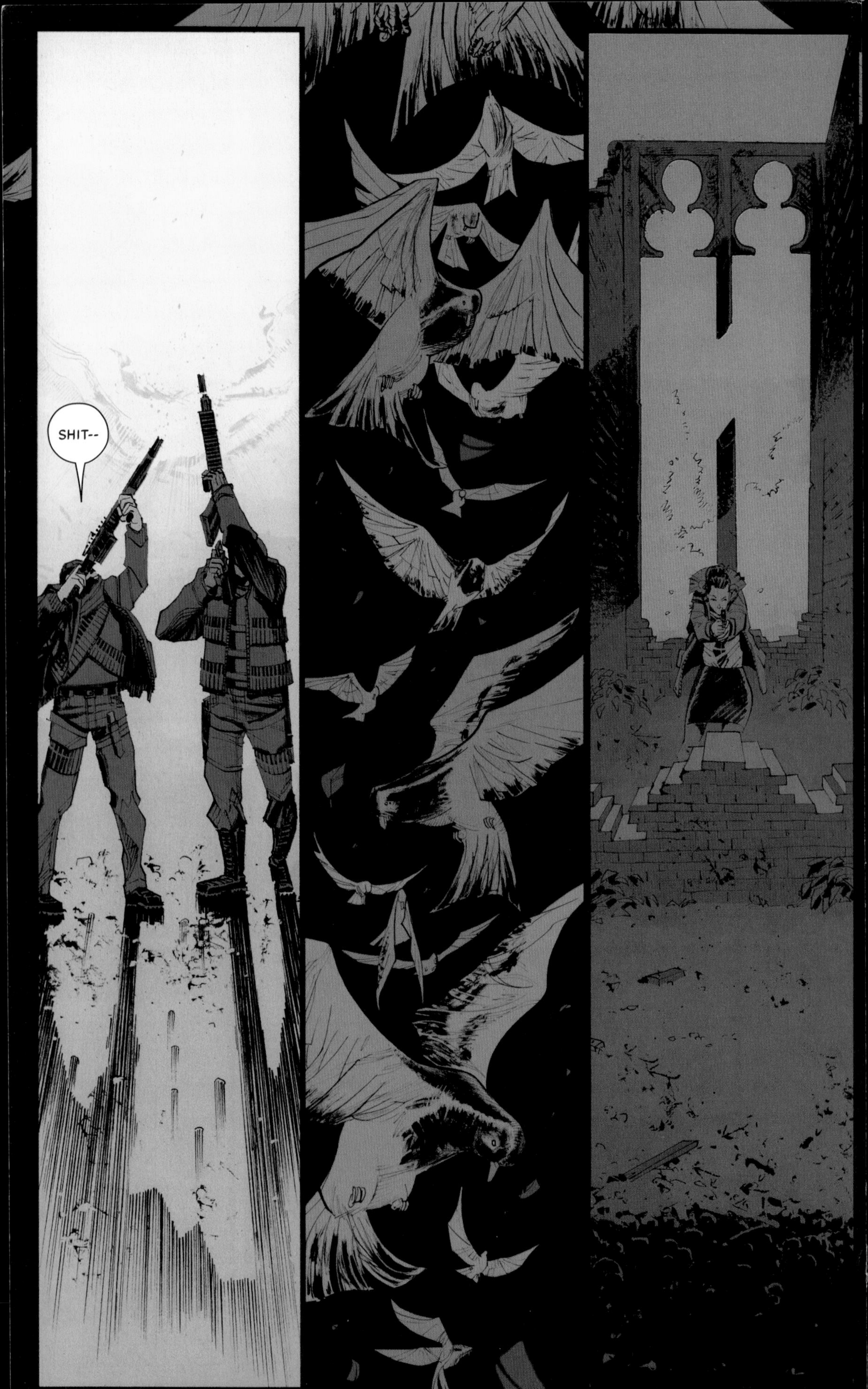
SHIT--

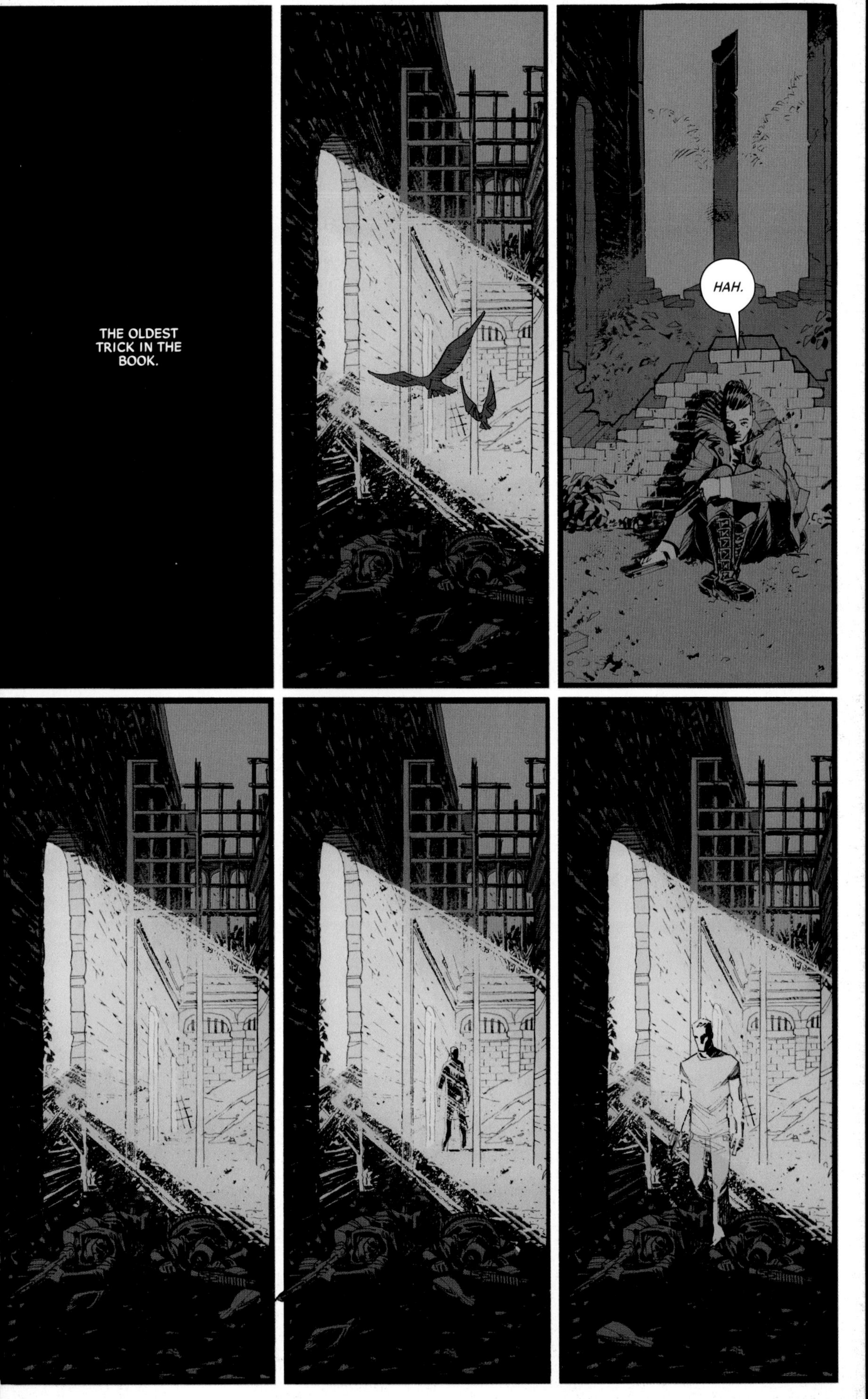
THE OLDEST TRICK IN THE BOOK.
HAH.

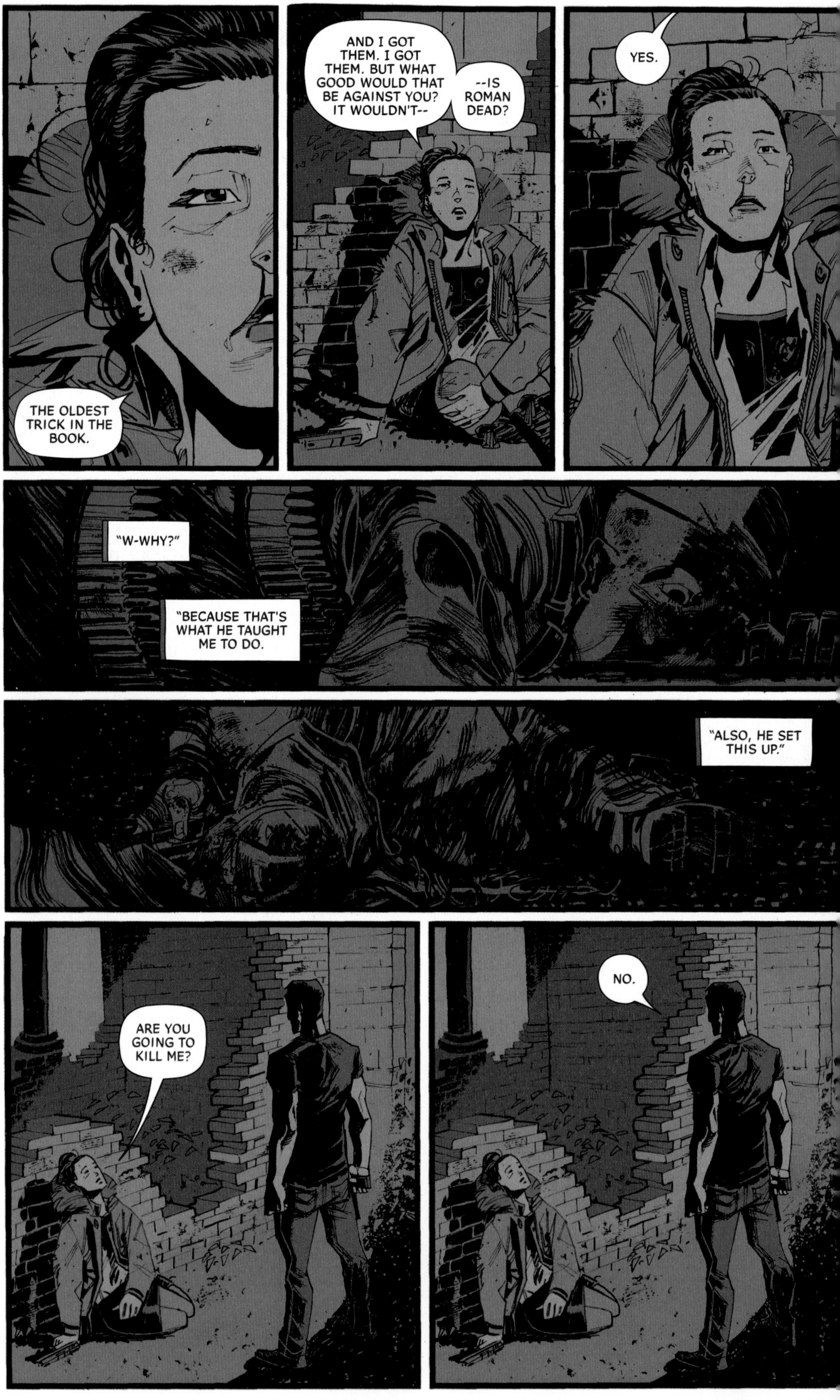
THE OLDEST TRICK IN THE BOOK.
AND I GOT THEM. I GOT THEM. BUT WHAT GOOD WOULD THAT BE AGAINST YOU? IT WOULDN'T--
--IS ROMAN DEAD?
YES.
"W-WHY?"
"BECAUSE THAT'S WHAT HE TAUGHT ME TO DO.
"ALSO, HE SET THIS UP."
ARE YOU GOING TO KILL ME?
NO.

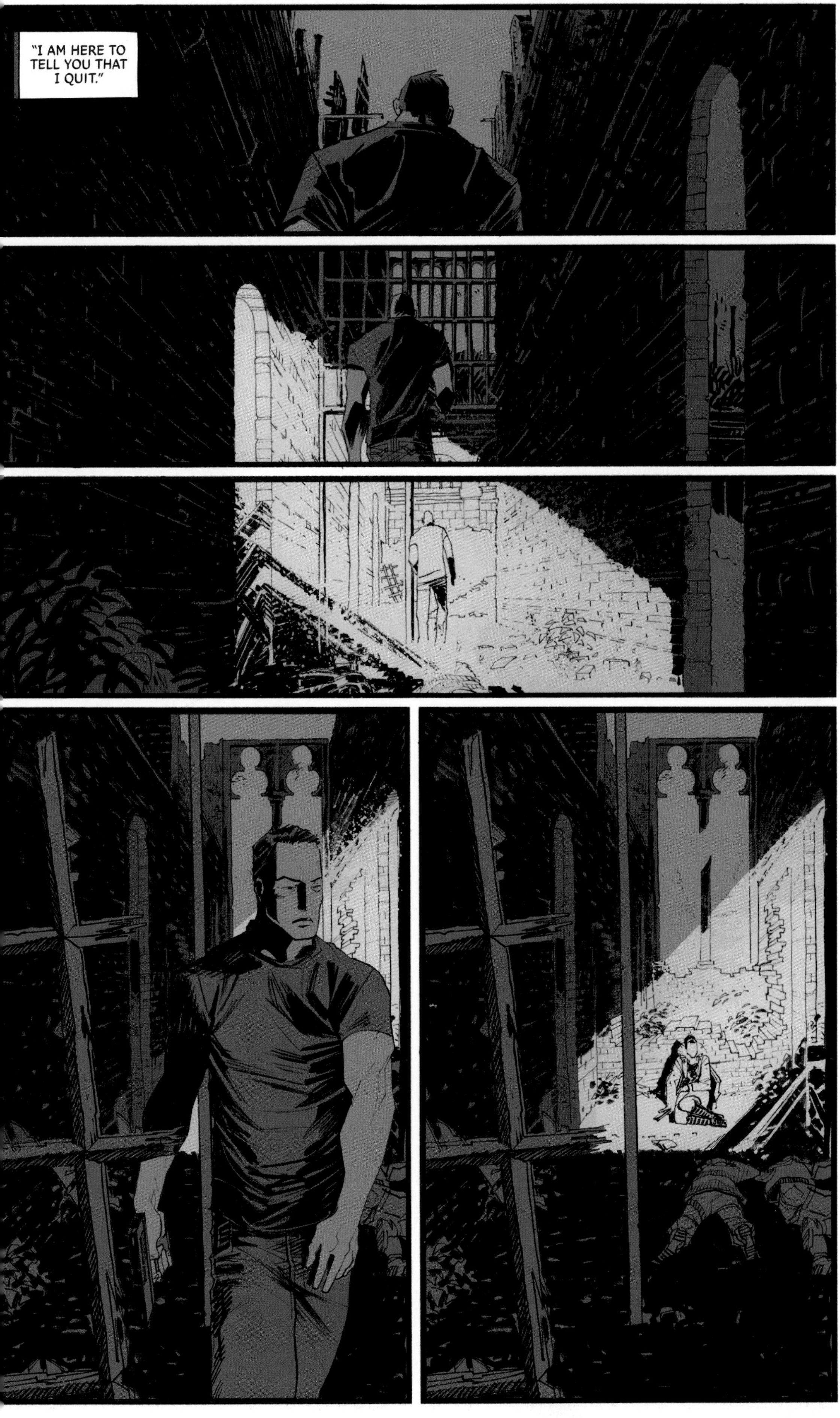
"I AM HERE TO TELL YOU THAT I QUIT."

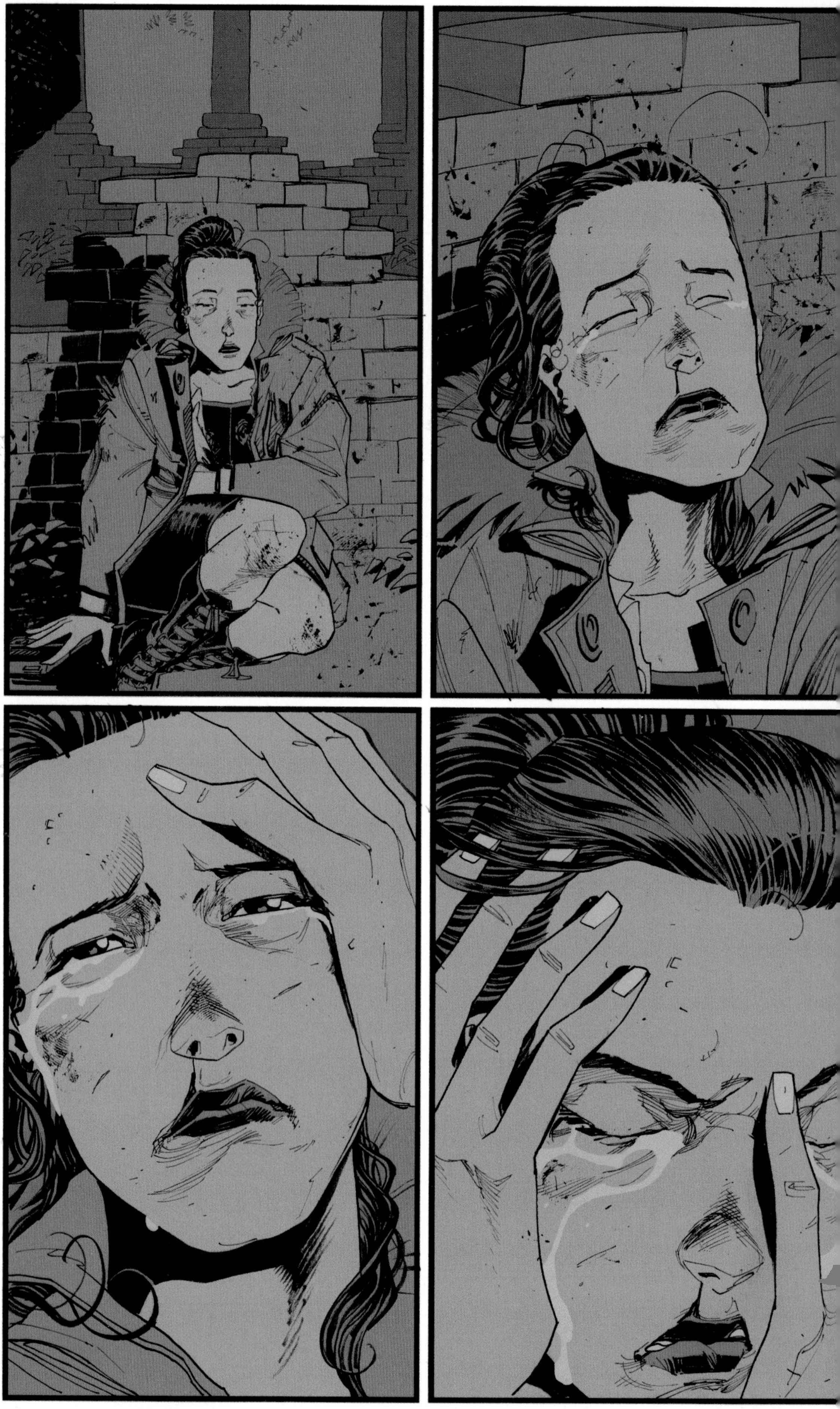

CHAPTER 8: SHAME AS THE INCITING FACTOR OF VIOLENCE.

INTERROGATION OF SARA COOKE, 18 HOURS AFTER THE INCIDENT
"SHADOW LINE"

1 COX: WHO SENT YOU ON THIS MISSION?

2 COOKE: AGENT ZIZEK.

3 COX: AND AGENT ZIZEK IS CURRENTLY...?

4 COOKE: MISSING AND PRESUMED DEAD. YOU KNOW THAT. I TOLD YOU THAT ALREADY.

5 COX: I UNDERSTAND THIS IS HARD. STILL. AVOID FURTHER COMMENTS. ANSWER SIMPLY AND TO THE POINT.

6 COOKE: YES, SIR.

7 COX: WHAT WAS THE PURPOSE OF THE MISSION?

8 COOKE: THE PURPOSE OF THE MISSION WAS TO MEET AGENT ZIZEK'S SOURCE, CODENAME "BODIE", WHO AGENT ZIZEK WORKED WITH, UTILIZING THE CODENAME "MCGOOHAN."

9 COX: WOULD YOU SAY THAT IT'S POSSIBLE AGENT ZIZEK'S SOURCE WAS IN FACT A HIRED KILLER?

10 COOKE: NO. "BODIE" WAS GENUINELY DISTURBED BY THE TRAP AND ATTEMPTED TO FLEE.

11 COX: AT WHICH POINT HE ACCIDENTALLY CAUGHT A BULLET.

12 COOKE: PRECISELY.

13 COX: DO YOU HAVE ANY KNOWLEDGE OF THE WHEREABOUTS OF AGENT EDWARD ZERO?

14 COOKE: I KNOW THAT HE WENT TO MEXICO WITH AGENT ZIZEK.

15 COX: AGENT ZERO IS ALSO CURRENTLY UNAVAILABLE.

16 COX: IS THERE ANYTHING YOU WOULD LIKE TO ADD?

17 COOKE: NO.

18 COX: IS IT TRUE YOU AND AGENT ZIZEK WERE HAVING AN AFFAIR?

19 COOKE: YES.

20 COX: WOULD YOU SAY THAT THIS AFFAIR HAD, AT ANY POINT, CLOUDED YOUR JUDGEMENT?

21 COOKE: ABSOLUTELY NOT.

22 COX: NO?

23 COOKE: NO. WE JUST FUCKED. THAT IS ALL IT WAS.

INTERROGATION OF SARA COOKE, 18 HOURS AFTER THE INCIDENT
"SHADOW LINE"

24 COX: ARE YOU AWARE OF THE IDENTITY OF THE PERSON WHO KILLED THE ENEMY SNIPER?

25 COOKE: I THOUGHT AGENT THOMPSON WAS RESPONSIBLE. HOW DID IT--

26 COX: ...SIMPLE ANSWERS. TO THE POINT, PLEASE. NO QUESTIONS.

27 COOKE: I APOLOGIZE.

28 COX: ARE YOU AWARE OF THE EXTRA SET OF BOOTS ON THE GROUND DURING YOUR FAILED OPERATION?

29 COOKE: I DON'T UNDERSTAND THE QUESTION.

30 COX: ARE YOU AWARE THAT SOMEONE BESIDES THE NOW DECEASED AGENT THOMPSON WAS...HOW TO PUT IT BLUNTLY...THAT SOMEONE THERE, ON THE GROUND, SAVED YOUR DUMB ASS, DIRECTOR COOKE?

31 COOKE: I AM NOT AWARE OF ANY SUCH PERSON, SIR.

32 COX: DO YOU UNDERSTAND THAT THERE WILL BE AN INQUIRY?

33 COOKE: I DO, SIR.

34 COX: DO YOU HAVE ANYTHING ELSE TO ADD?

35 COOKE: I DO NOT.

---

1.   Director Cooke, while clearly shaken by the events, seems to be telling the truth, however shakily. That said, we will have to examine everything further, as certain elements of the case point in the direction of her deeper involvement.

2.   Roman Zizek's body is being examined locally by our trusted operators. The wild fauna of the area did not leave us much to inspect, but it is clear that he died of a single gunshot wound in the neck area.

3.   Agent Zero is presumed missing at this time. Director Cooke suggested he could be either directly involved in the murder of Roman Zizek, or kidnapped and tortured so information about the Agency can be extracted. Cooke believes in the second version, but does not discount the first one, perhaps because she is smart enough to understand that pushing the second version too hard could point at her and Zero's involvement in Zizek's death.

4.   In light of recent events, I recommend Director Sara Cooke to be placed under surveillance. While there is no proof of her direct involvement in the events surrounding Roman Zizek's demise and Edward Zero's disappearance, we need to keep an eye on her.

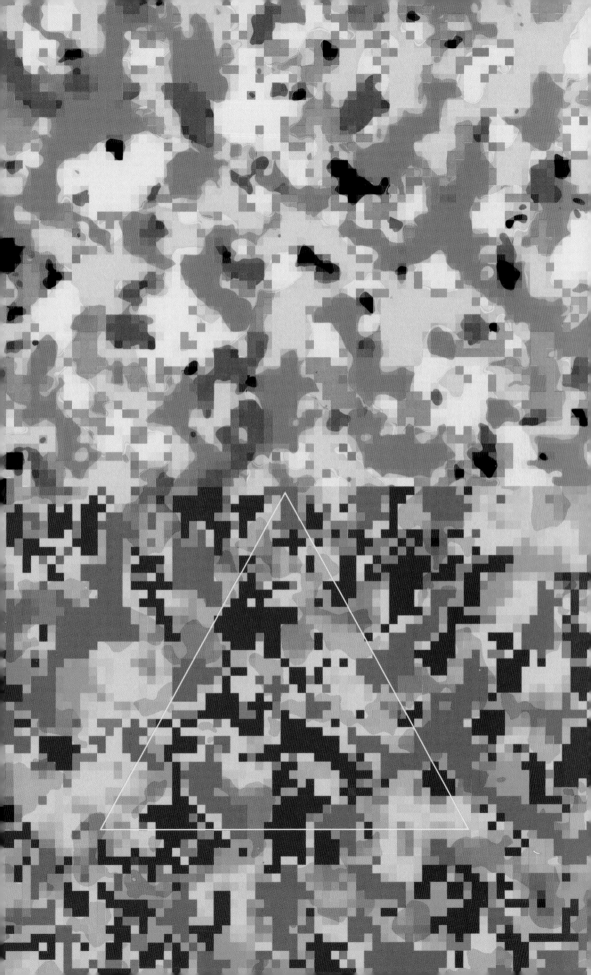

CHAPTER 9

MARINA
Illustrated by Tonči Zonjić

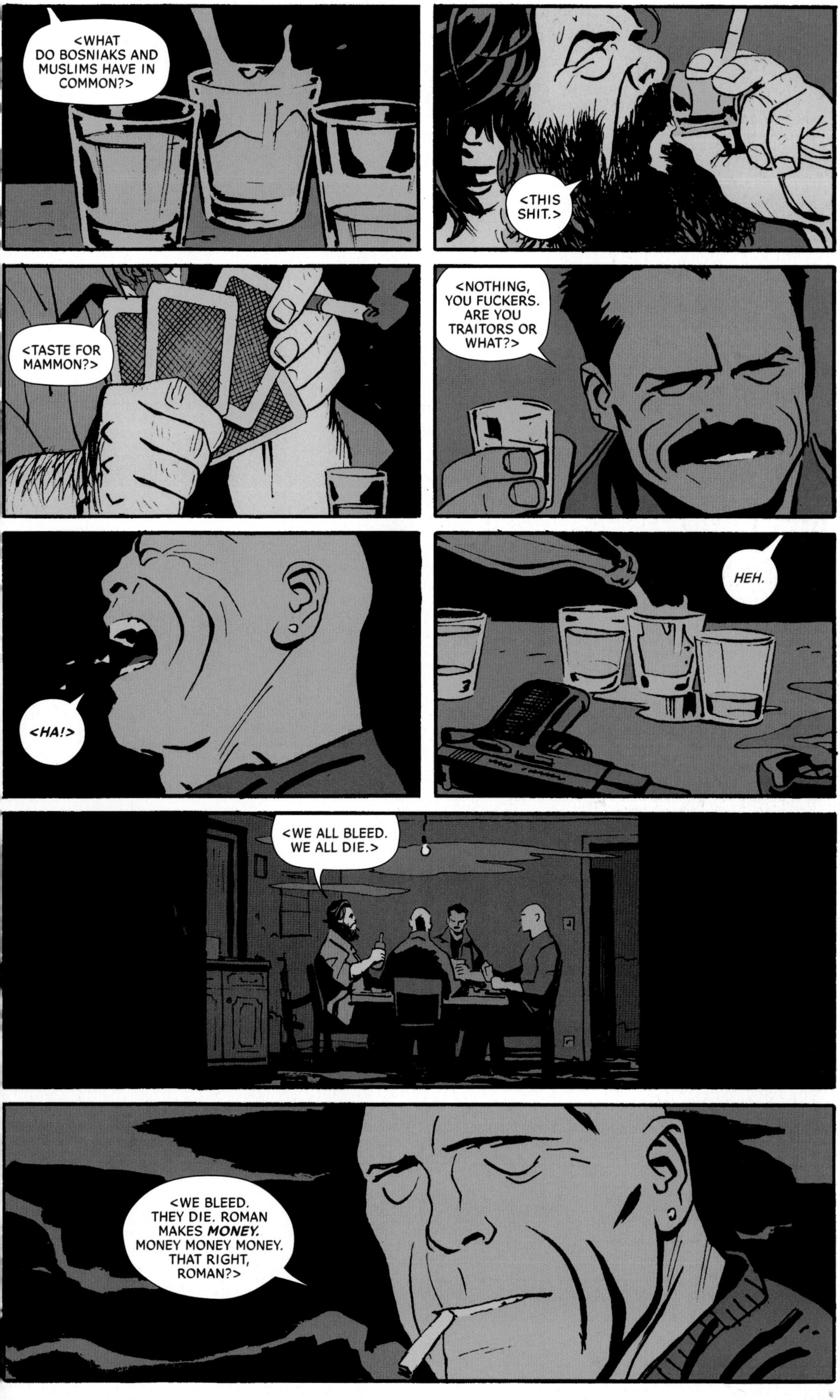
<WHAT DO BOSNIAKS AND MUSLIMS HAVE IN COMMON?>
<THIS SHIT.>
<TASTE FOR MAMMON?>
<NOTHING, YOU FUCKERS. ARE YOU TRAITORS OR WHAT?>
<HA!>
HEH.
<WE ALL BLEED. WE ALL DIE.>
<WE BLEED. THEY DIE. ROMAN MAKES MONEY. MONEY MONEY MONEY. THAT RIGHT, ROMAN?>

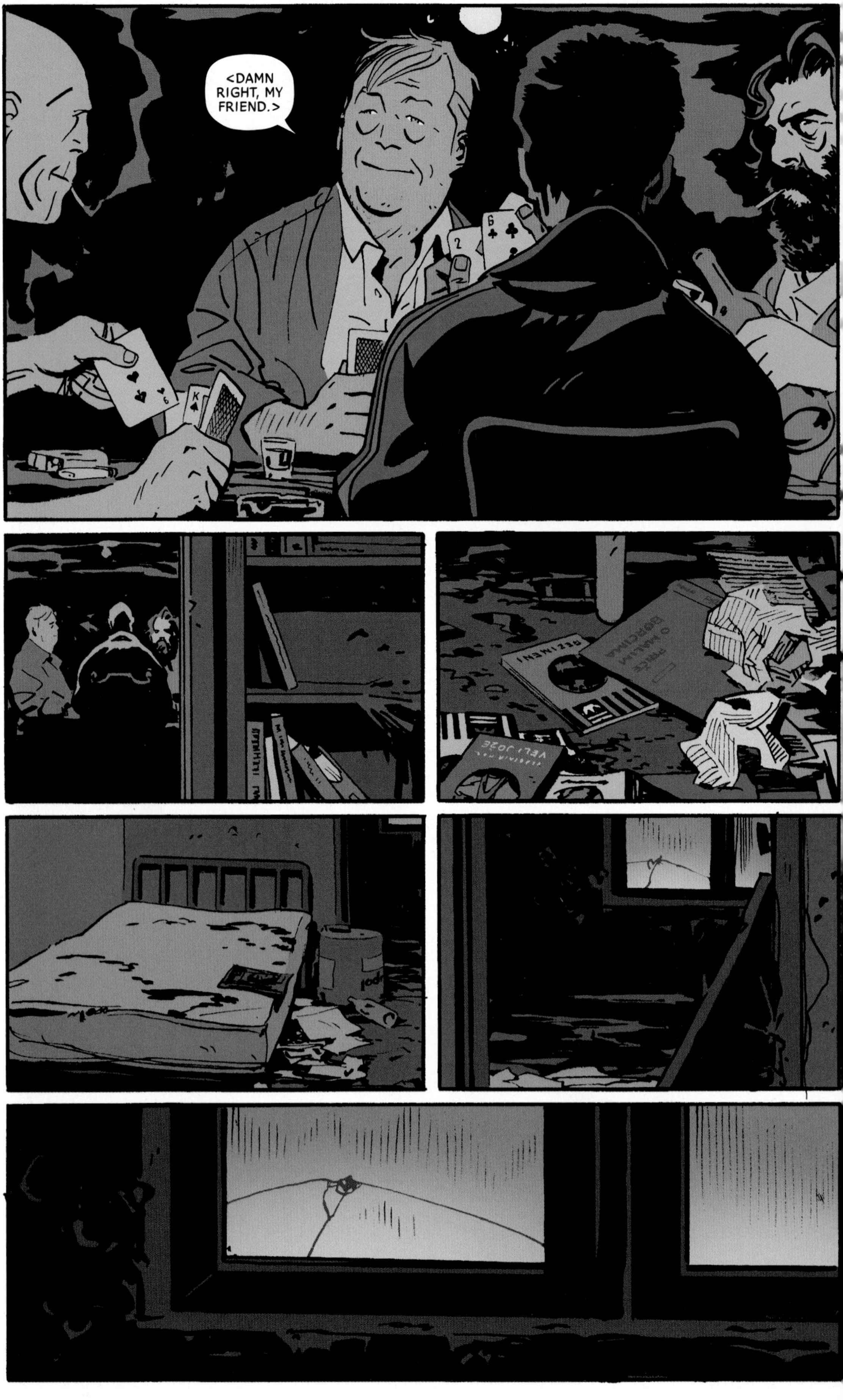
<DAMN RIGHT, MY FRIEND.>

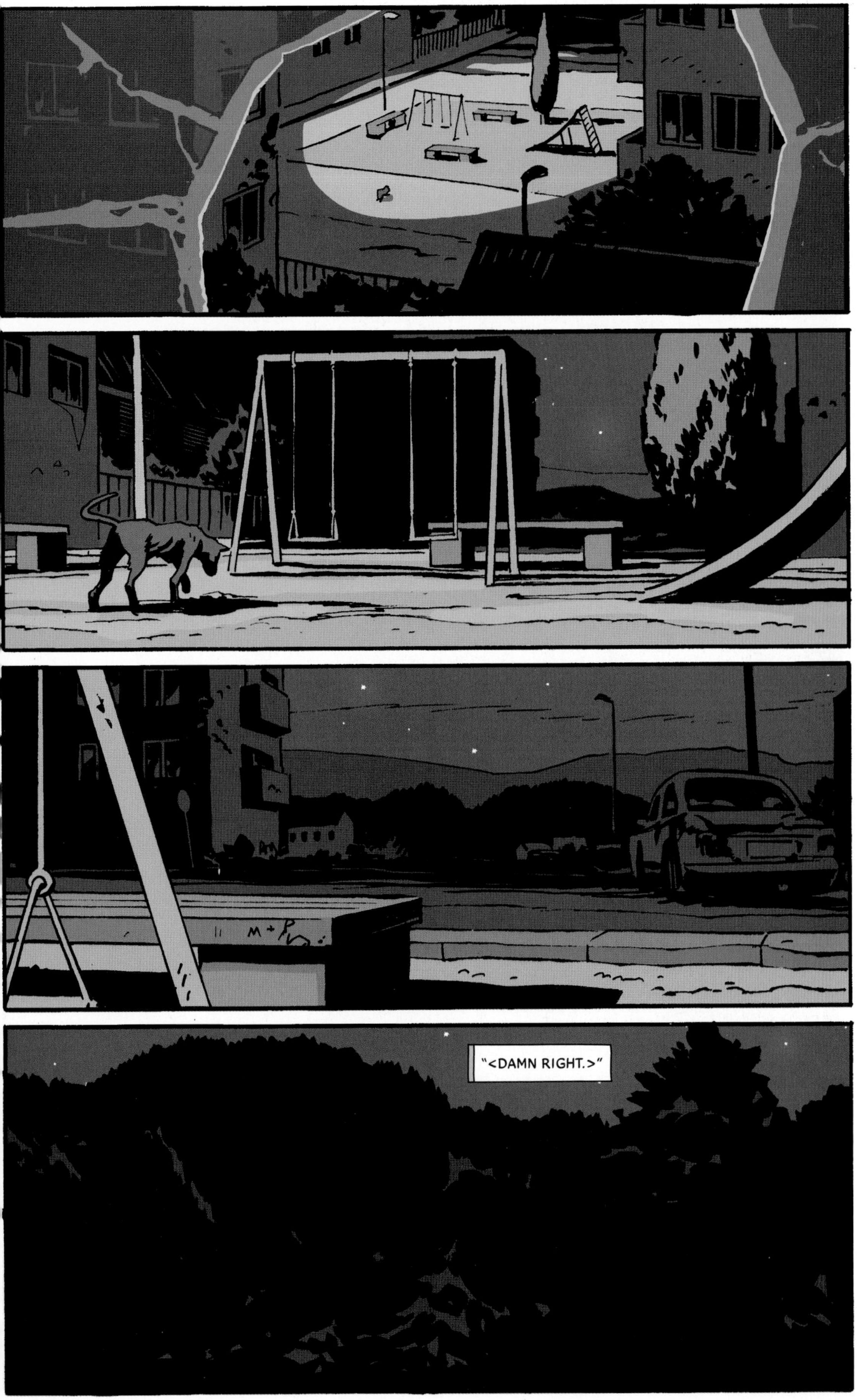
"<DAMN RIGHT.>"

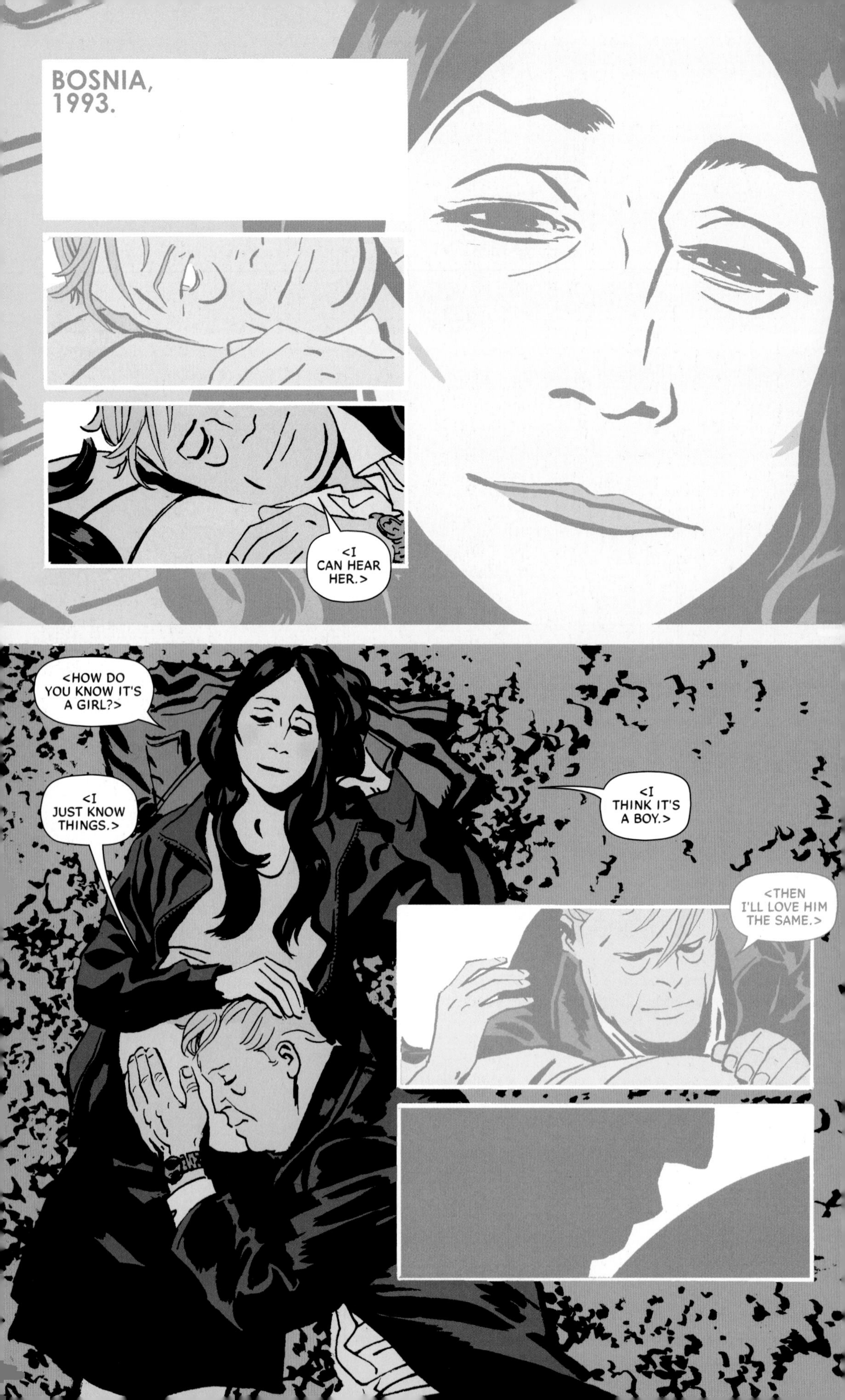
BOSNIA, 1993.
<I CAN HEAR HER.>
<HOW DO YOU KNOW IT'S A GIRL?>
<I JUST KNOW THINGS.>
<I THINK IT'S A BOY.>
<THEN I'LL LOVE HIM THE SAME.>

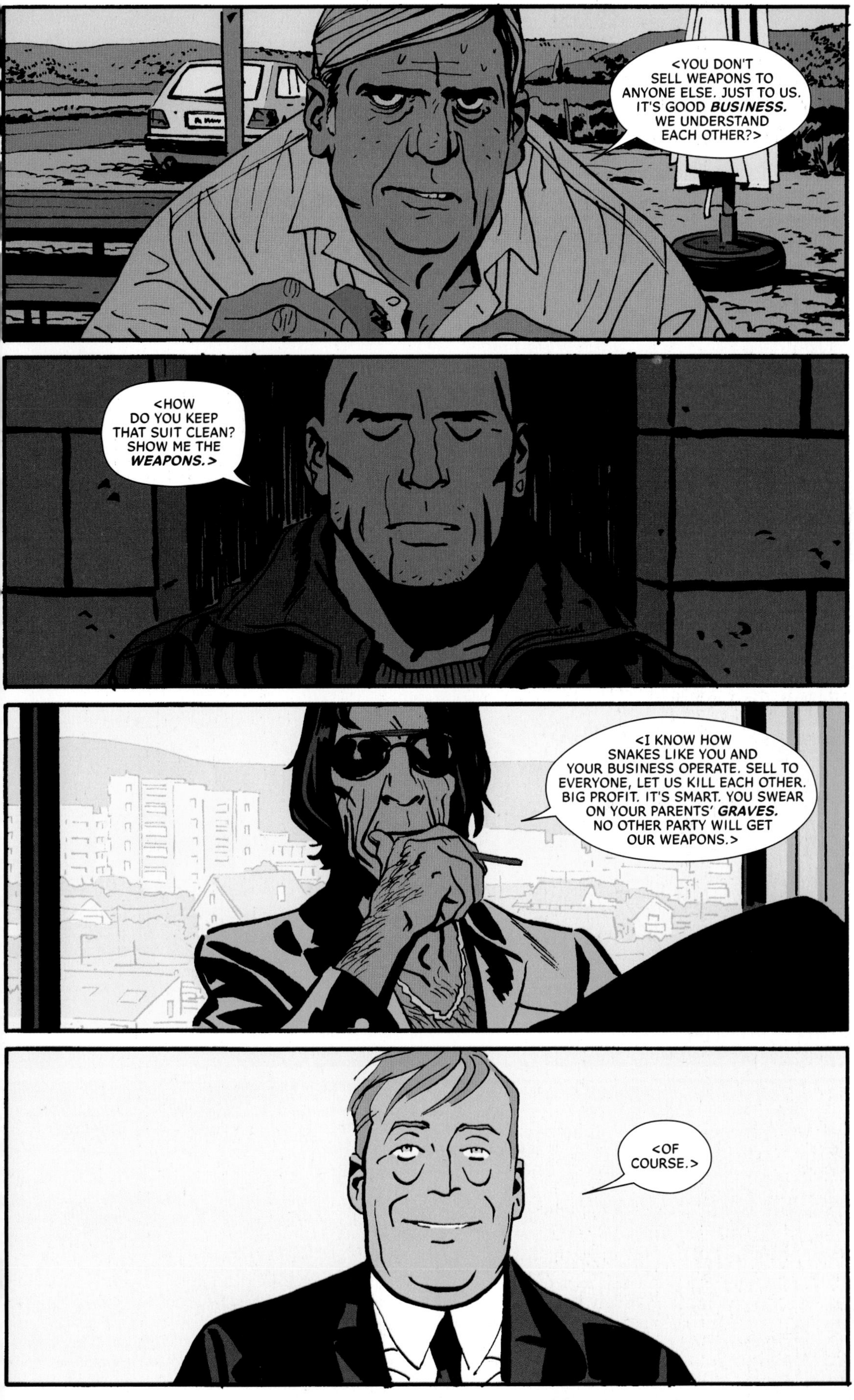
<YOU DON'T SELL WEAPONS TO ANYONE ELSE. JUST TO US. IT'S GOOD **BUSINESS.** WE UNDERSTAND EACH OTHER?>
<HOW DO YOU KEEP THAT SUIT CLEAN? SHOW ME THE **WEAPONS.**>
<I KNOW HOW SNAKES LIKE YOU AND YOUR BUSINESS OPERATE. SELL TO EVERYONE, LET US KILL EACH OTHER. BIG PROFIT. IT'S SMART. YOU SWEAR ON YOUR PARENTS' **GRAVES.** NO OTHER PARTY WILL GET OUR WEAPONS.>
<OF COURSE.>

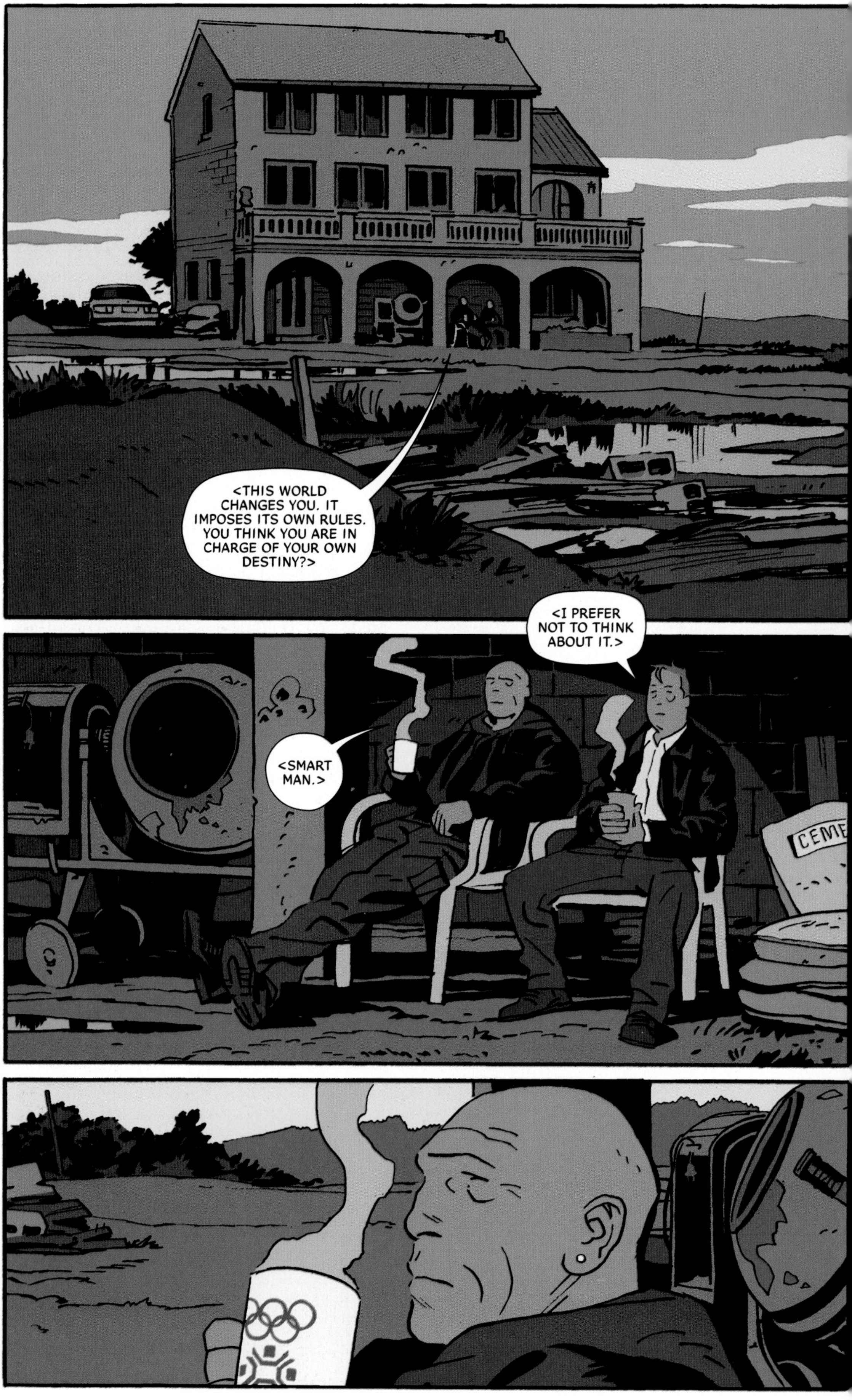
<THIS WORLD CHANGES YOU. IT IMPOSES ITS OWN RULES. YOU THINK YOU ARE IN CHARGE OF YOUR OWN DESTINY?>
<I PREFER NOT TO THINK ABOUT IT.>
<SMART MAN.>

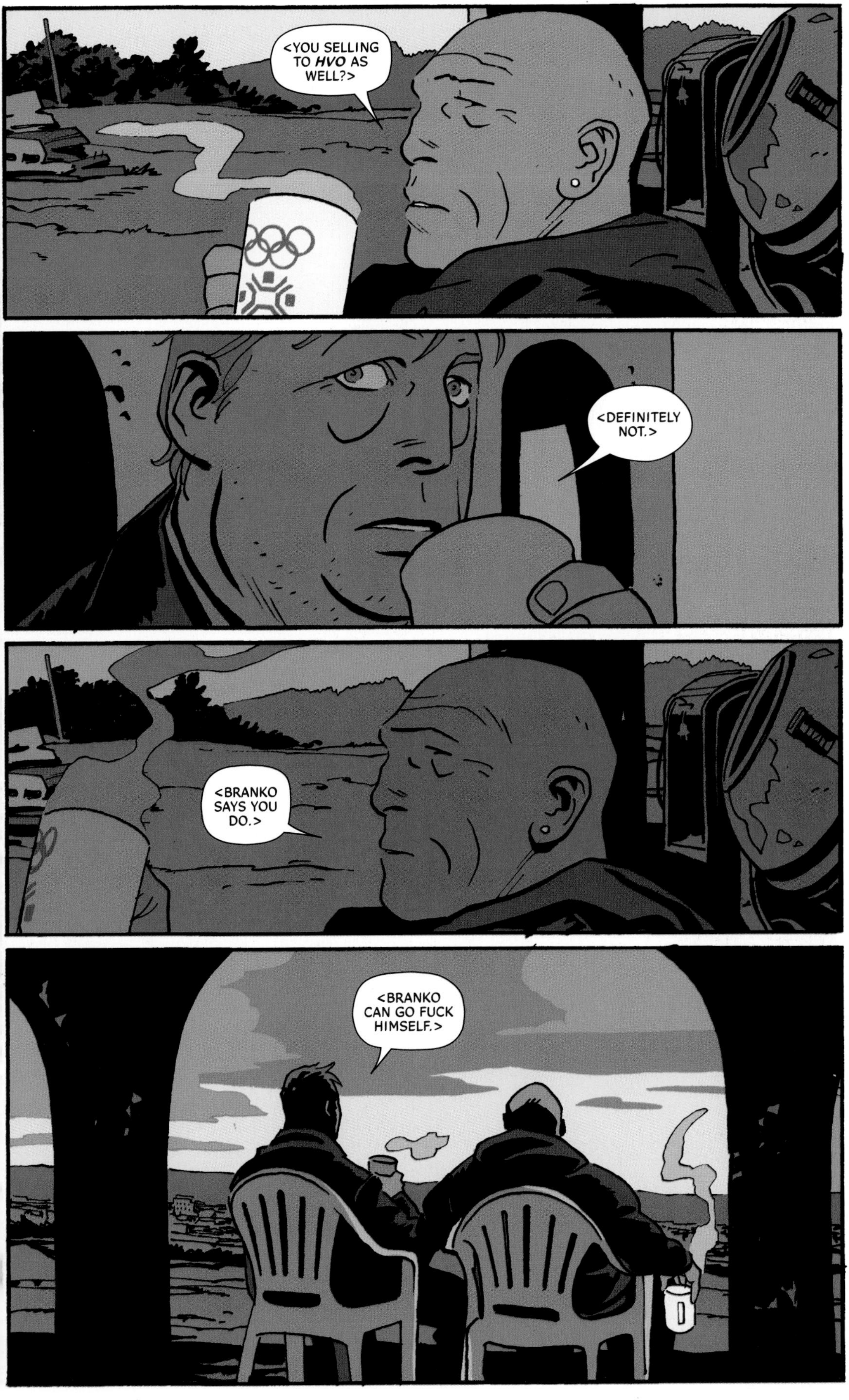
<YOU SELLING TO *HVO* AS WELL?>
<DEFINITELY NOT.>
<BRANKO SAYS YOU DO.>
<BRANKO CAN GO FUCK HIMSELF.>

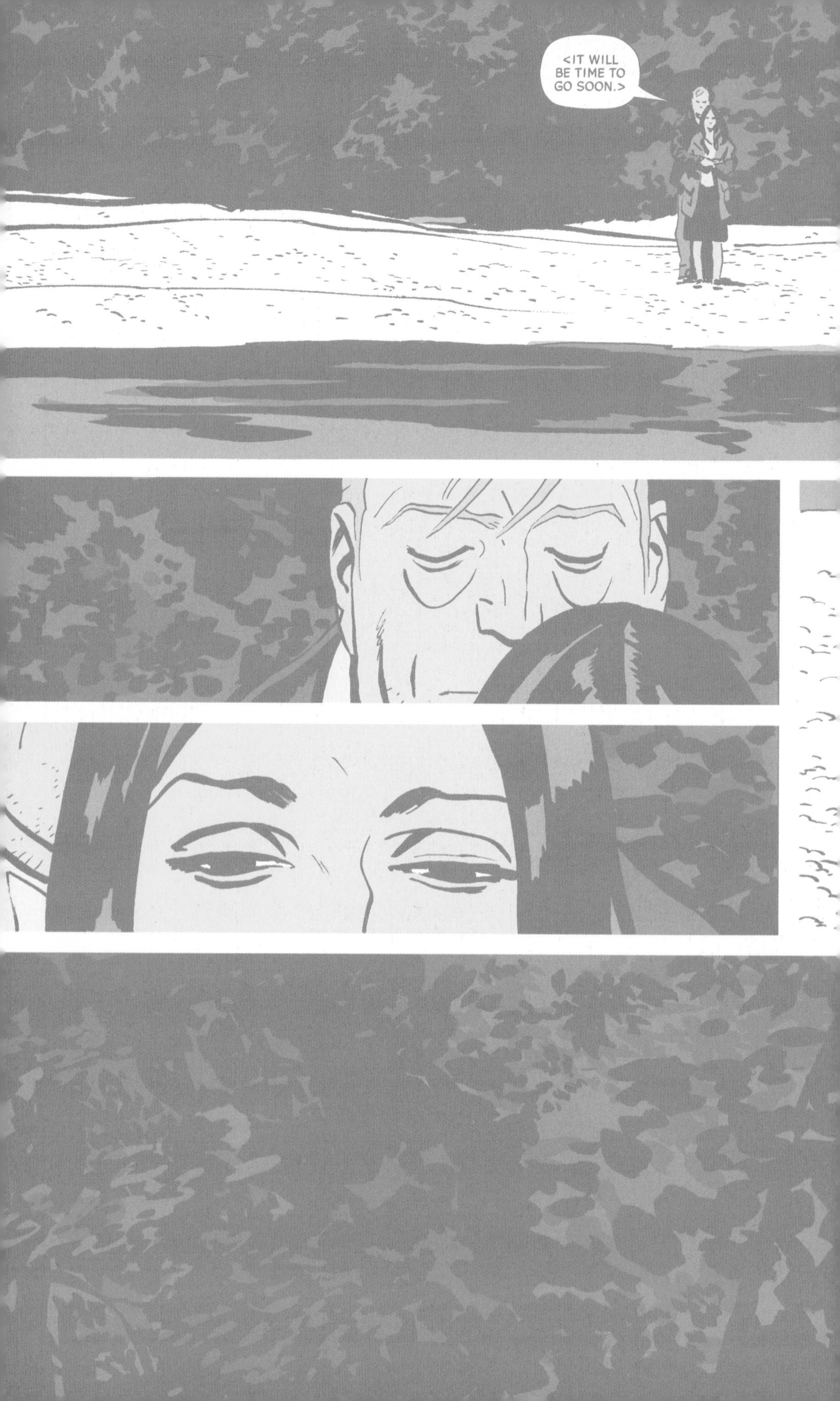
<IT WILL BE TIME TO GO SOON.>

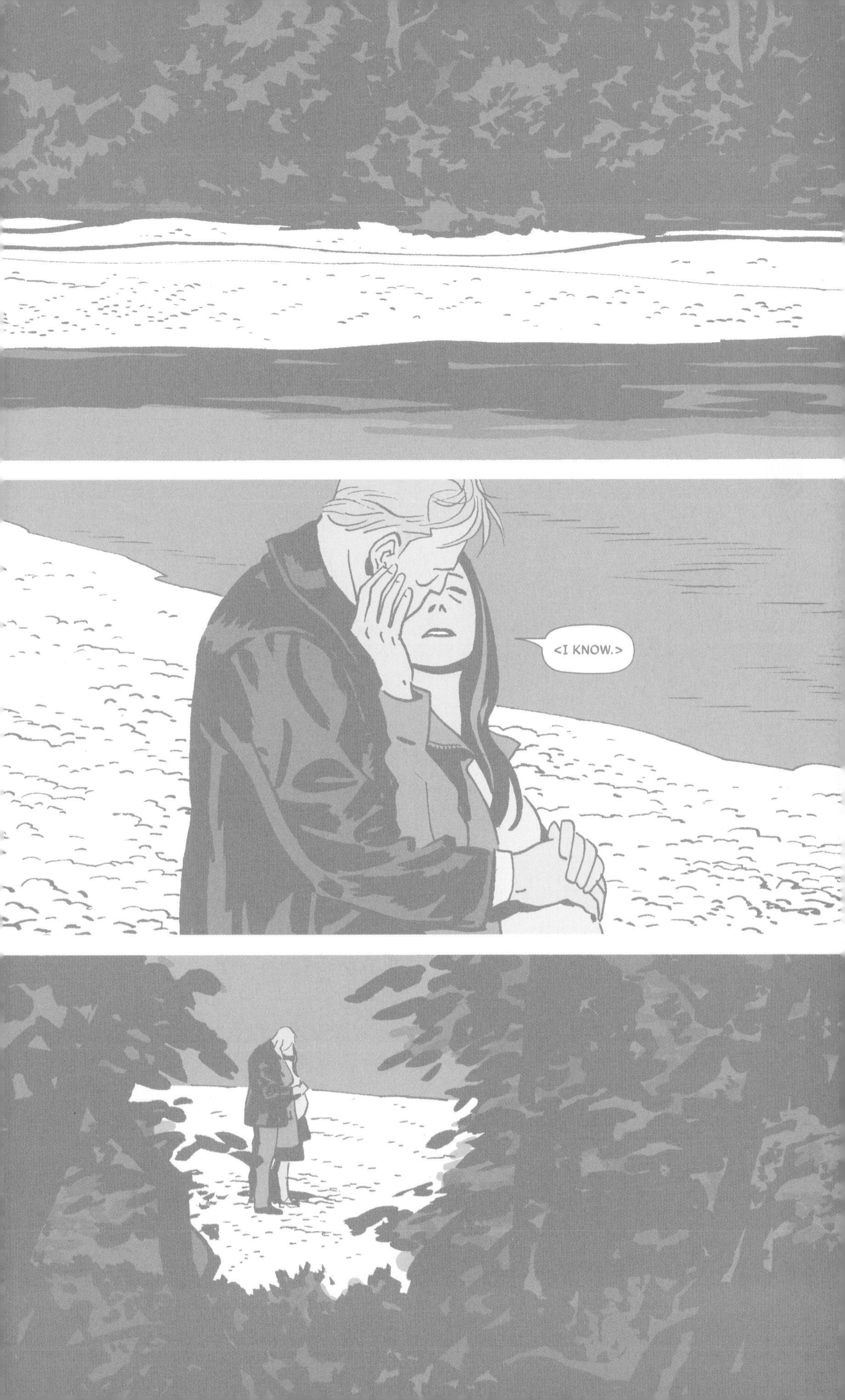
<I KNOW.>

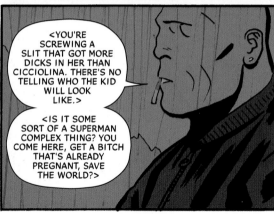

<YOU'RE SCREWING A SLIT THAT GOT MORE DICKS IN HER THAN CICCIOLINA. THERE'S NO TELLING WHO THE KID WILL LOOK LIKE.>

<IS IT SOME SORT OF A SUPERMAN COMPLEX THING? YOU COME HERE, GET A BITCH THAT'S ALREADY PREGNANT, SAVE THE WORLD?>

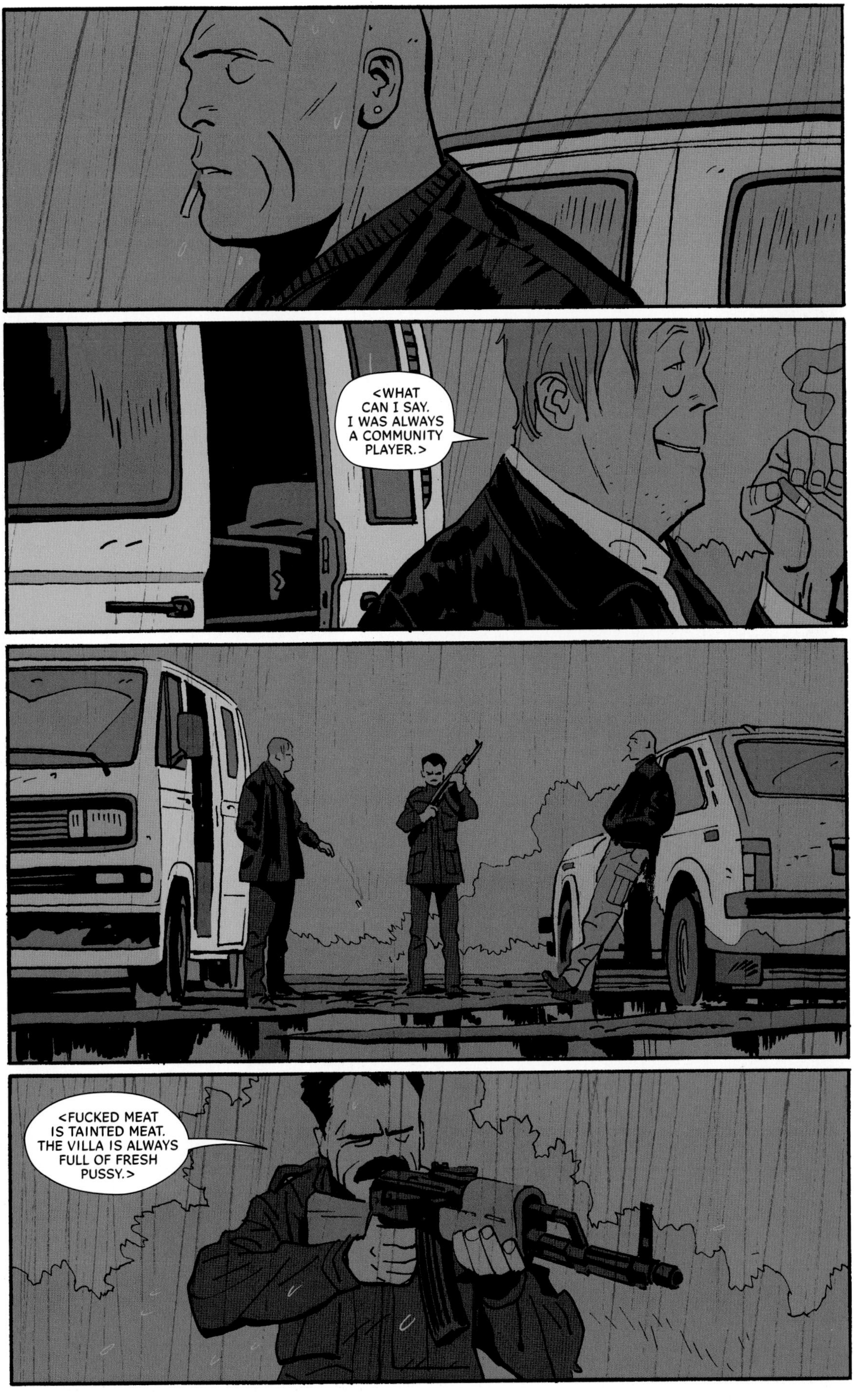
<WHAT CAN I SAY. I WAS ALWAYS A COMMUNITY PLAYER.>
<FUCKED MEAT IS TAINTED MEAT. THE VILLA IS ALWAYS FULL OF FRESH PUSSY.>

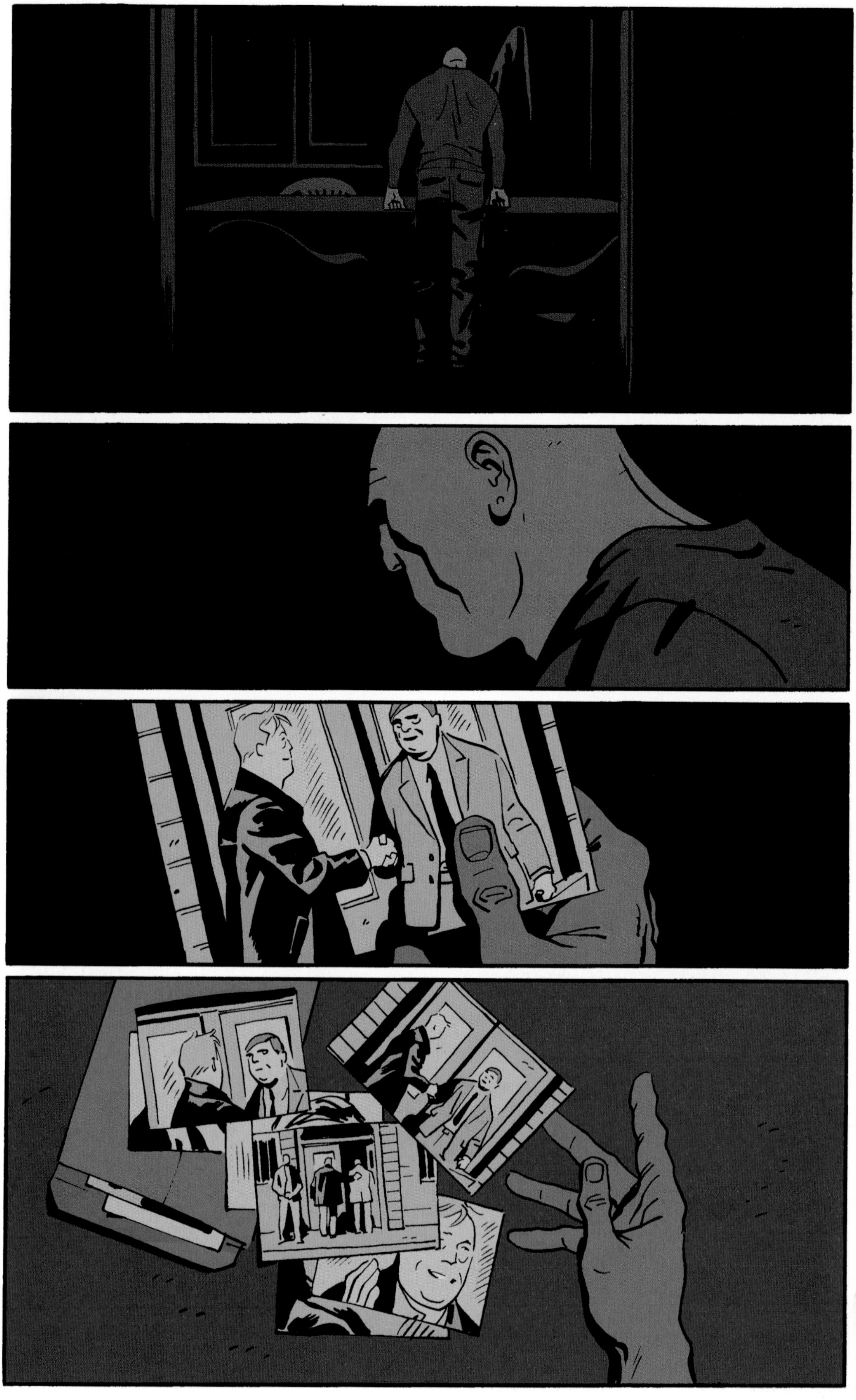

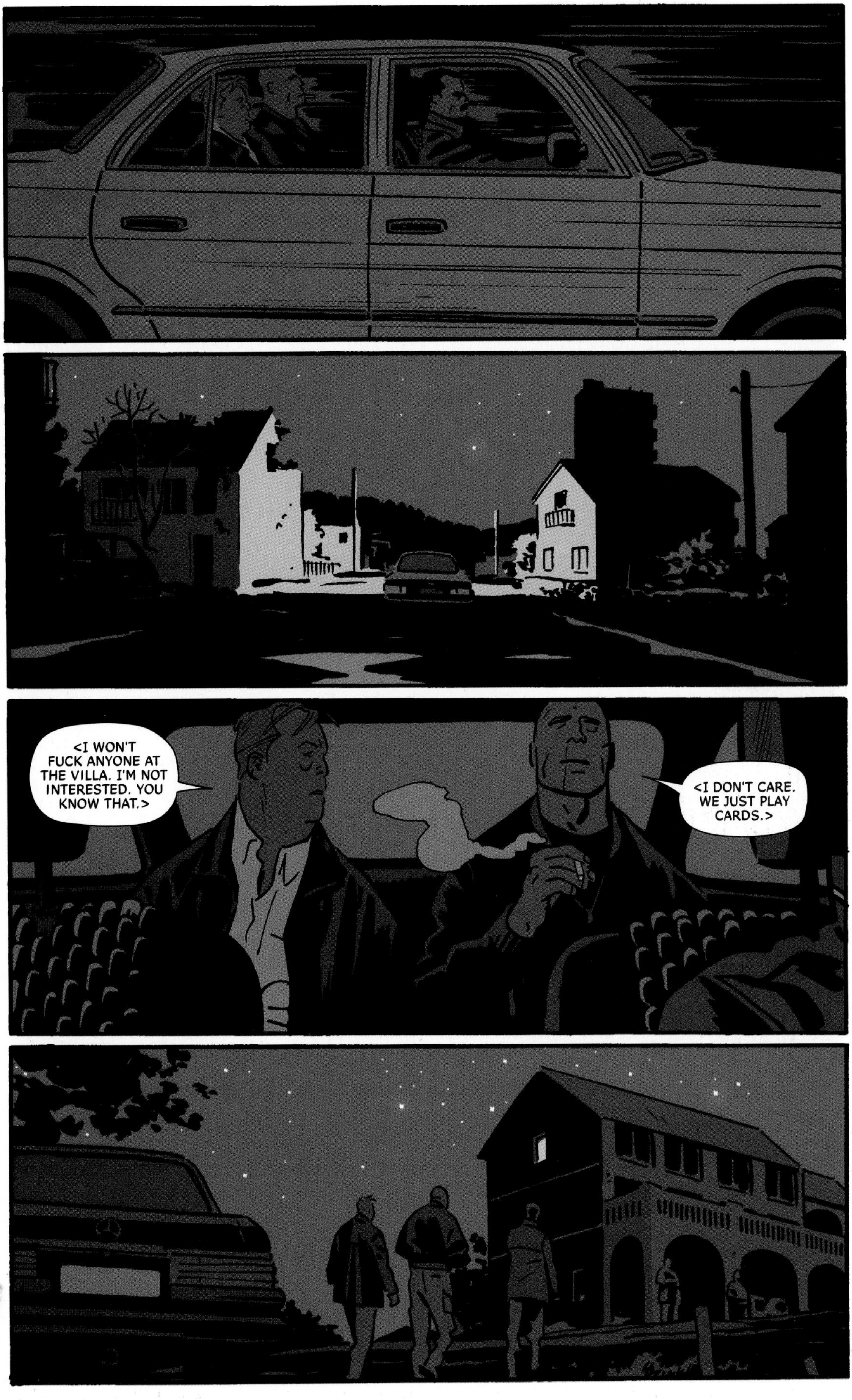
<I WON'T FUCK ANYONE AT THE VILLA. I'M NOT INTERESTED. YOU KNOW THAT.>
<I DON'T CARE. WE JUST PLAY CARDS.>

<MAN, I FEEL LIKE PUTTING MY DICK IN SOMETHING.>

<NO, YOU FUCKING STAY HERE, VEDRAN. WE PLAY CARDS.>

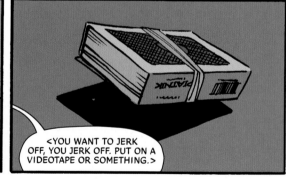

<YOU WANT TO JERK OFF, YOU JERK OFF. PUT ON A VIDEOTAPE OR SOMETHING.>

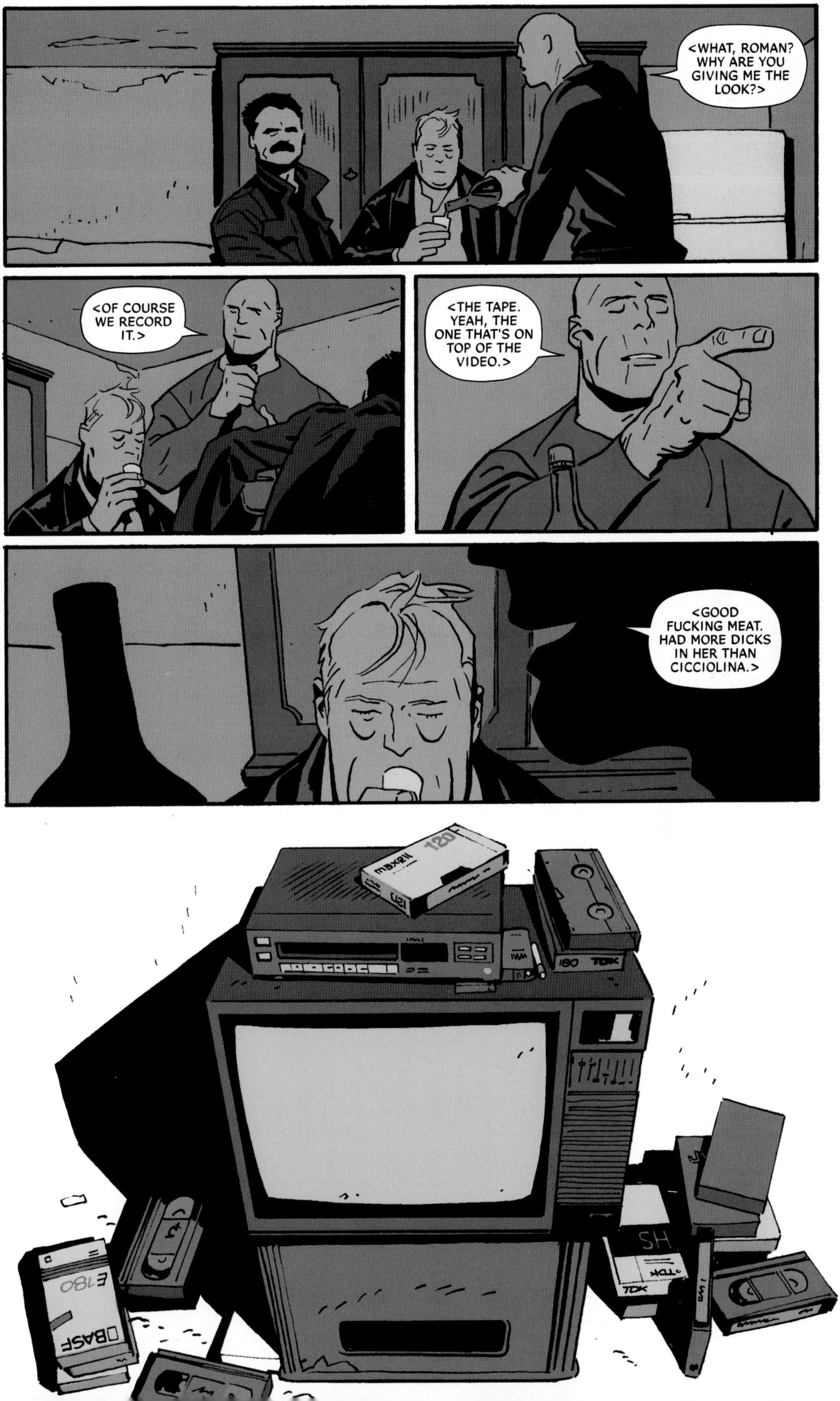

<WHAT, ROMAN? WHY ARE YOU GIVING ME THE LOOK?>
<OF COURSE WE RECORD IT.>
<THE TAPE. YEAH, THE ONE THAT'S ON TOP OF THE VIDEO.>
<GOOD FUCKING MEAT. HAD MORE DICKS IN HER THAN CICCIOLINA.>

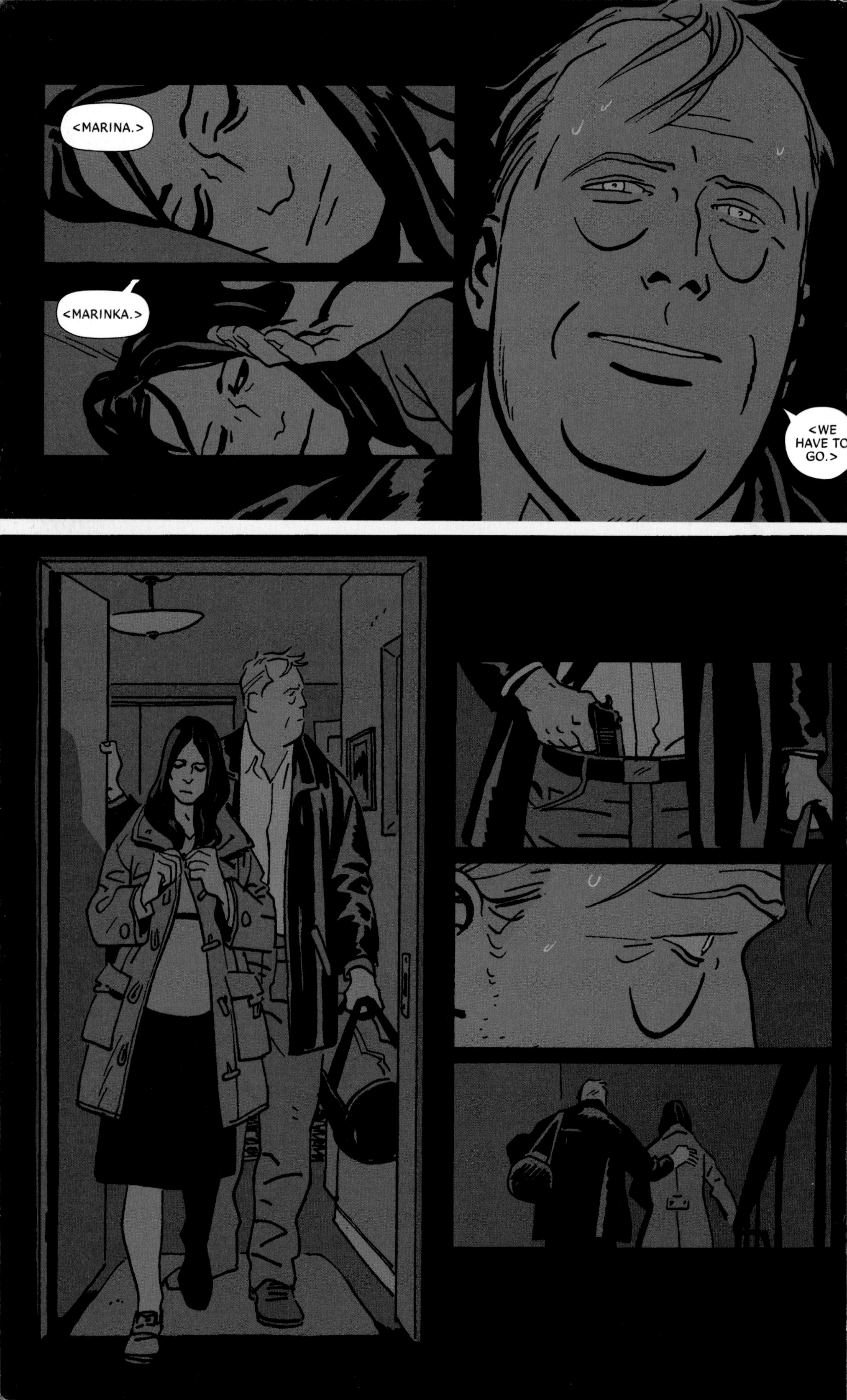
<MARINA.>
<MARINKA.>
<WE HAVE TO GO.>

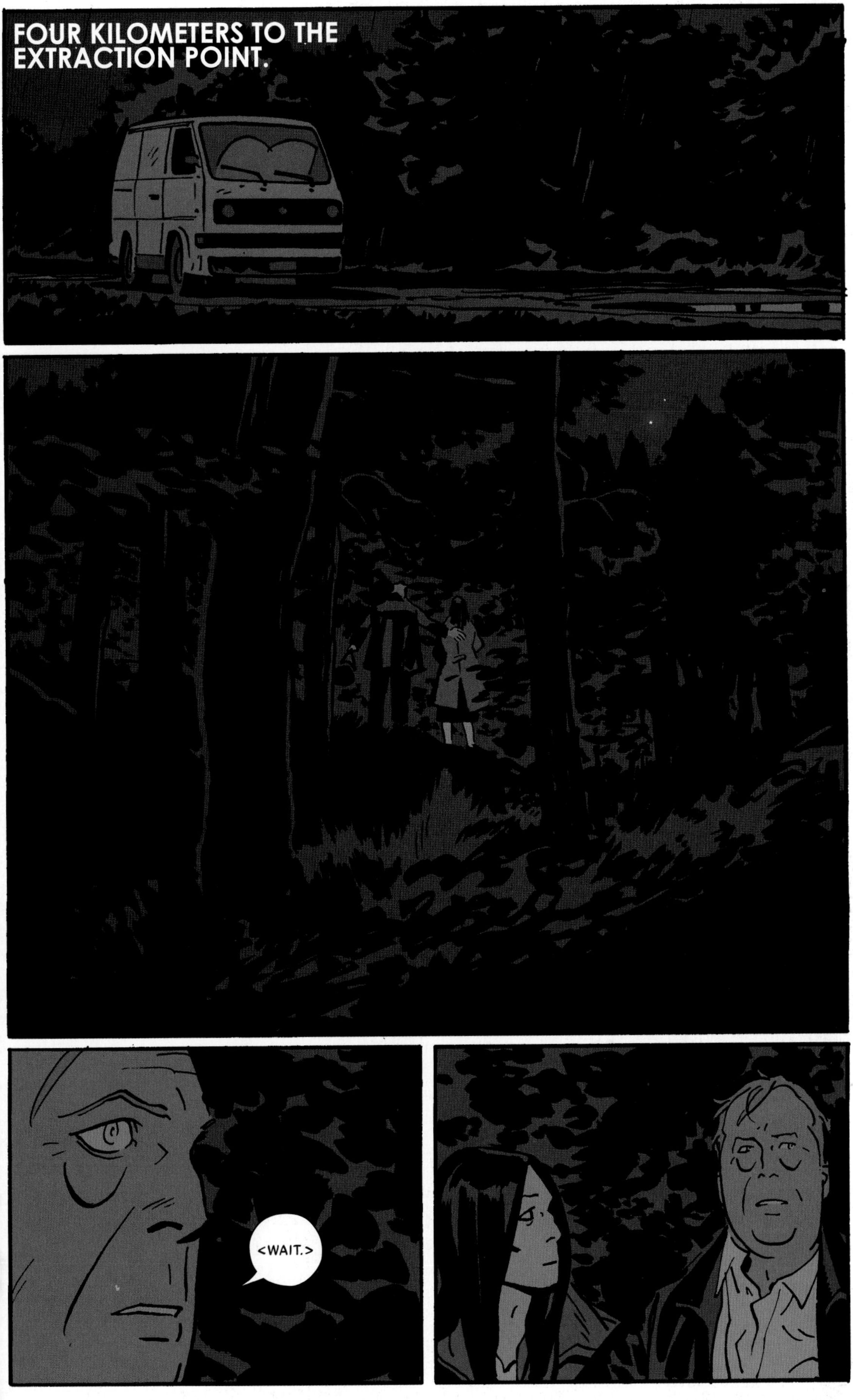
FOUR KILOMETERS TO THE EXTRACTION POINT.
<WAIT.>

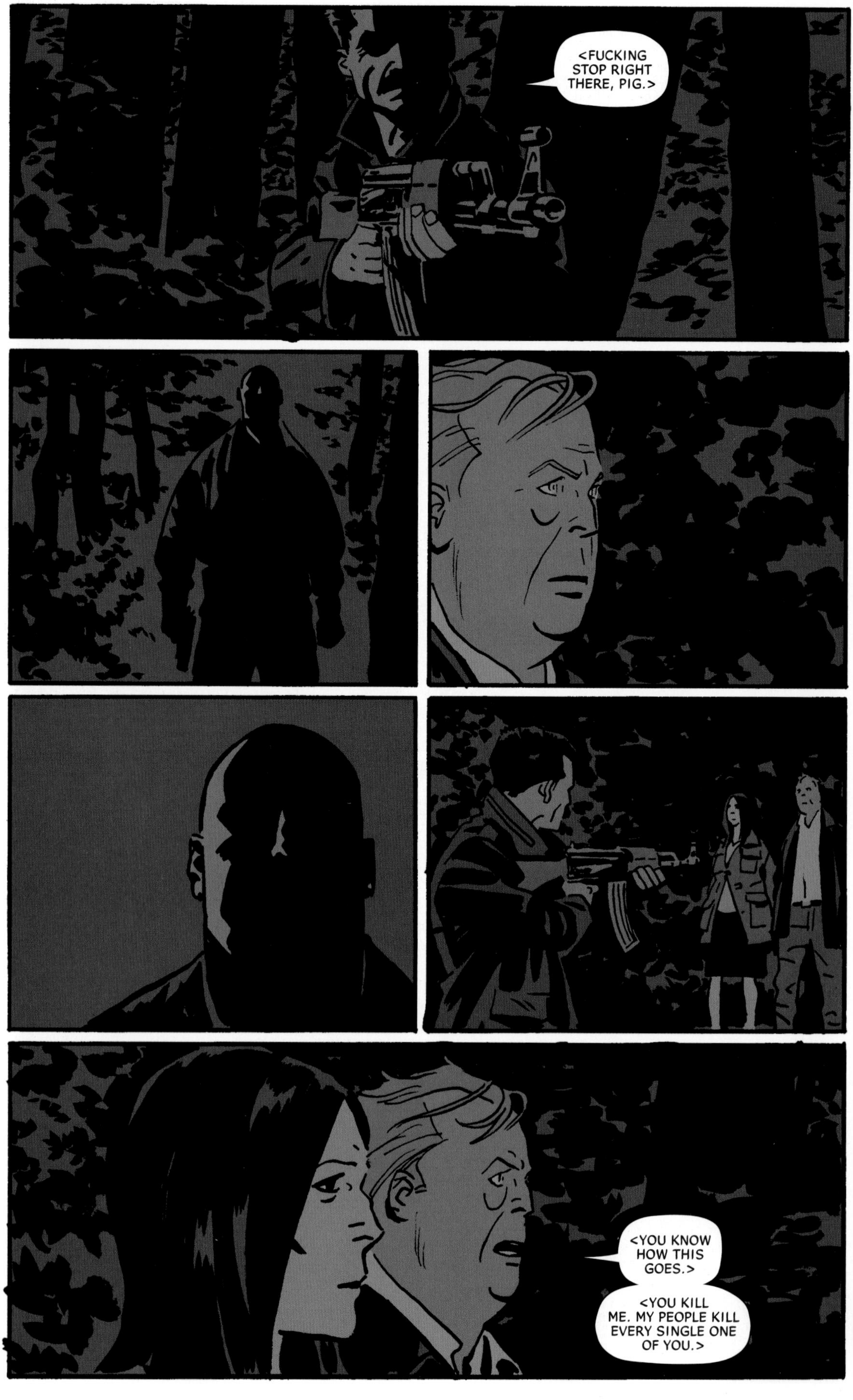
<FUCKING STOP RIGHT THERE, PIG.>
<YOU KNOW HOW THIS GOES.>
<YOU KILL ME. MY PEOPLE KILL EVERY SINGLE ONE OF YOU.>

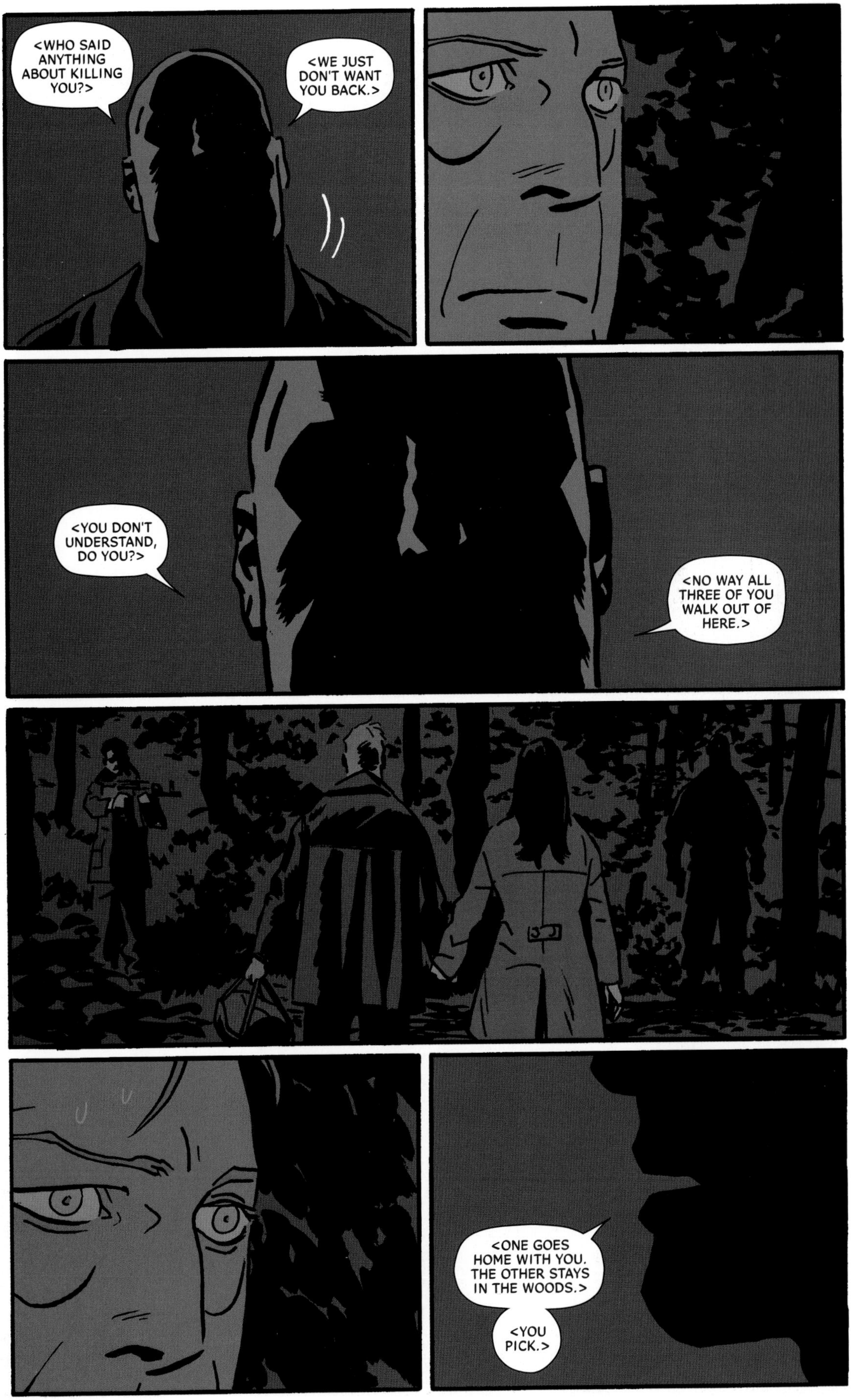

<WHO SAID ANYTHING ABOUT KILLING YOU?>
<WE JUST DON'T WANT YOU BACK.>
<YOU DON'T UNDERSTAND, DO YOU?>
<NO WAY ALL THREE OF YOU WALK OUT OF HERE.>
<ONE GOES HOME WITH YOU. THE OTHER STAYS IN THE WOODS.>
<YOU PICK.>

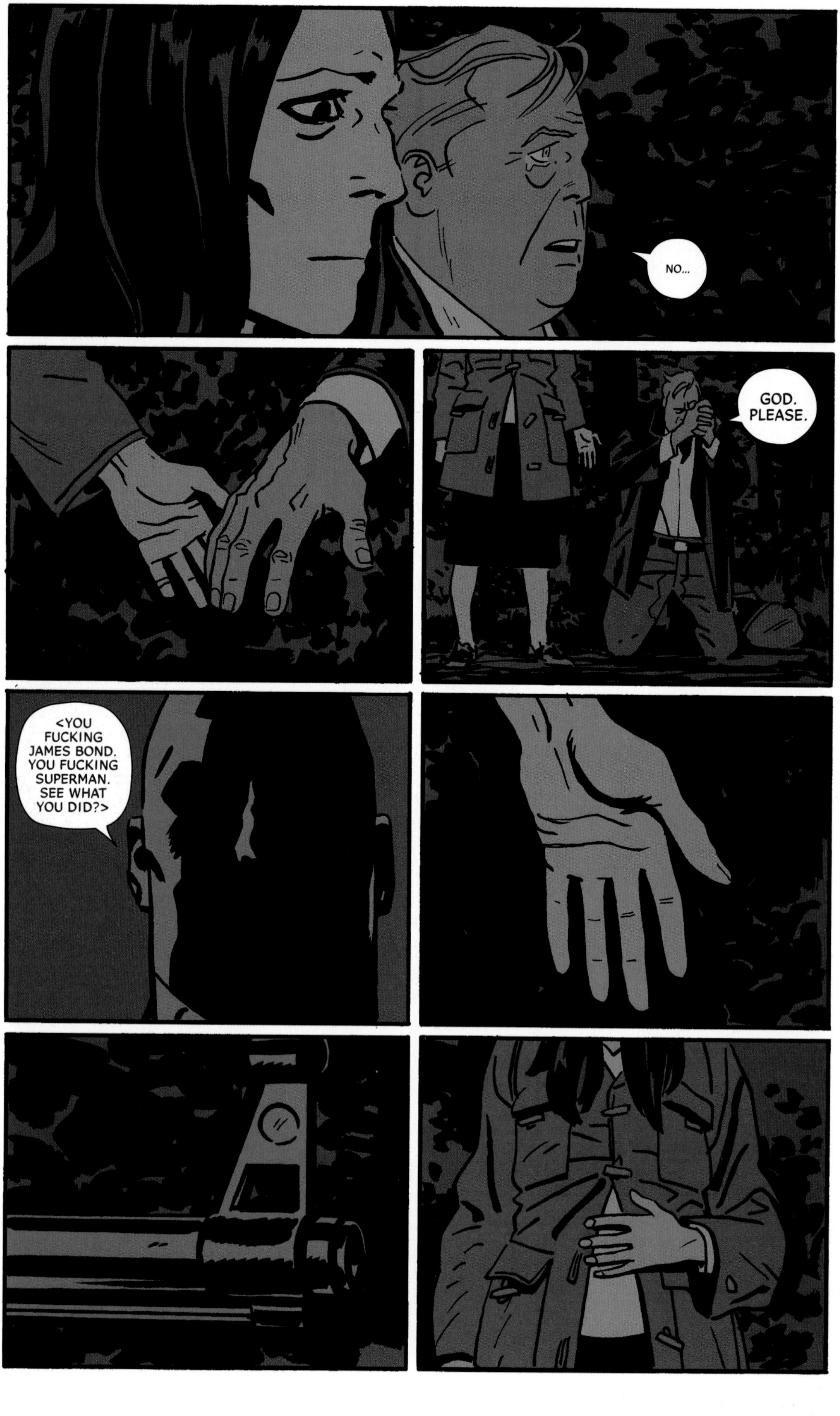
NO...
GOD. PLEASE.
<YOU FUCKING JAMES BOND. YOU FUCKING SUPERMAN. SEE WHAT YOU DID?>

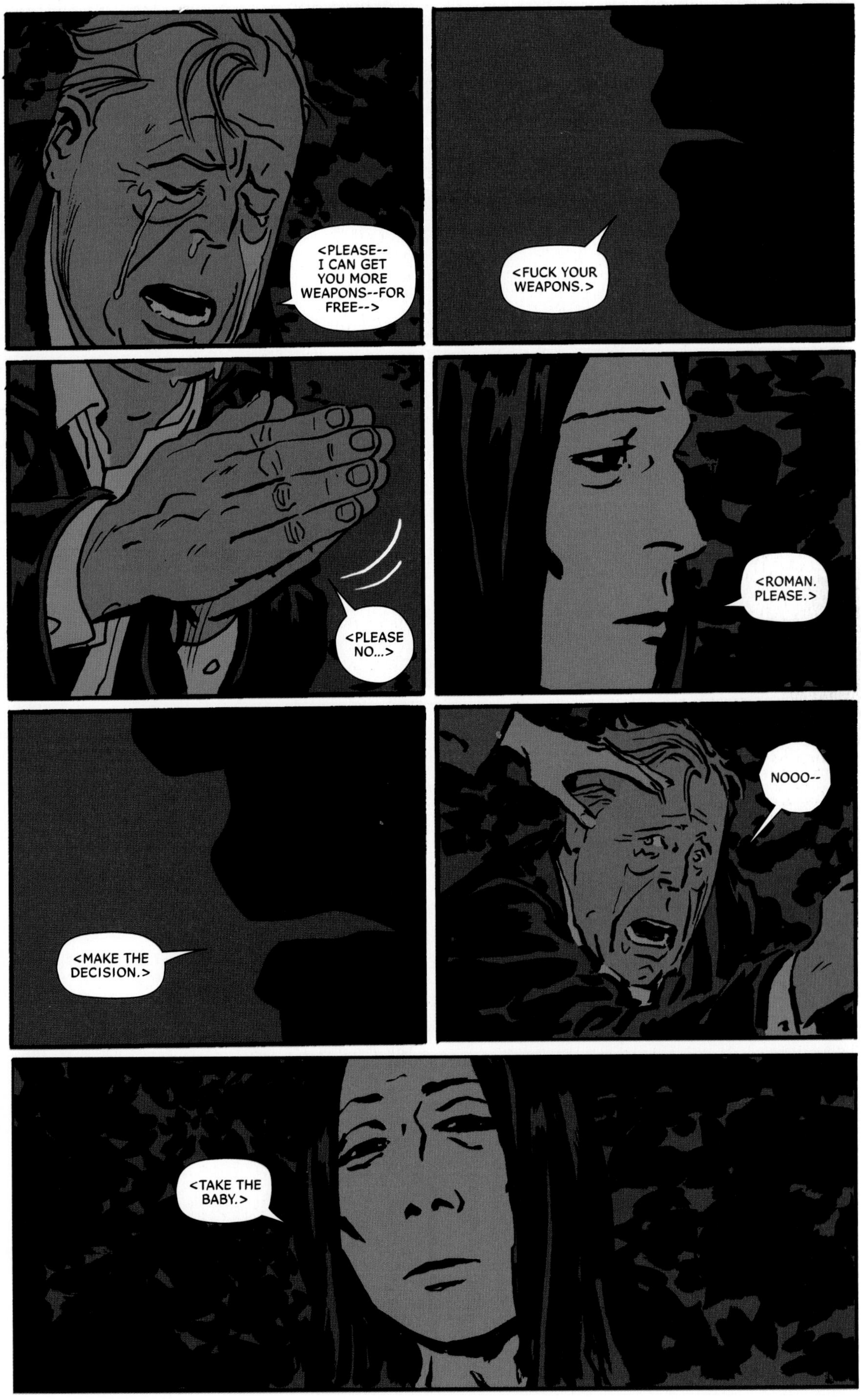
<PLEASE-- I CAN GET YOU MORE WEAPONS--FOR FREE-->
<FUCK YOUR WEAPONS.>
<PLEASE NO...>
<ROMAN. PLEASE.>
<MAKE THE DECISION.>
NOOO--
<TAKE THE BABY.>

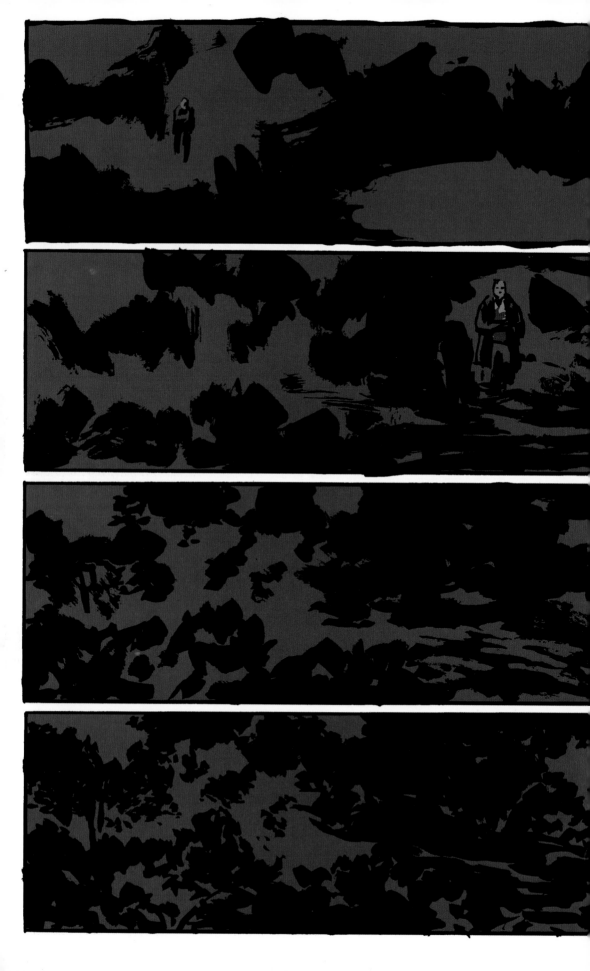

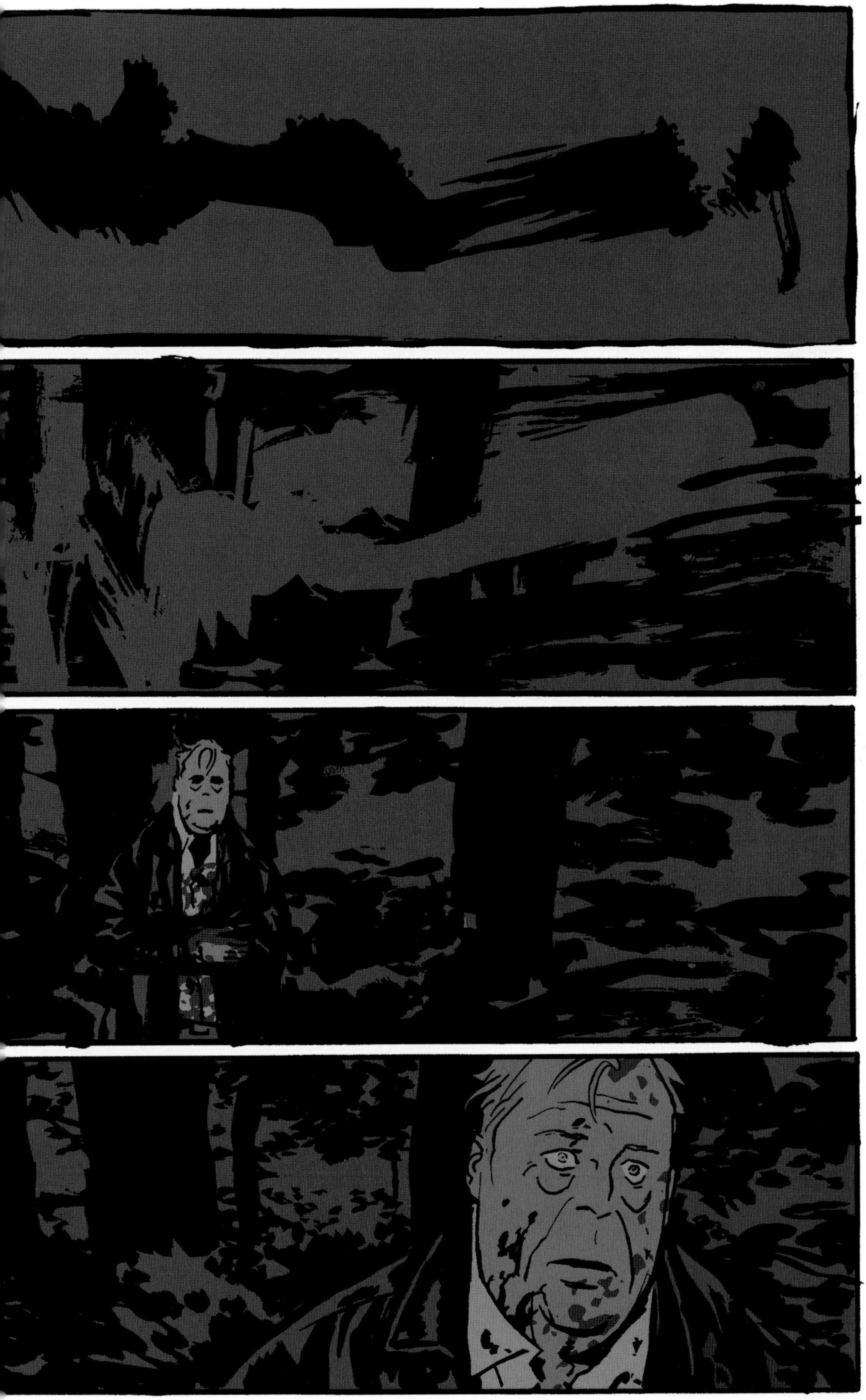

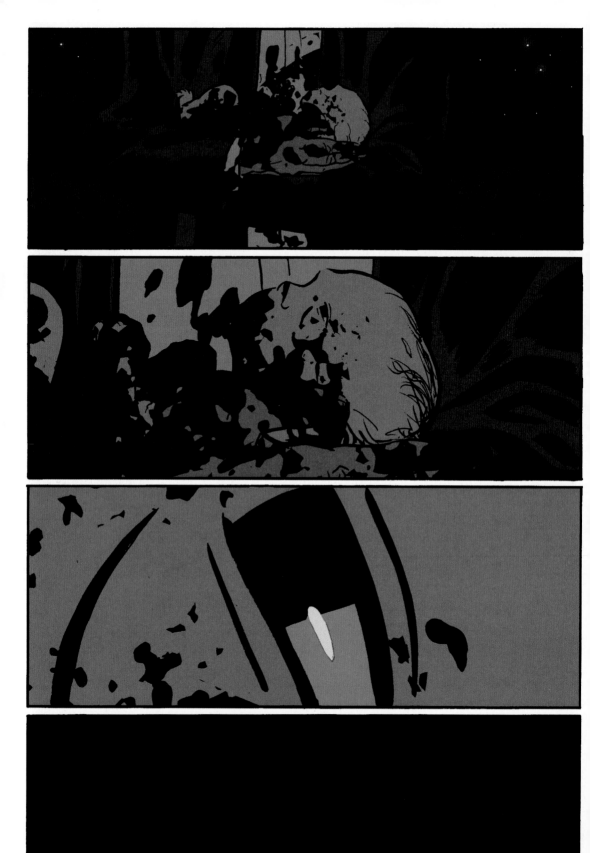

CHAPTER 9:
MARINA

ESTIMATES FOR THE
TOTAL NUMBER OF
WOMEN RAPED DURING
THE BOSNIAN WAR
RANGE FROM
20,000 TO **50,000**.

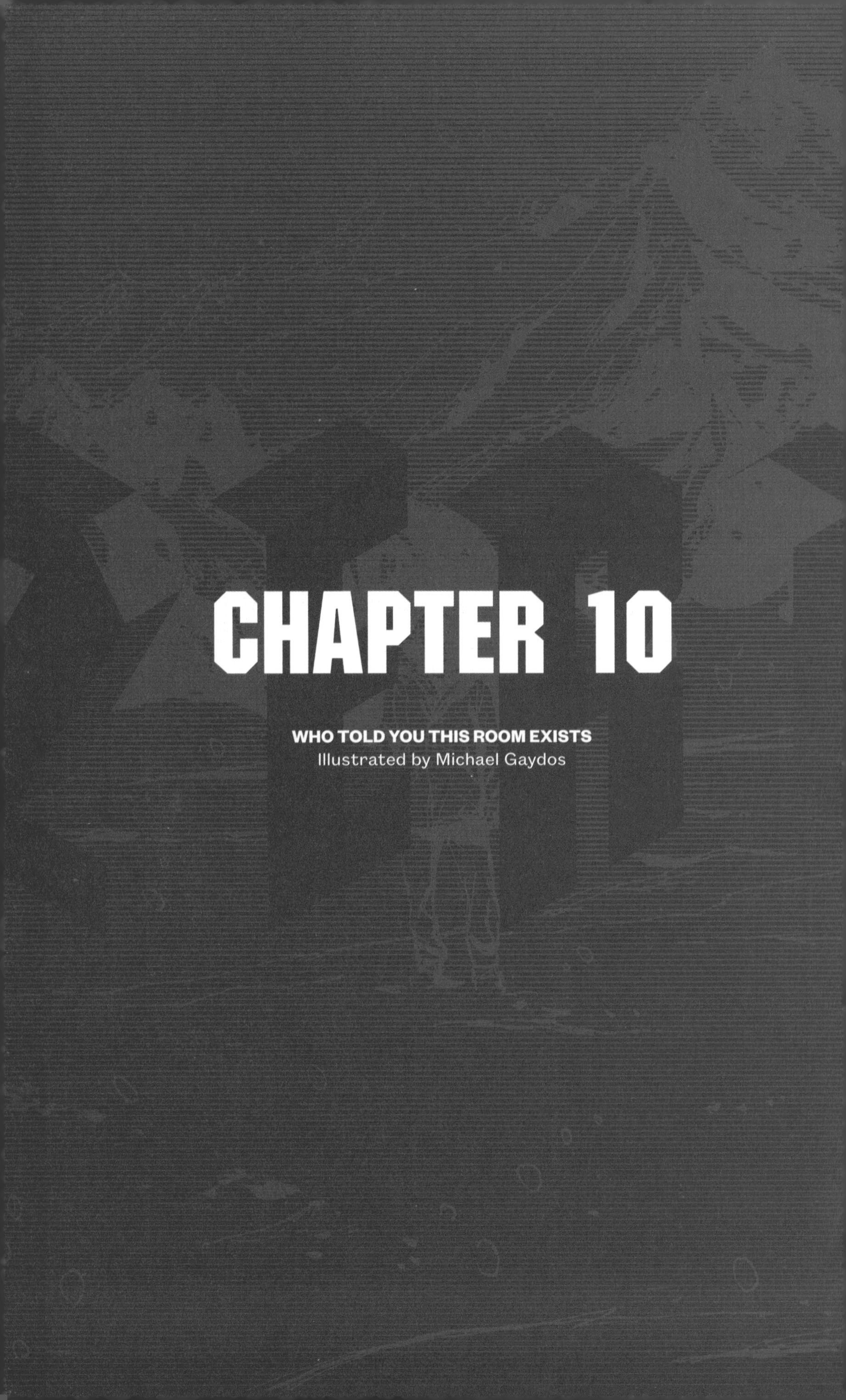

CHAPTER 10

WHO TOLD YOU THIS ROOM EXISTS

Illustrated by Michael Gaydos

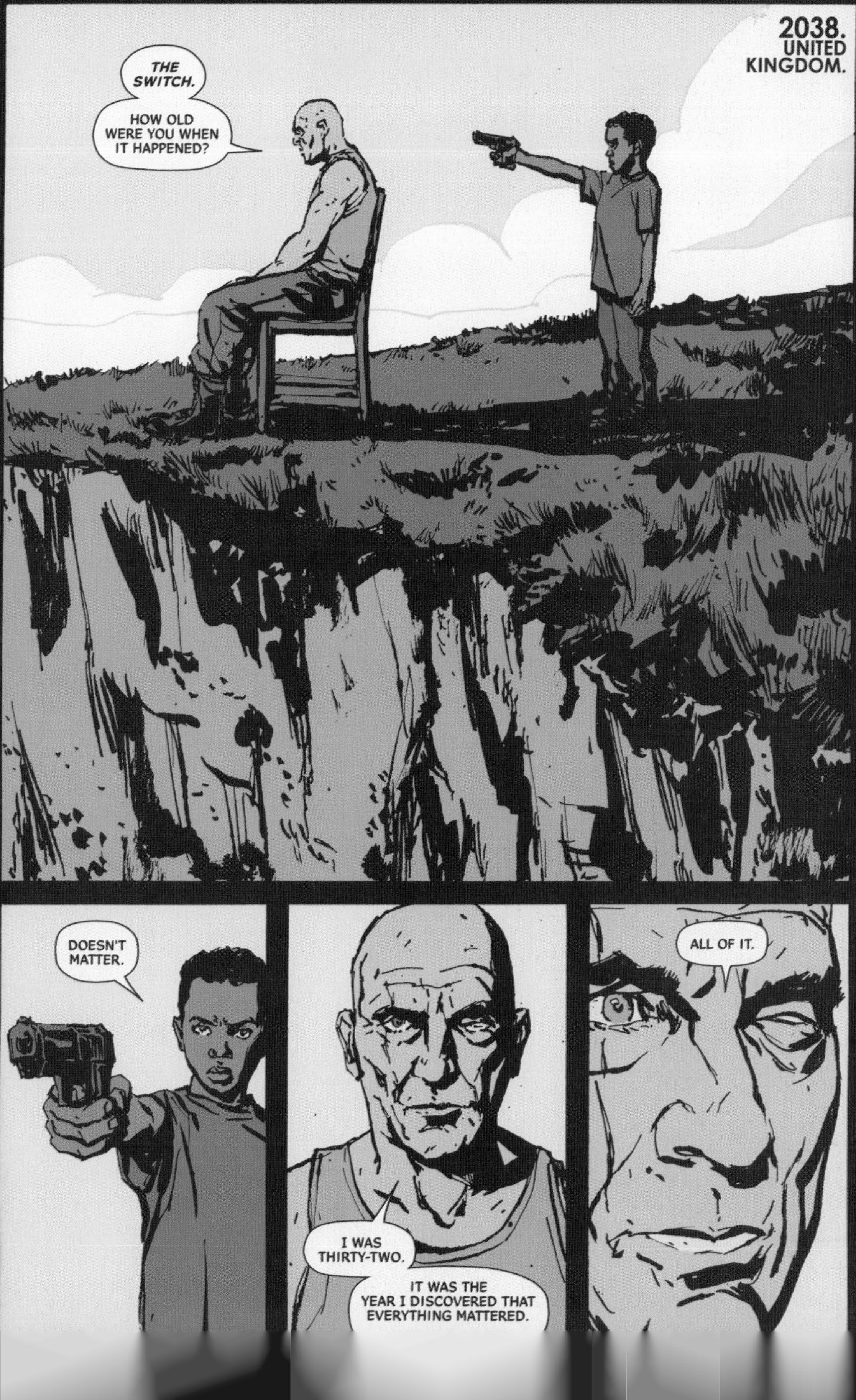
2038. UNITED KINGDOM.
THE SWITCH.
HOW OLD WERE YOU WHEN IT HAPPENED?
DOESN'T MATTER.
I WAS THIRTY-TWO.
IT WAS THE YEAR I DISCOVERED THAT EVERYTHING MATTERED.
ALL OF IT.

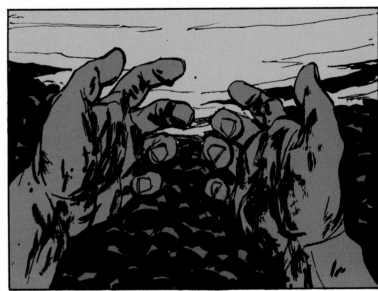

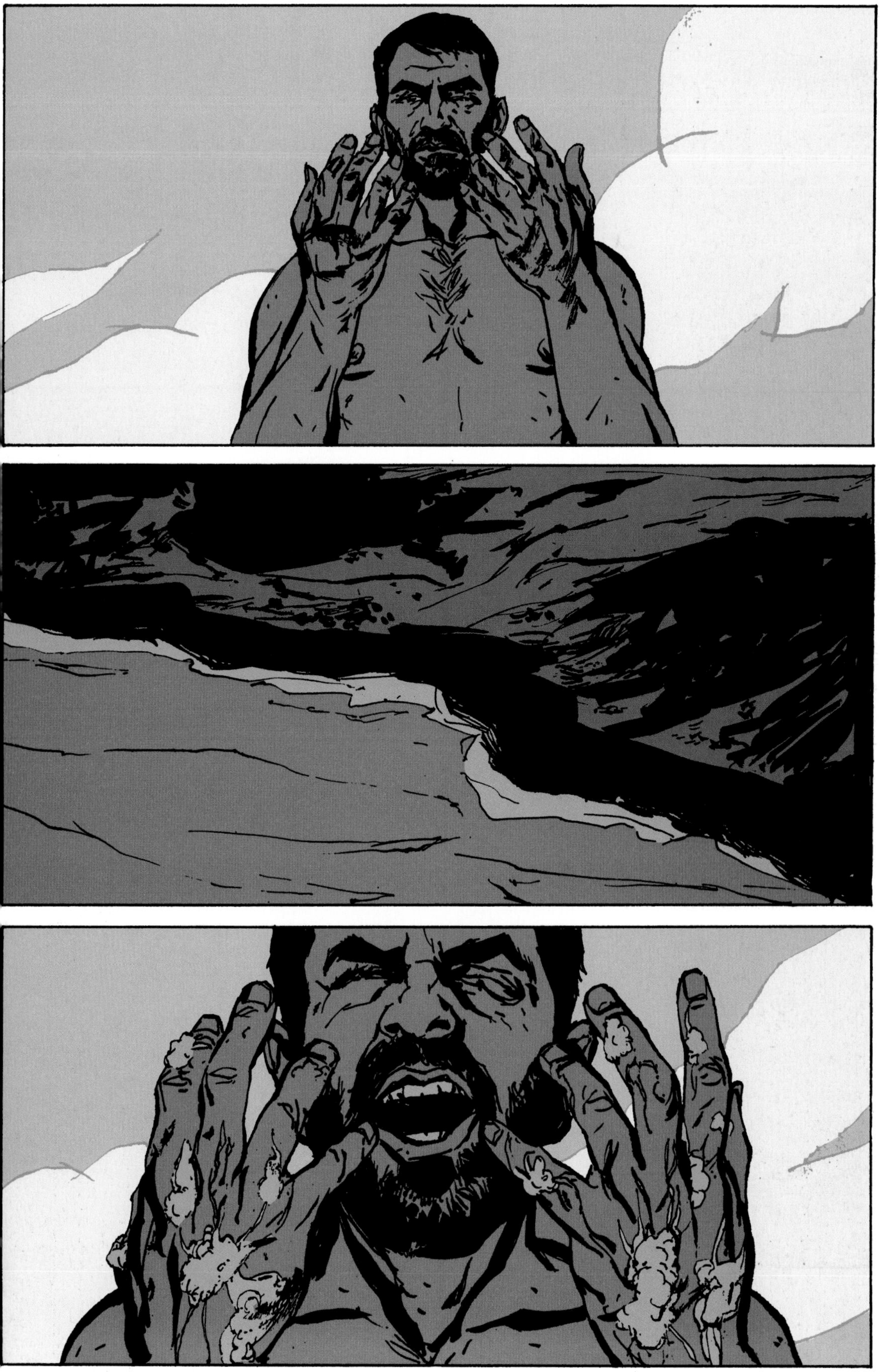

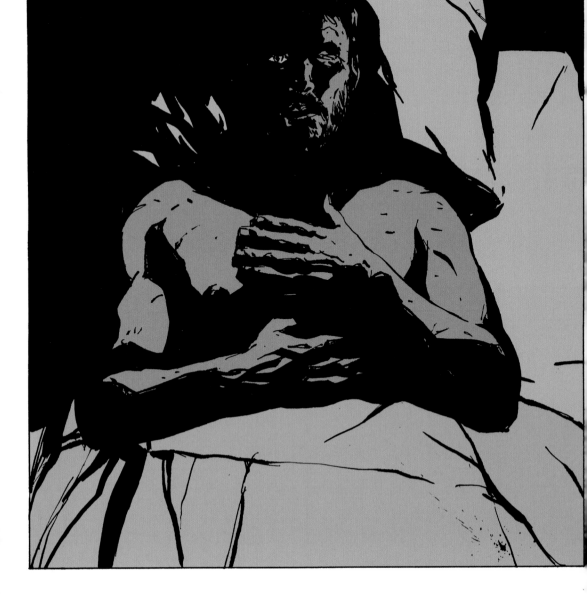

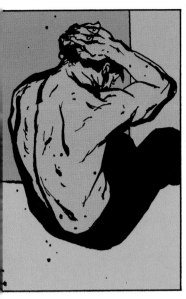

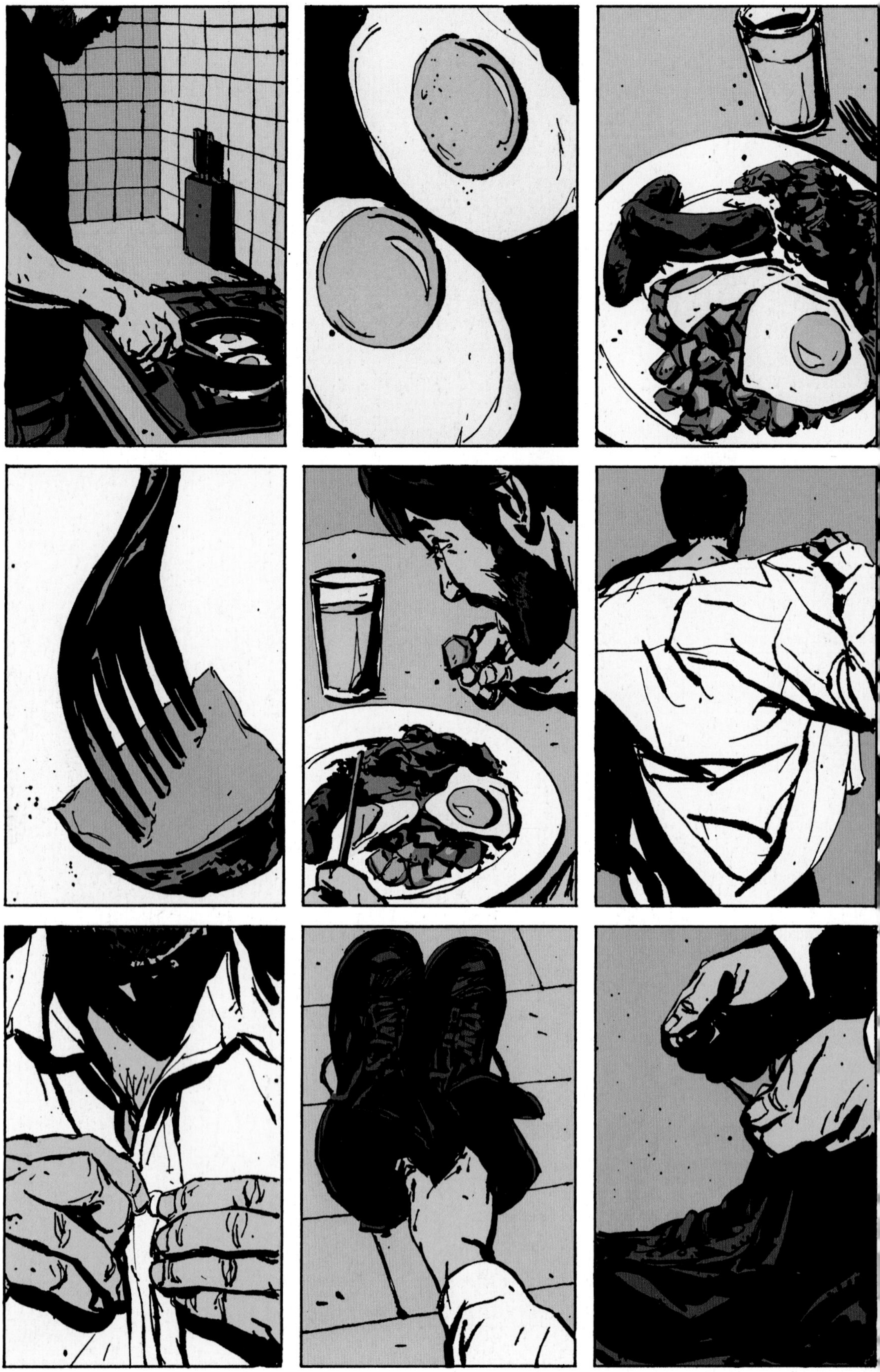

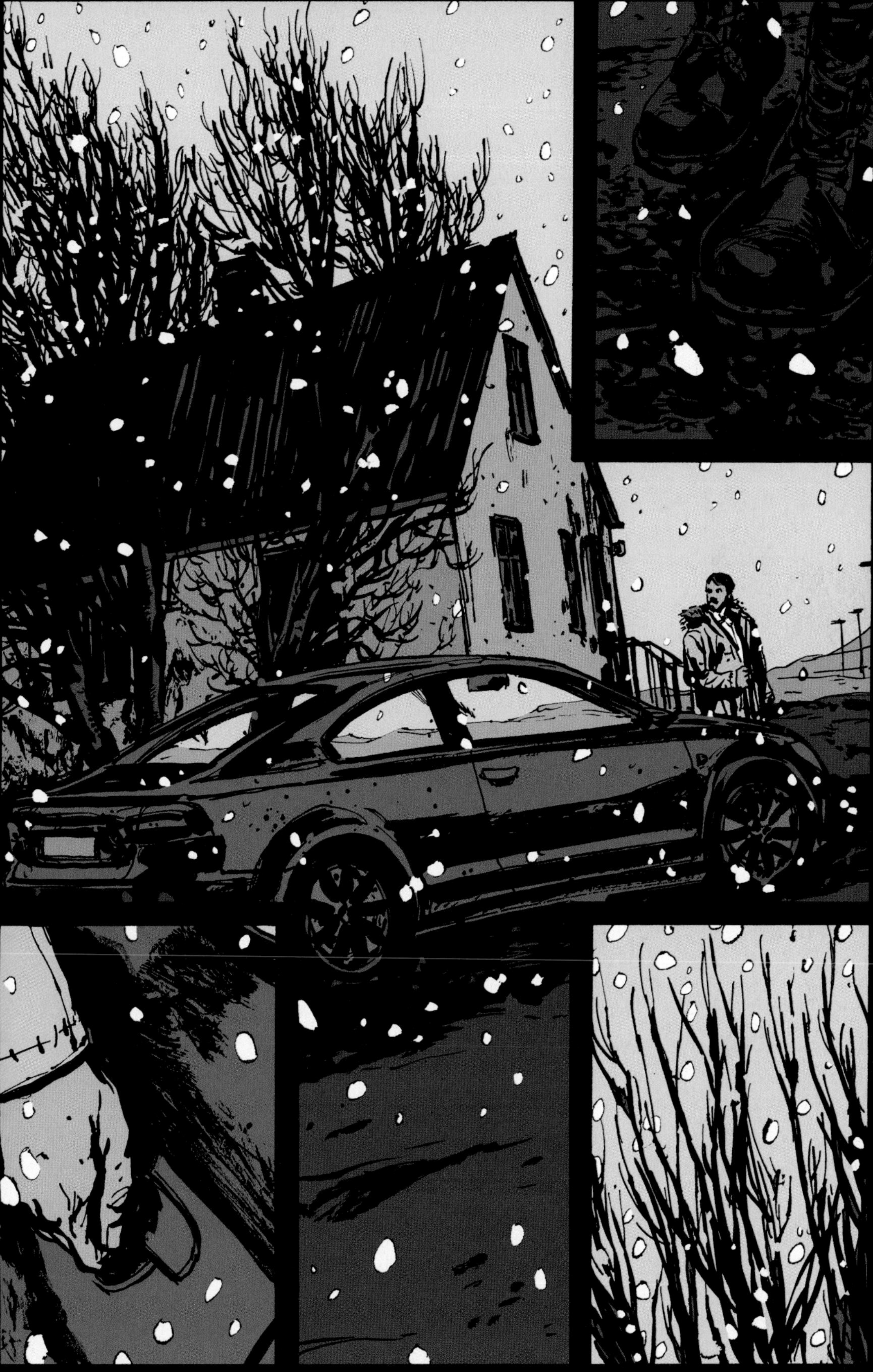

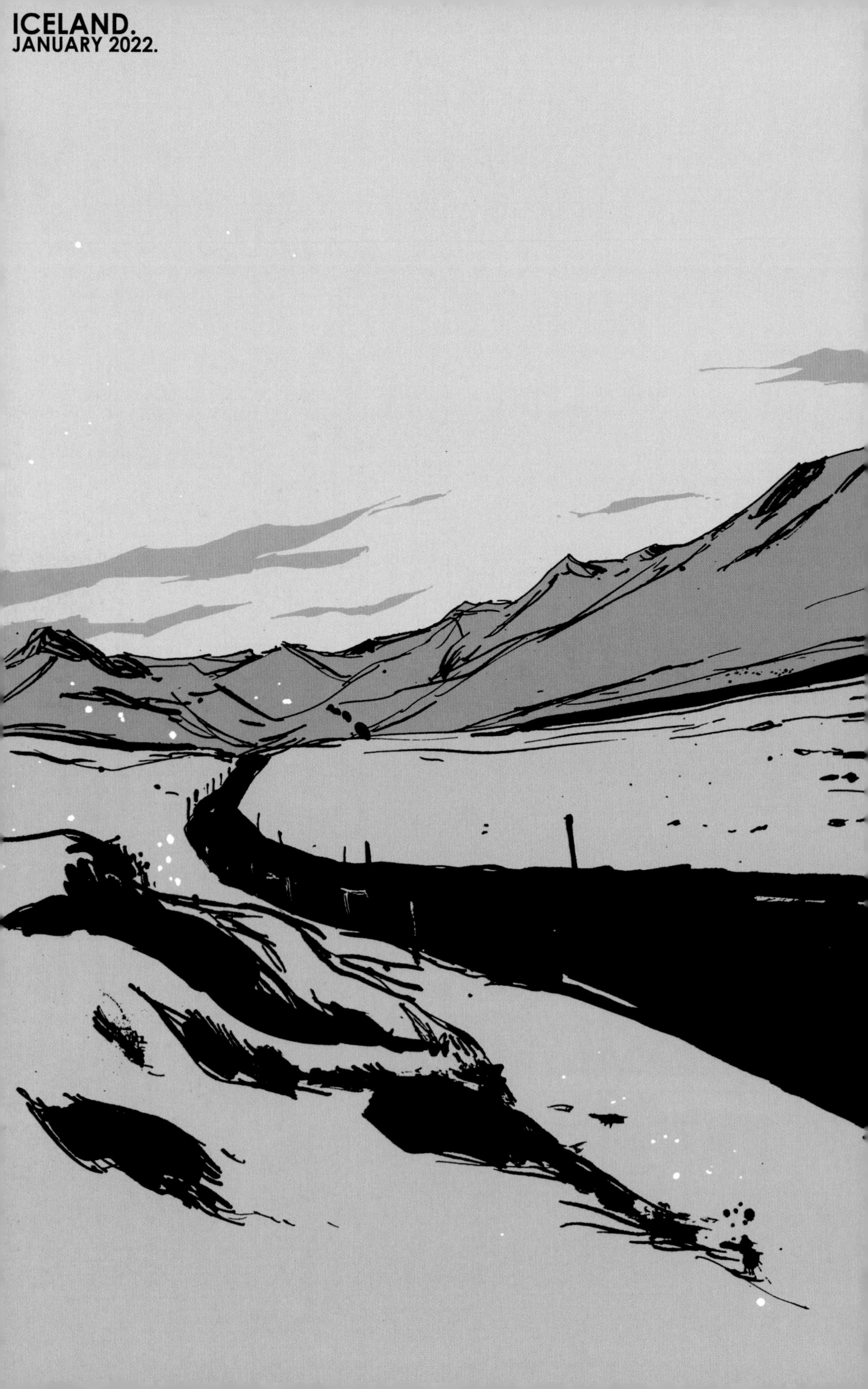
ICELAND.
JANUARY 2022.

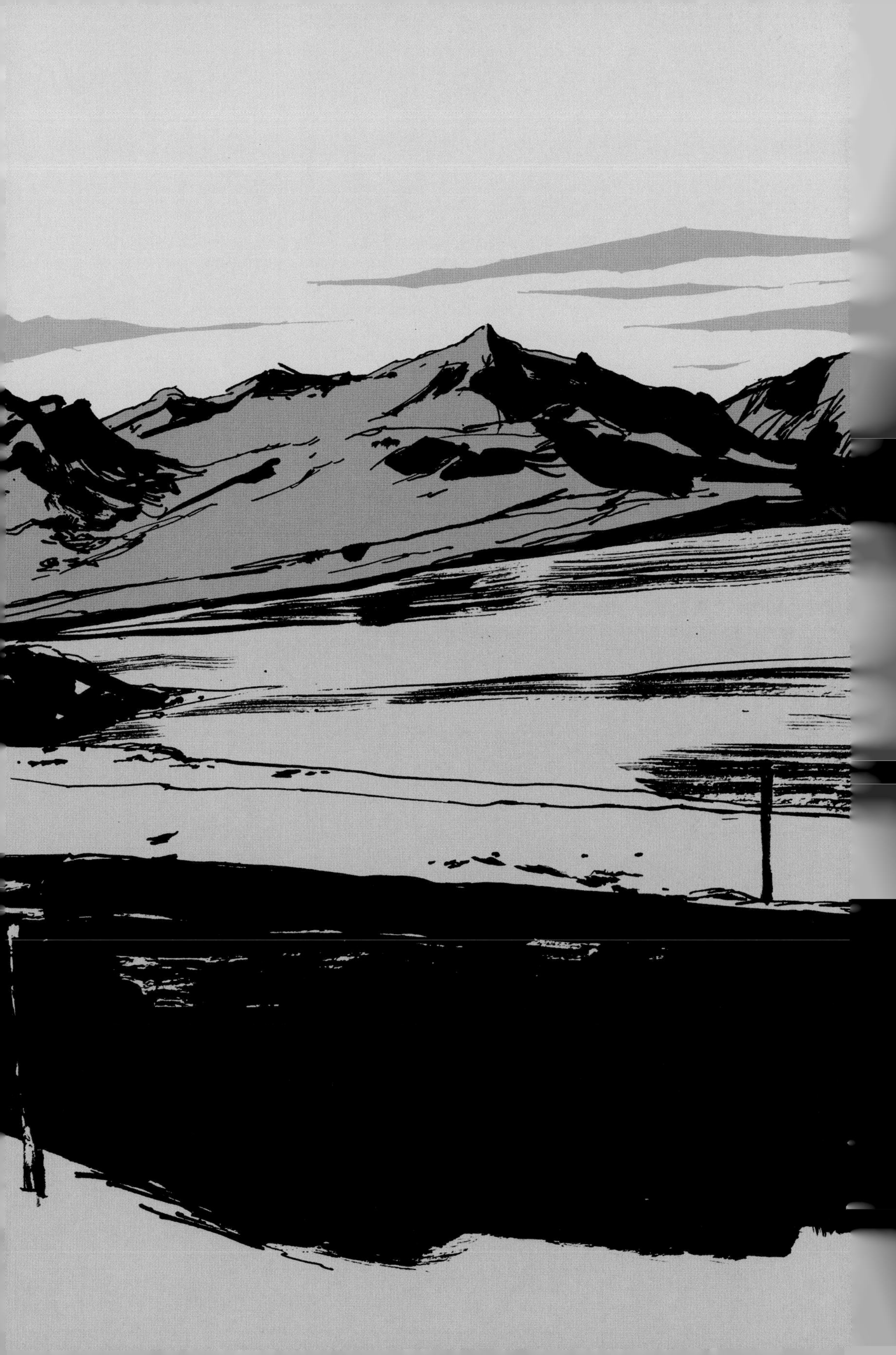

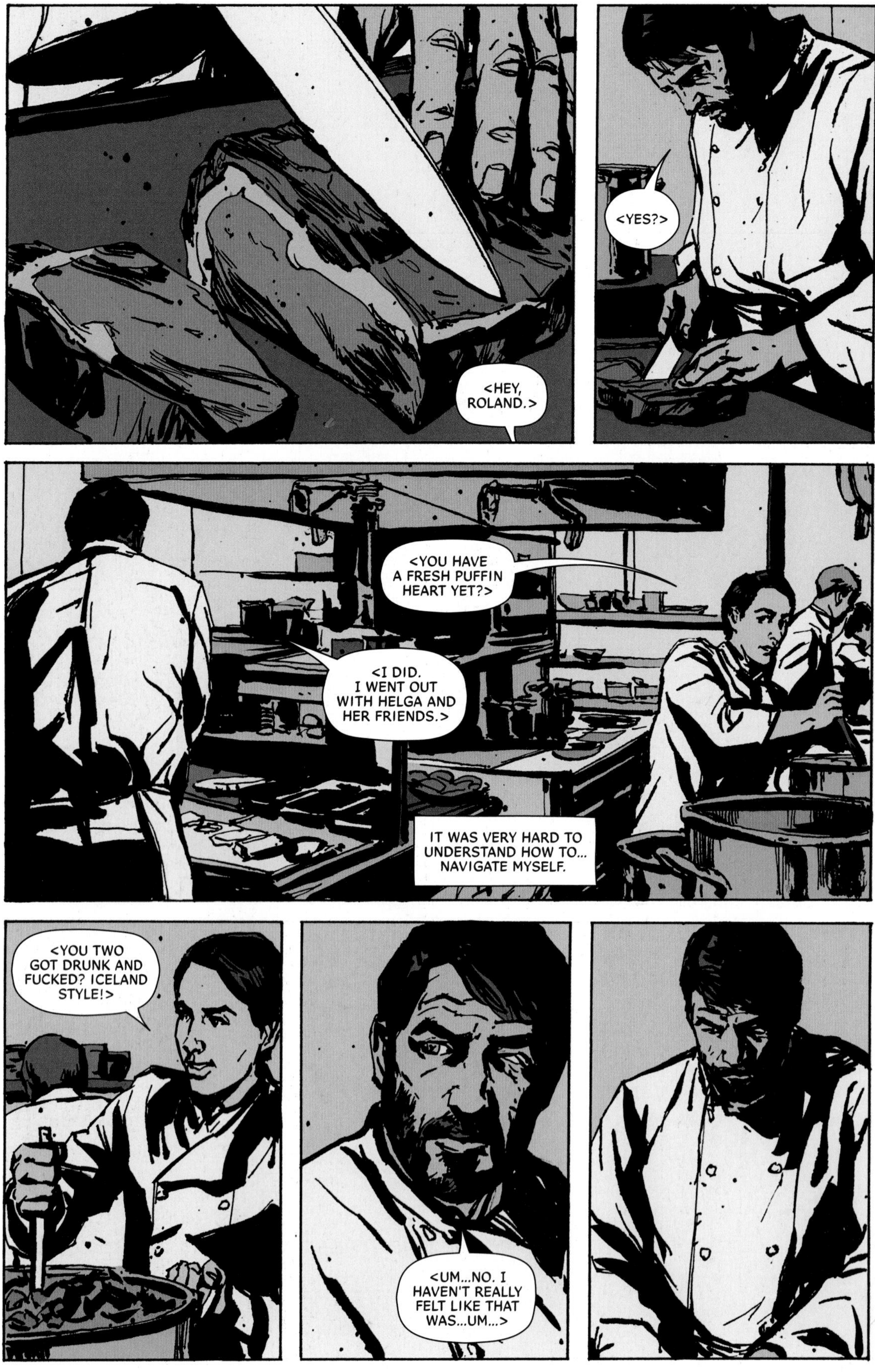
<HEY, ROLAND.>
<YES?>
<YOU HAVE A FRESH PUFFIN HEART YET?>
<I DID. I WENT OUT WITH HELGA AND HER FRIENDS.>
IT WAS VERY HARD TO UNDERSTAND HOW TO... NAVIGATE MYSELF.
<YOU TWO GOT DRUNK AND FUCKED? ICELAND STYLE!>
<UM...NO. I HAVEN'T REALLY FELT LIKE THAT WAS...UM...>

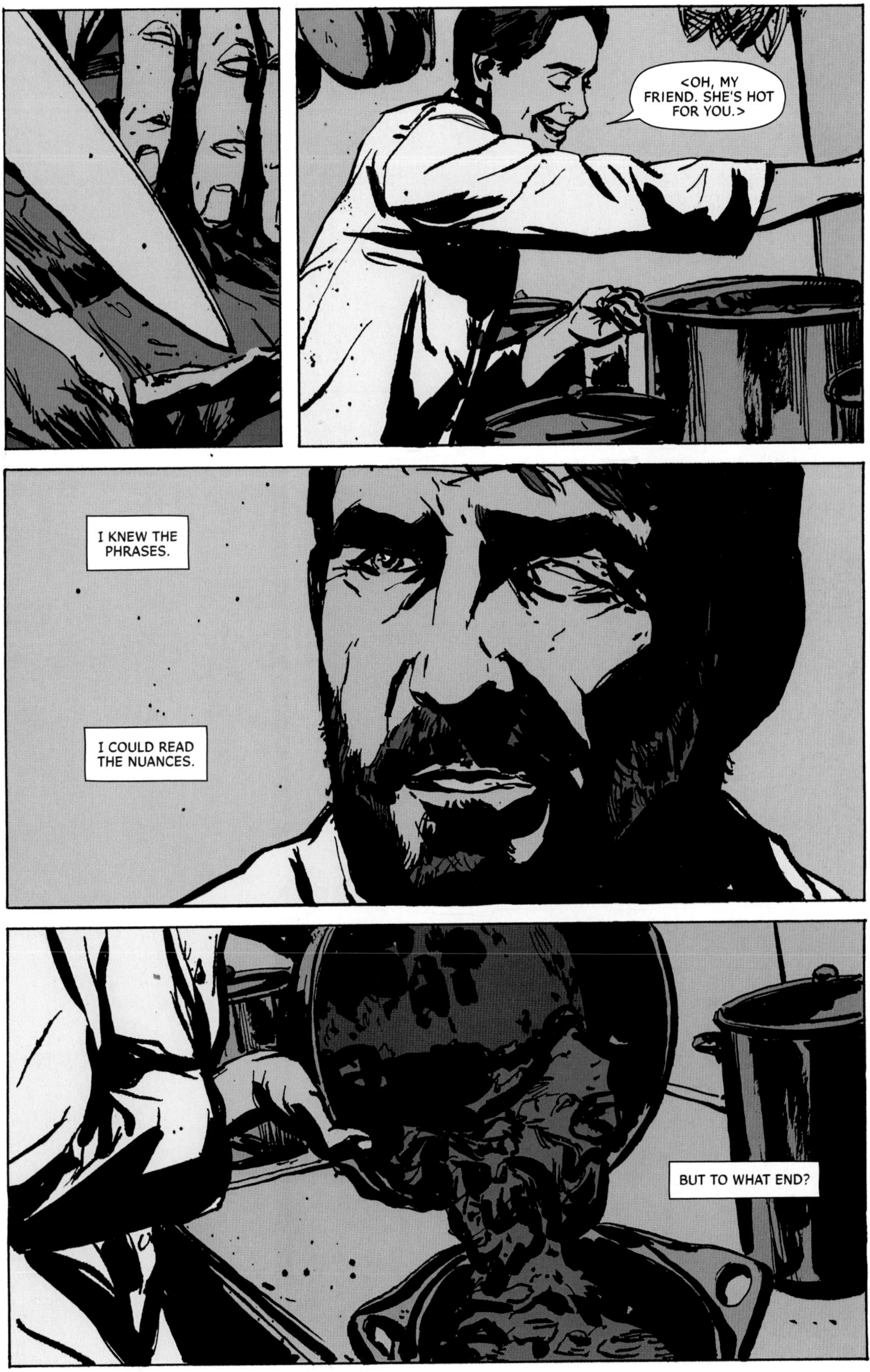
<OH, MY FRIEND. SHE'S HOT FOR YOU.>
I KNEW THE PHRASES.
I COULD READ THE NUANCES.
BUT TO WHAT END?

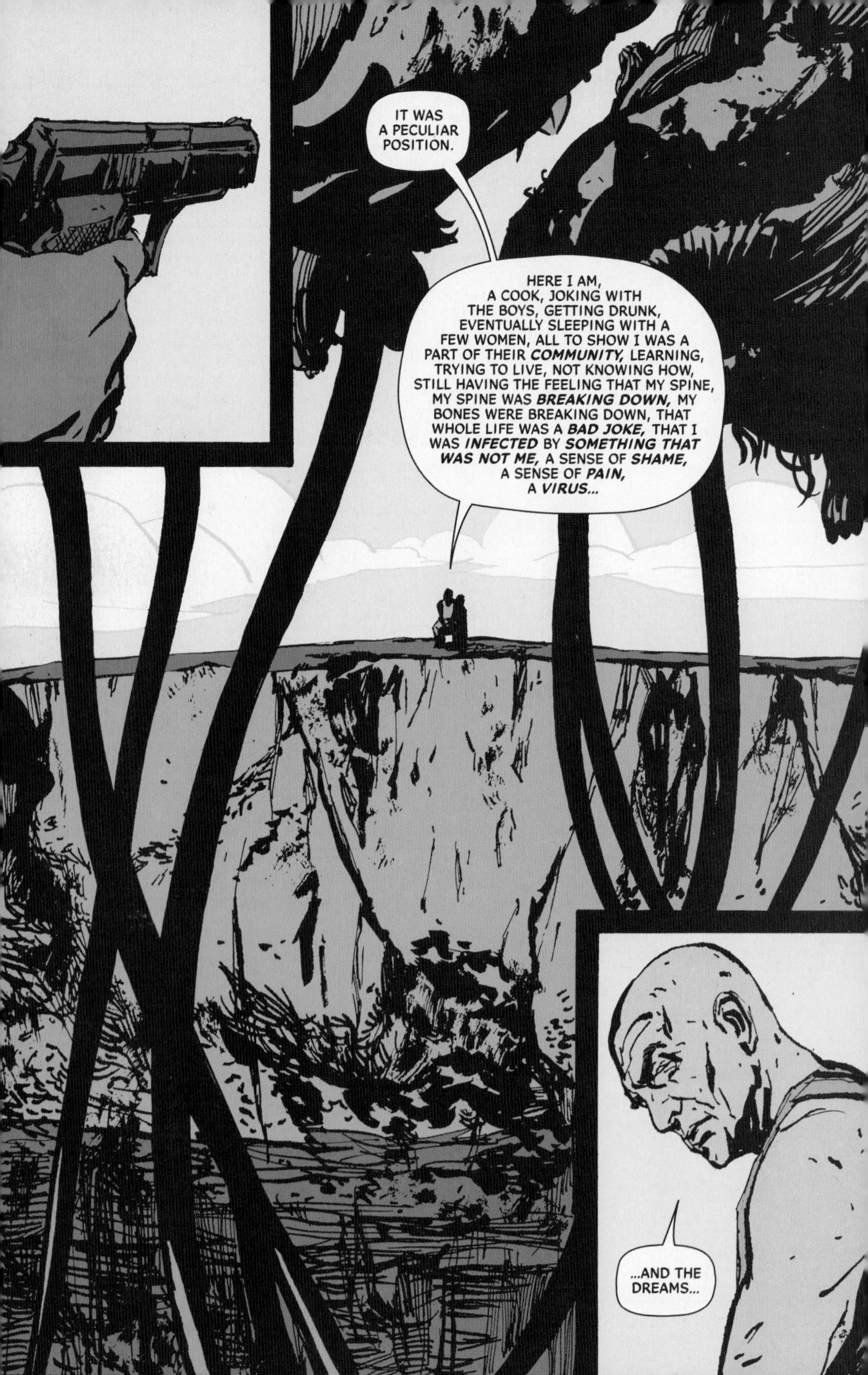
IT WAS A PECULIAR POSITION.
HERE I AM, A COOK, JOKING WITH THE BOYS, GETTING DRUNK, EVENTUALLY SLEEPING WITH A FEW WOMEN, ALL TO SHOW I WAS A PART OF THEIR *COMMUNITY,* LEARNING, TRYING TO LIVE, NOT KNOWING HOW, STILL HAVING THE FEELING THAT MY SPINE, MY SPINE WAS *BREAKING DOWN,* MY BONES WERE BREAKING DOWN, THAT WHOLE LIFE WAS A *BAD JOKE,* THAT I WAS *INFECTED* BY *SOMETHING THAT WAS NOT ME,* A SENSE OF *SHAME,* A SENSE OF *PAIN,* A *VIRUS*...
...AND THE DREAMS...

THE DREAMS
JUST

<IT'S
OKAY.>

<IT'S
OKAY, HONEY.
I'M FINE.>

DROVE

IT

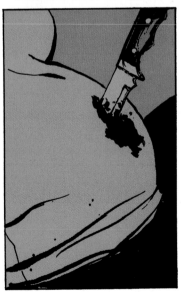

IN.

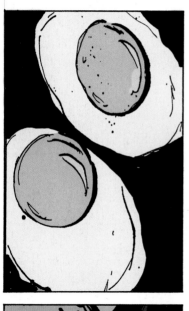

ROUTINE HELPED.

READING HELPED.

PROGRAM OR BE PROGRAMMED

TEN COMMANDS
R A DIGITAL AGE

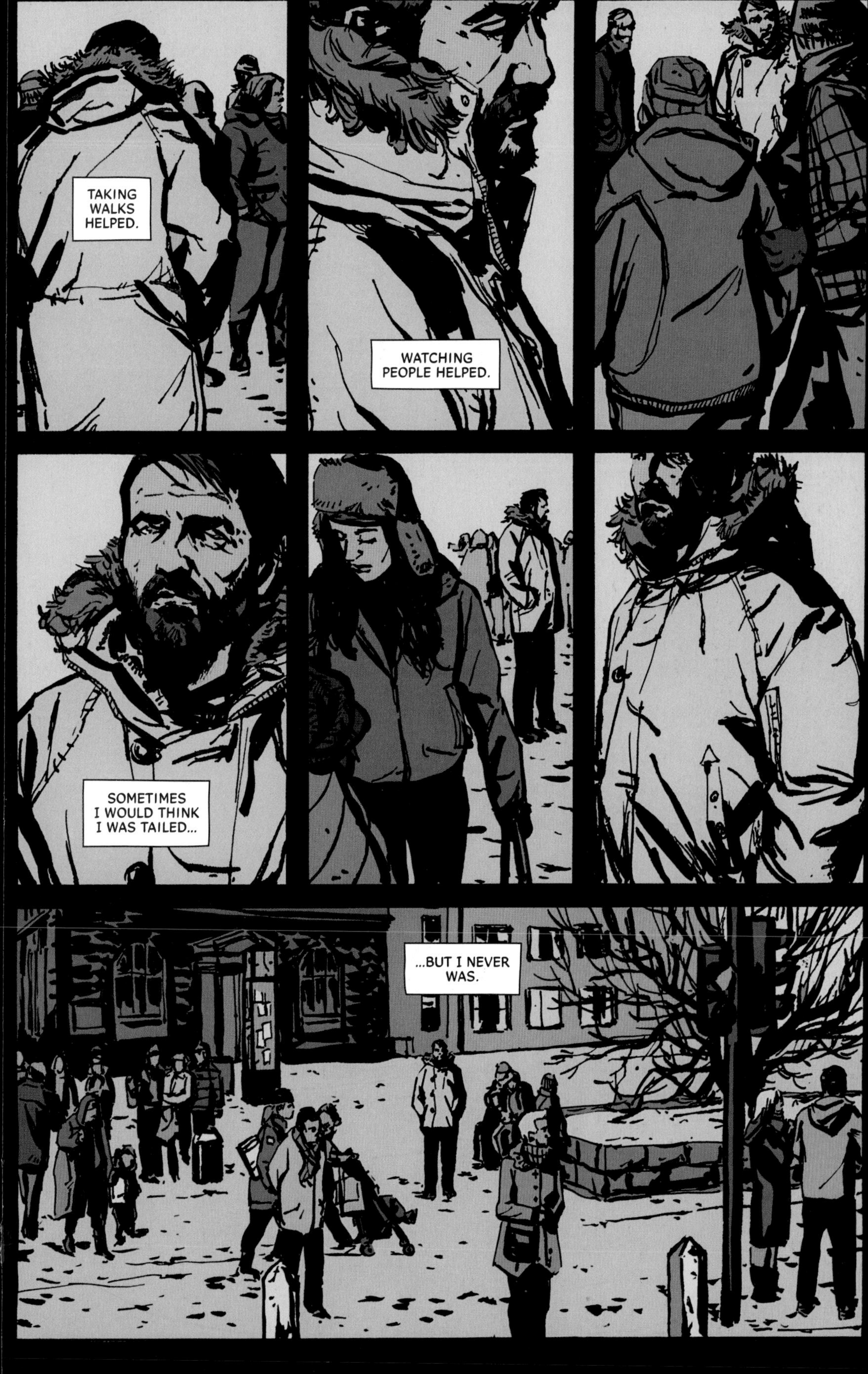
TAKING WALKS HELPED.
WATCHING PEOPLE HELPED.
SOMETIMES I WOULD THINK I WAS TAILED...
...BUT I NEVER WAS.

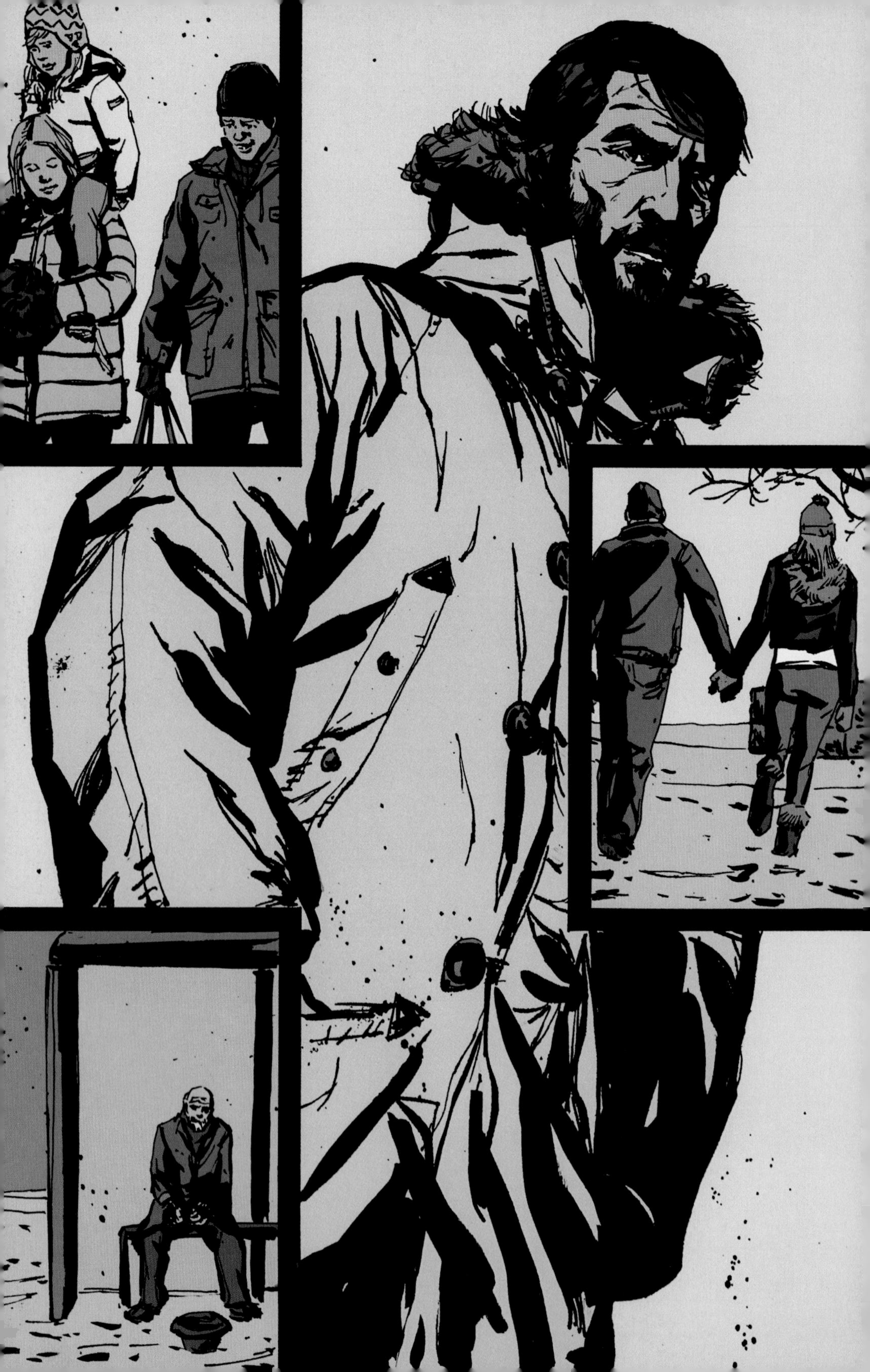

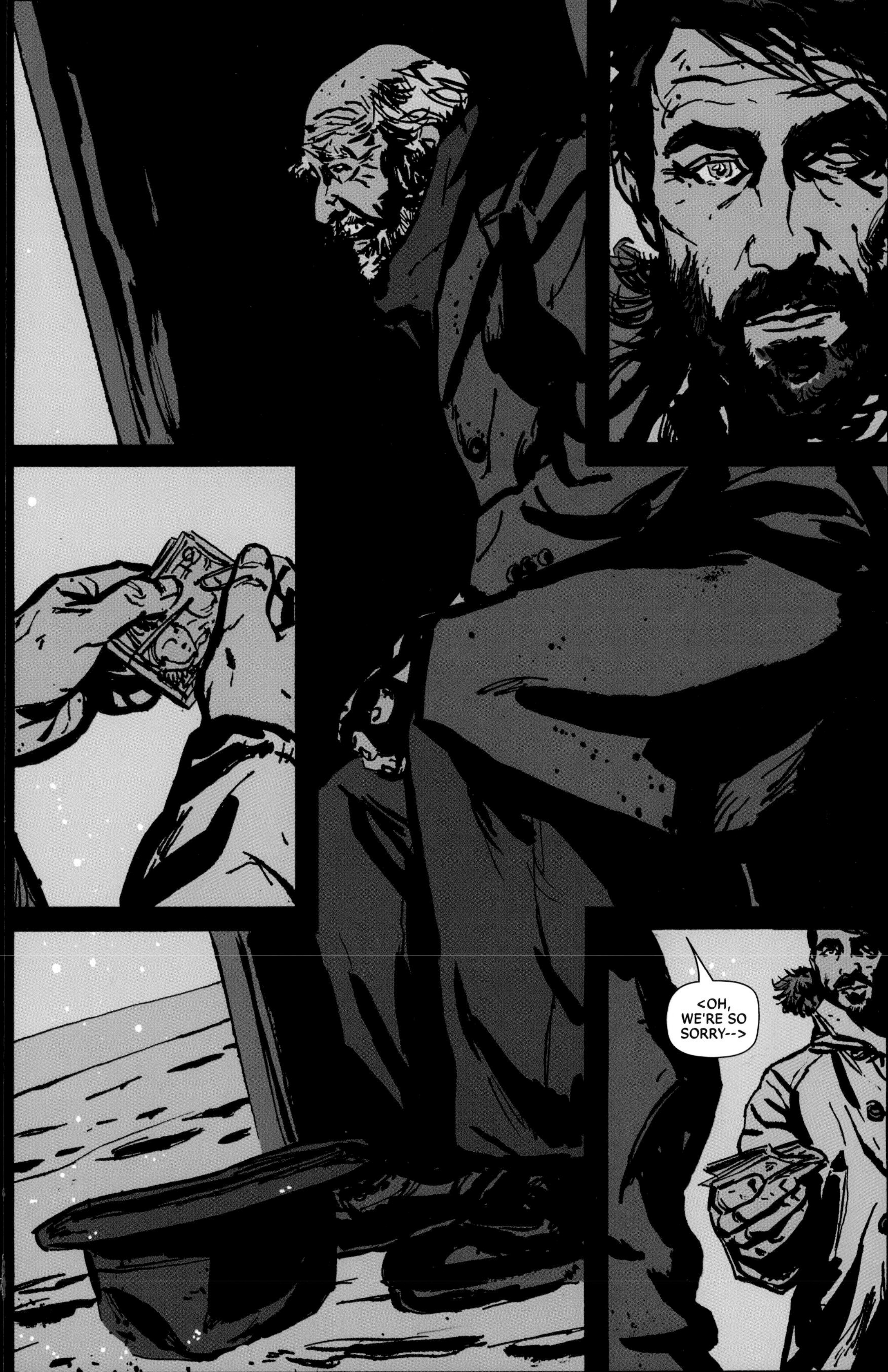
<OH, WE'RE SO SORRY-->

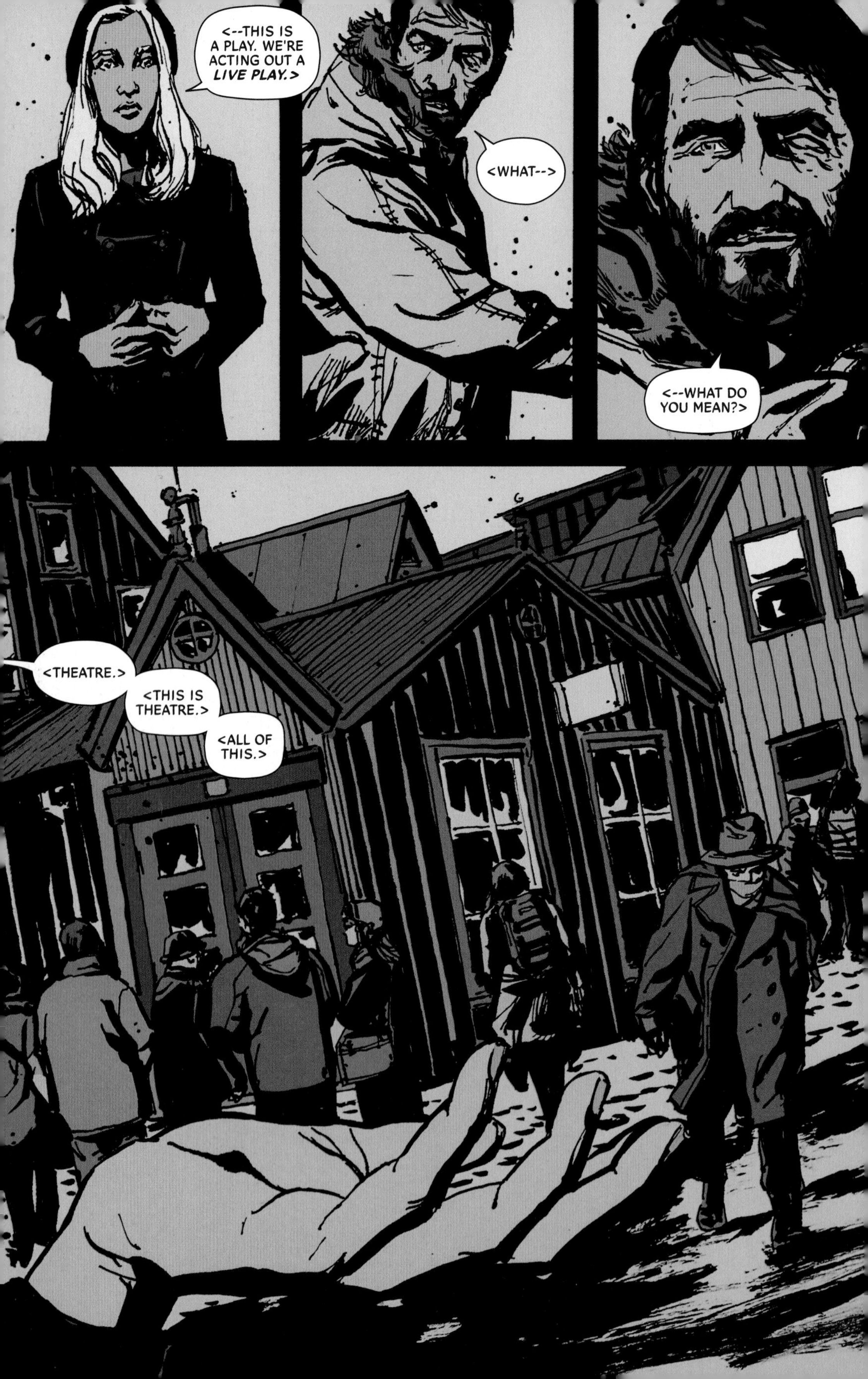
<--THIS IS A PLAY. WE'RE ACTING OUT A *LIVE PLAY.*>
<WHAT-->
<--WHAT DO YOU MEAN?>
<THEATRE.>
<THIS IS THEATRE.>
<ALL OF THIS.>

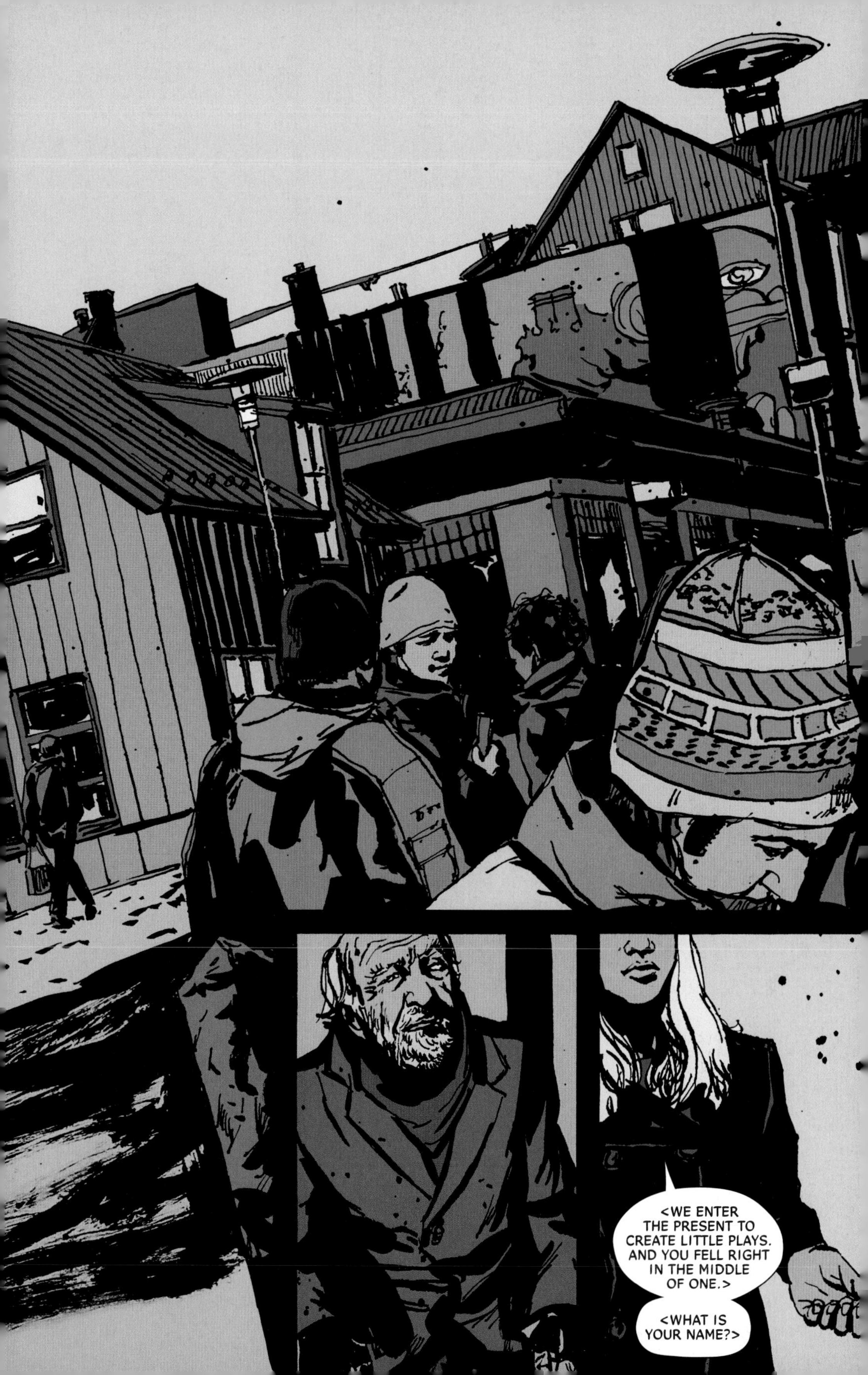
<WE ENTER THE PRESENT TO CREATE LITTLE PLAYS. AND YOU FELL RIGHT IN THE MIDDLE OF ONE.>
<WHAT IS YOUR NAME?>

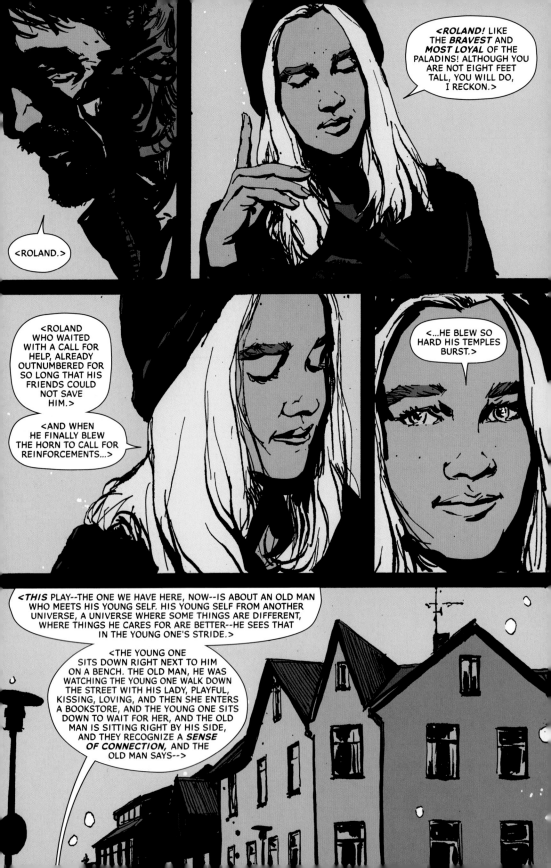

\<ROLAND! LIKE THE *BRAVEST* AND *MOST LOYAL* OF THE PALADINS! ALTHOUGH YOU ARE NOT EIGHT FEET TALL, YOU WILL DO, I RECKON.\>

\<ROLAND.\>

\<ROLAND WHO WAITED WITH A CALL FOR HELP, ALREADY OUTNUMBERED FOR SO LONG THAT HIS FRIENDS COULD NOT SAVE HIM.\>

\<AND WHEN HE FINALLY BLEW THE HORN TO CALL FOR REINFORCEMENTS...\>

\<...HE BLEW SO HARD HIS TEMPLES BURST.\>

\<*THIS* PLAY--THE ONE WE HAVE HERE, NOW--IS ABOUT AN OLD MAN WHO MEETS HIS YOUNG SELF. HIS YOUNG SELF FROM ANOTHER UNIVERSE, A UNIVERSE WHERE SOME THINGS ARE DIFFERENT, WHERE THINGS HE CARES FOR ARE BETTER--HE SEES THAT IN THE YOUNG ONE'S STRIDE.\>

\<THE YOUNG ONE SITS DOWN RIGHT NEXT TO HIM ON A BENCH. THE OLD MAN, HE WAS WATCHING THE YOUNG ONE WALK DOWN THE STREET WITH HIS LADY, PLAYFUL, KISSING, LOVING, AND THEN SHE ENTERS A BOOKSTORE, AND THE YOUNG ONE SITS DOWN TO WAIT FOR HER, AND THE OLD MAN IS SITTING RIGHT BY HIS SIDE, AND THEY RECOGNIZE A *SENSE OF CONNECTION,* AND THE OLD MAN SAYS--\>

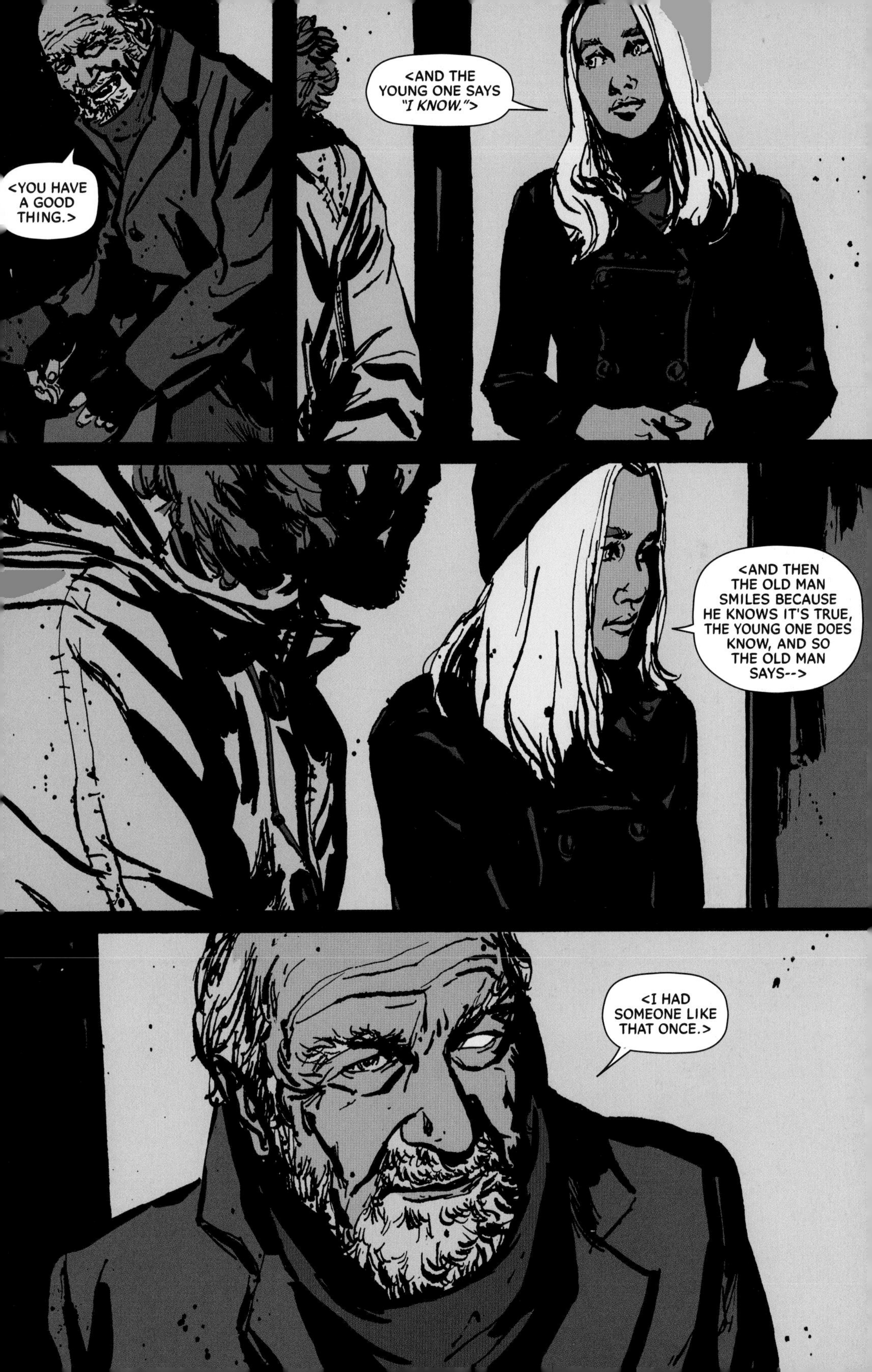
<AND THE YOUNG ONE SAYS *"I KNOW."*>
<YOU HAVE A GOOD THING.>
<AND THEN THE OLD MAN SMILES BECAUSE HE KNOWS IT'S TRUE, THE YOUNG ONE DOES KNOW, AND SO THE OLD MAN SAYS-->
<I HAD SOMEONE LIKE THAT ONCE.>

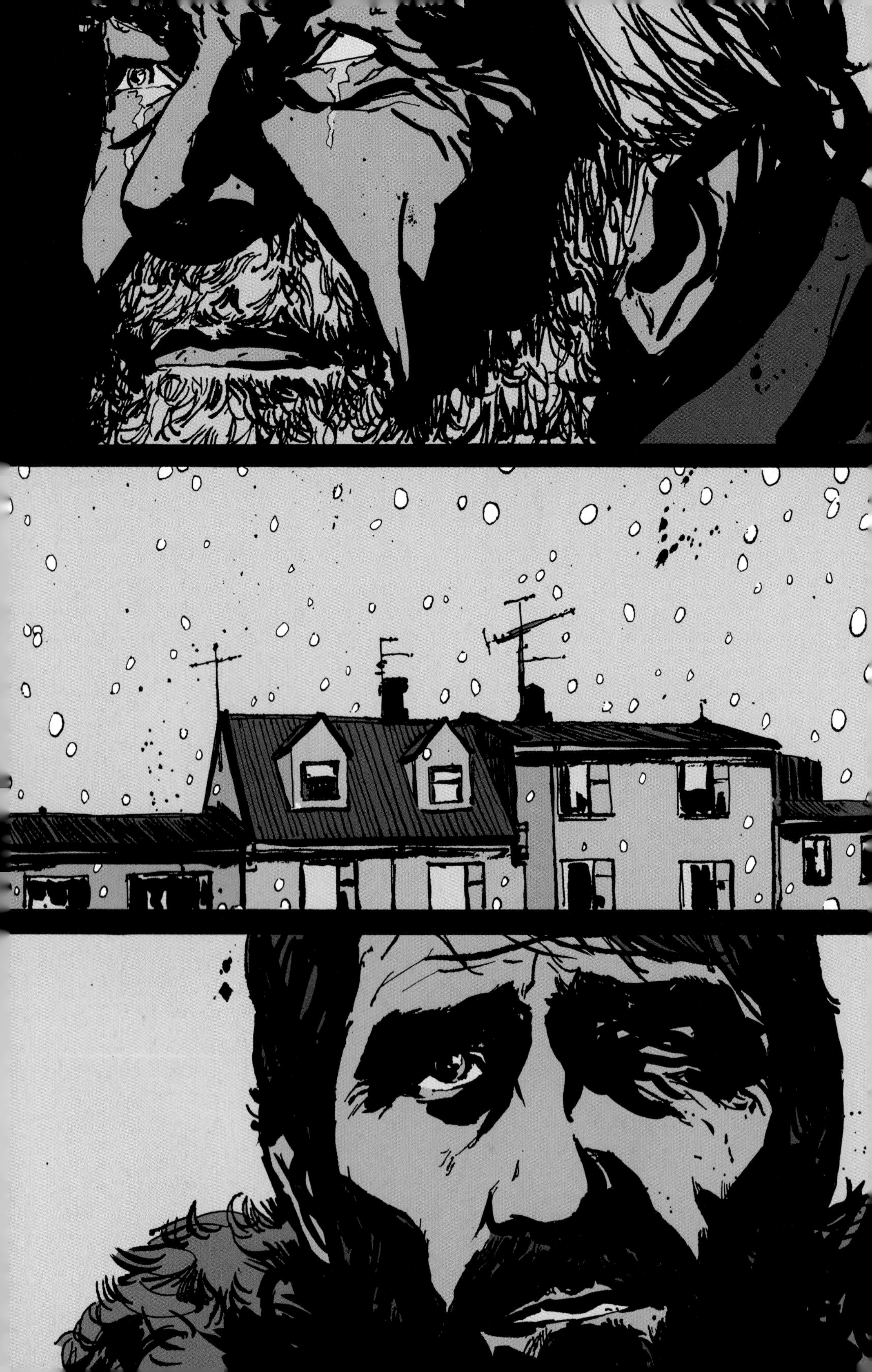

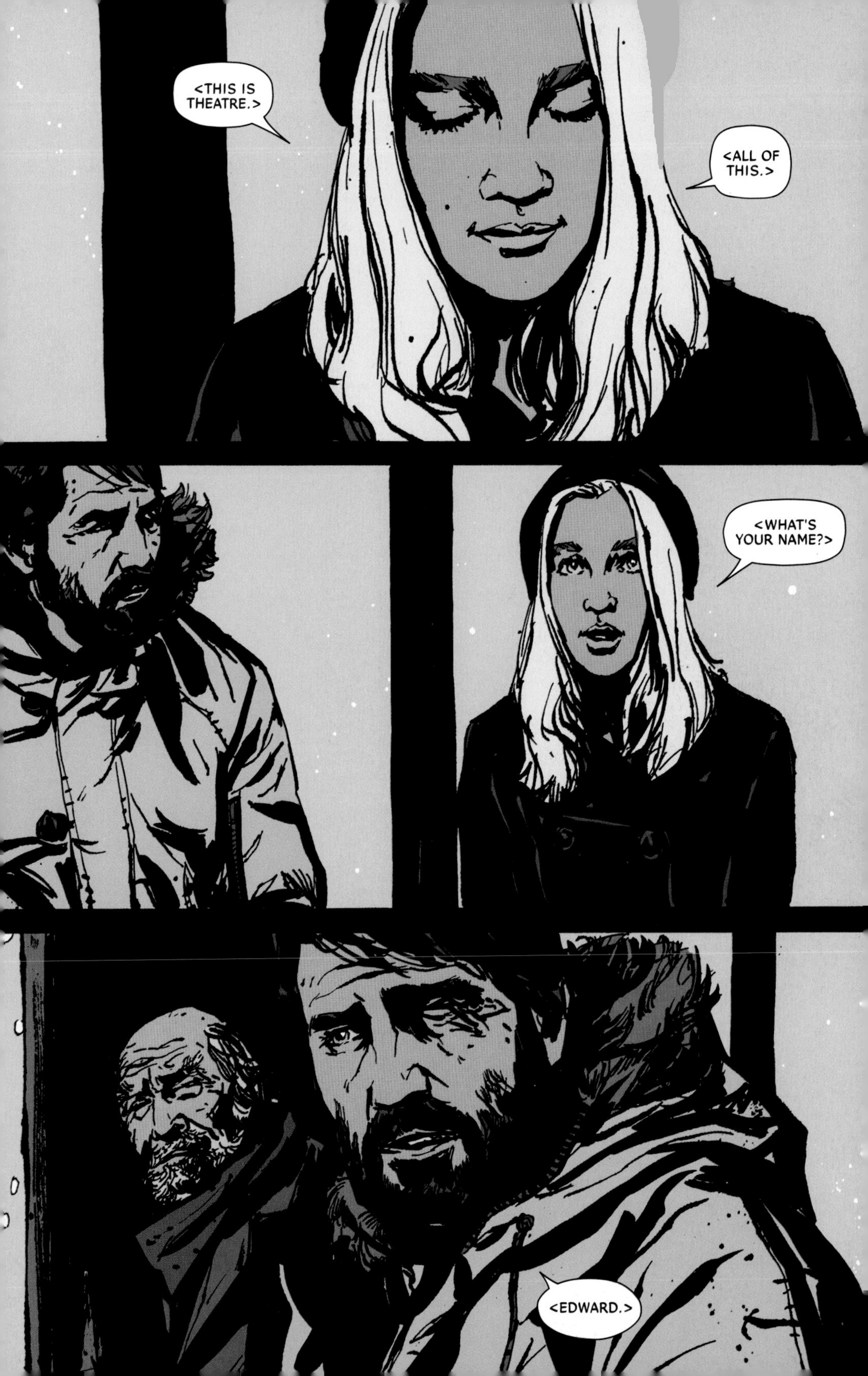
<THIS IS THEATRE.>
<ALL OF THIS.>
<WHAT'S YOUR NAME?>
<EDWARD.>

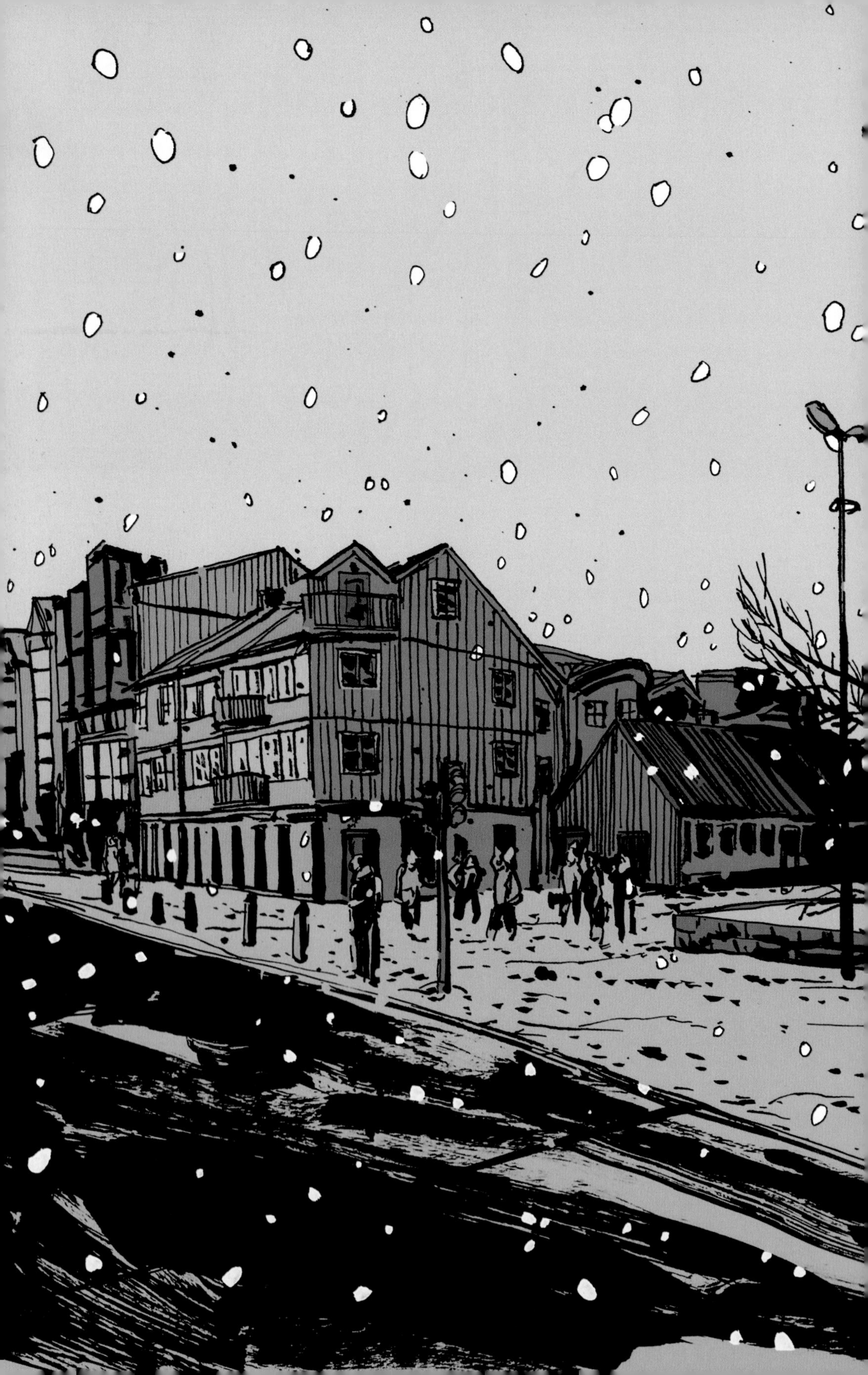

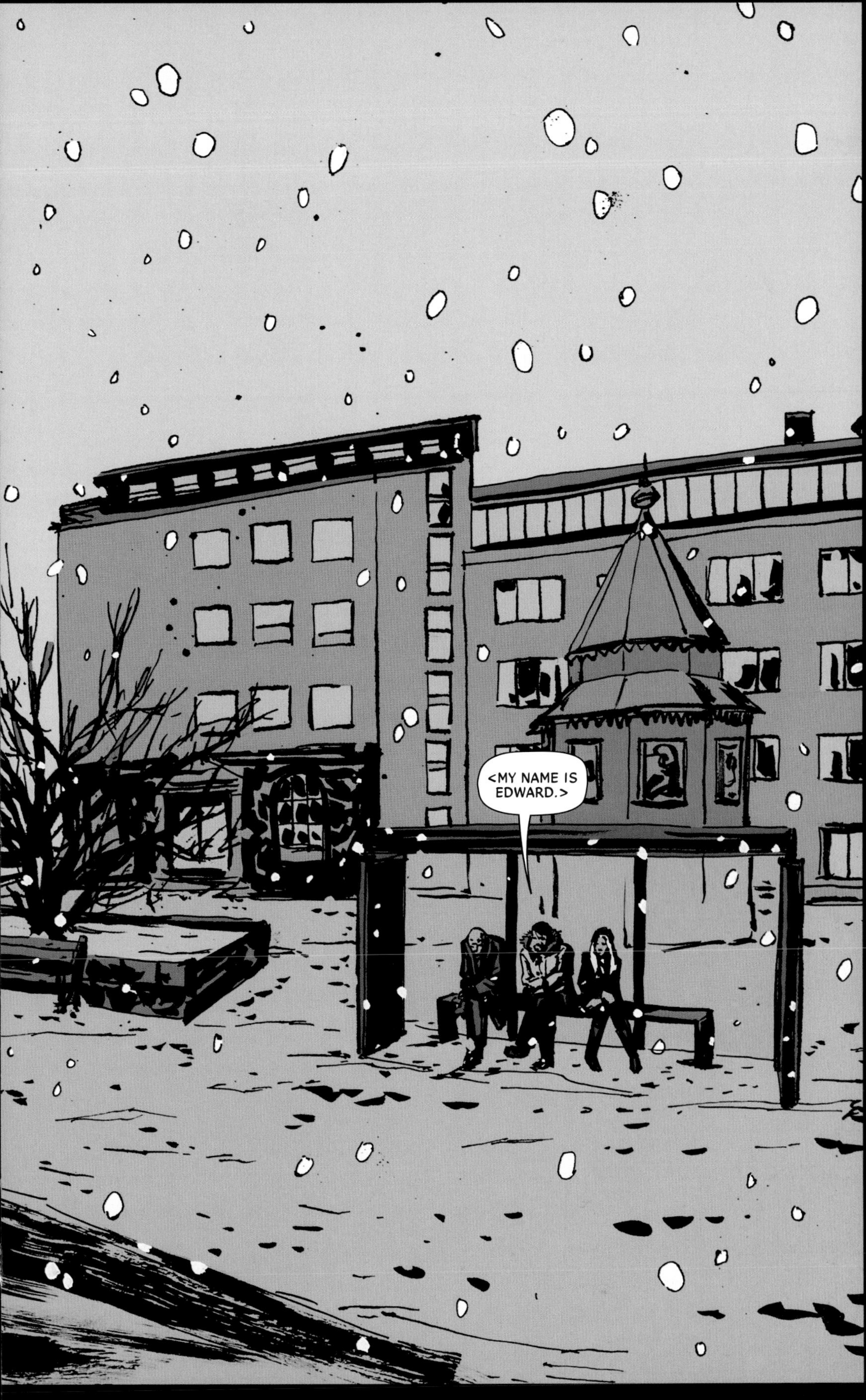
<MY NAME IS EDWARD.>

CHAPTER 10:

WHO TOLD YOU THIS ROOM EXISTS

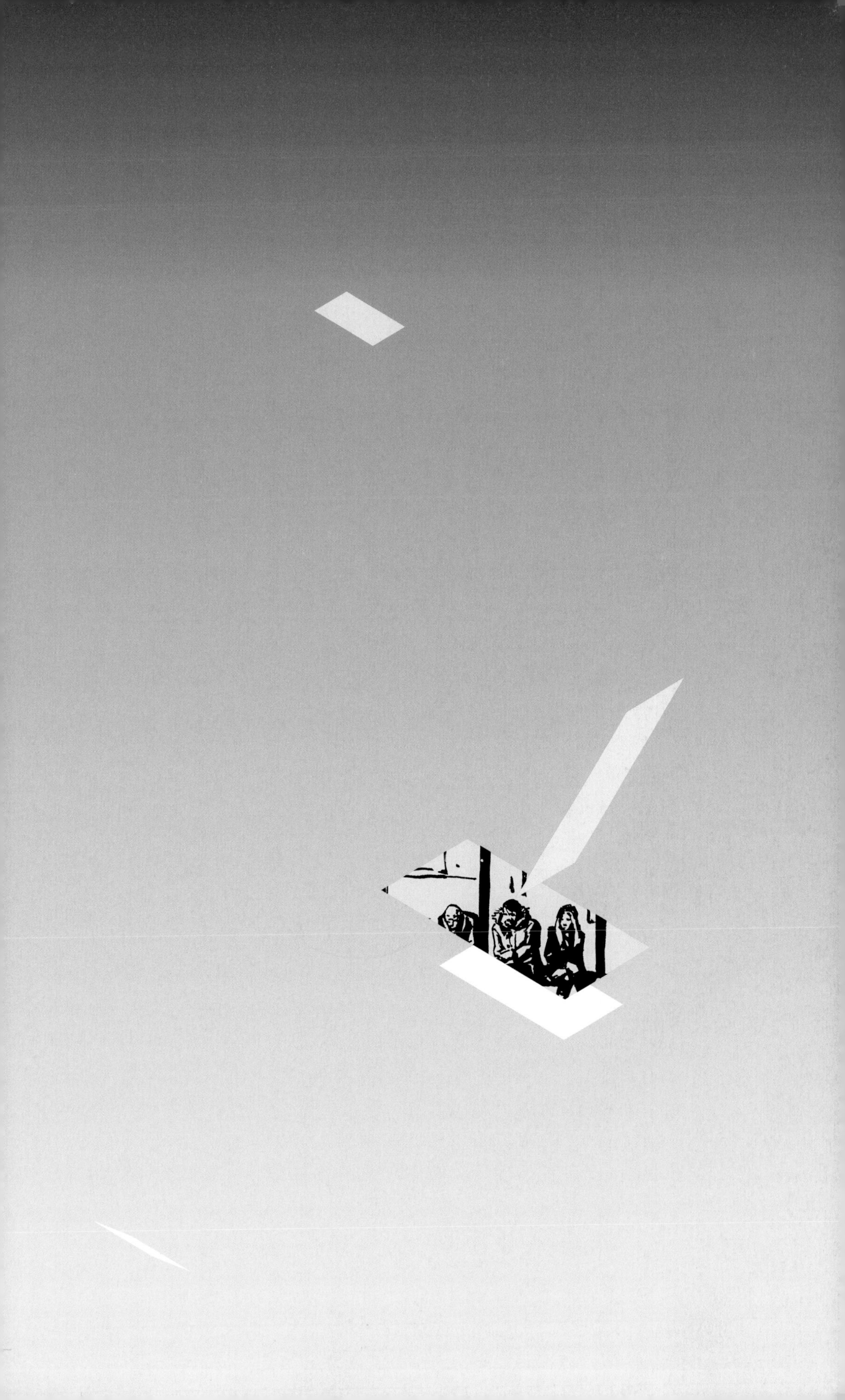

When all the numbers swim together
And all the shadows settle
When doors forced open shut again
A flytrap and a petal
My eyes burn and claws rush to fill them

And in the morning after the night
I fall in love with the light
It is so clear I realize
That here at last I have my eyes

PSYCHIC TV – 'THE ORCHIDS'

#6—10

PUBLICATION DESIGN

The original ZERO single issue
publication designs by Tom Muller,
with key art from series artists
Vanesa R. Del Rey, Matt Taylor,
Jorge Coelho, Tonči Zonjić, and
Michael Gaydos —
and variant cover art from
Francesco Francavilla,
Nick Dragotta, Cameron Stewart,
and Sean Phillips.

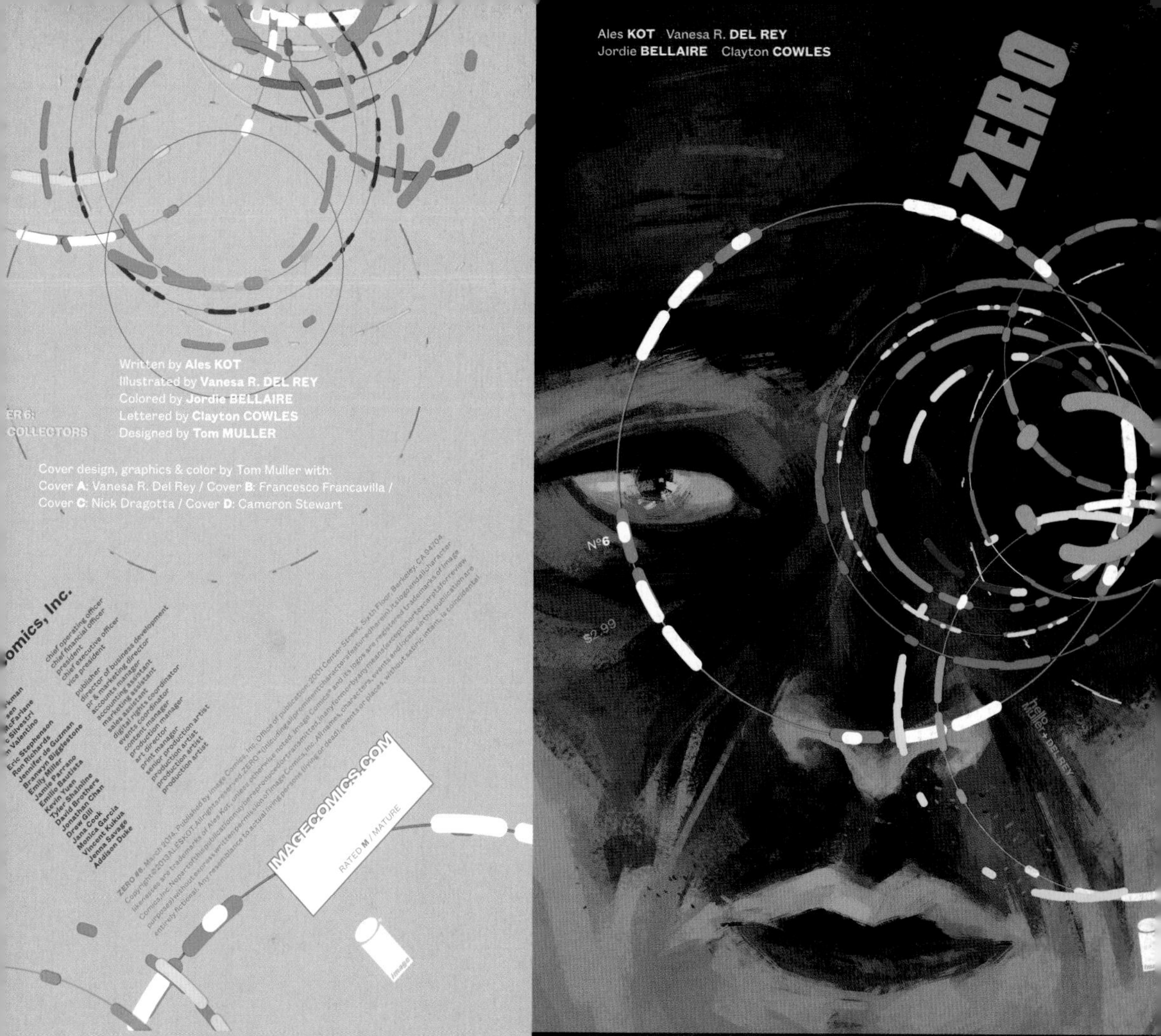

Ales KOT Vanesa R. DEL REY
Jordie BELLAIRE Clayton COWLES
ZERO™
No 6
$2.99
Written by Ales KOT
Illustrated by Vanesa R. DEL REY
Colored by Jordie BELLAIRE
Lettered by Clayton COWLES
Designed by Tom MULLER
Cover design, graphics & color by Tom Muller with:
Cover A: Vanesa R. Del Rey / Cover B: Francesco Francavilla /
Cover C: Nick Dragotta / Cover D: Cameron Stewart
omics, Inc.
Eric Stephenson publisher
Ron Richards director of business development
Jennifer de Guzman director of pr & marketing director
Branwyn Bigglestone accounts manager
Emily Miller accounting assistant
Jamie Parrano marketing assistant
Emilio Bautista sales assistant
Kevin Yuen digital rights coordinator
Tyler Shainline events coordinator
David Brothers content manager
Jonathan Chan production manager
Drew Gill art director
Jana Cook print manager
Monica Garcia senior production artist
Vincent Kukua production artist
Jenna Savage production artist
Addison Duke production artist
ZERO #6, March 2014. Published by Image Comics, Inc. Office of publication: 2001 Center Street, Sixth Floor, Berkeley, CA 94704. Copyright © 2013 ALES KOT. All rights reserved. ZERO™ (including all prominent characters featured herein), its logo and all character likenesses are trademarks of Ales Kot, unless otherwise noted. Image Comics® and its logos are registered trademarks of Image Comics, Inc. No part of this publication may be reproduced or transmitted, in any form or by any means (except for short excerpts for review purposes) without express written permission of Image Comics, Inc. All names, characters, events and locales in this publication are entirely fictional. Any resemblance to actual persons (living or dead), events or places, without satiric intent, is coincidental.
IMAGECOMICS.COM
RATED M / MATURE
image

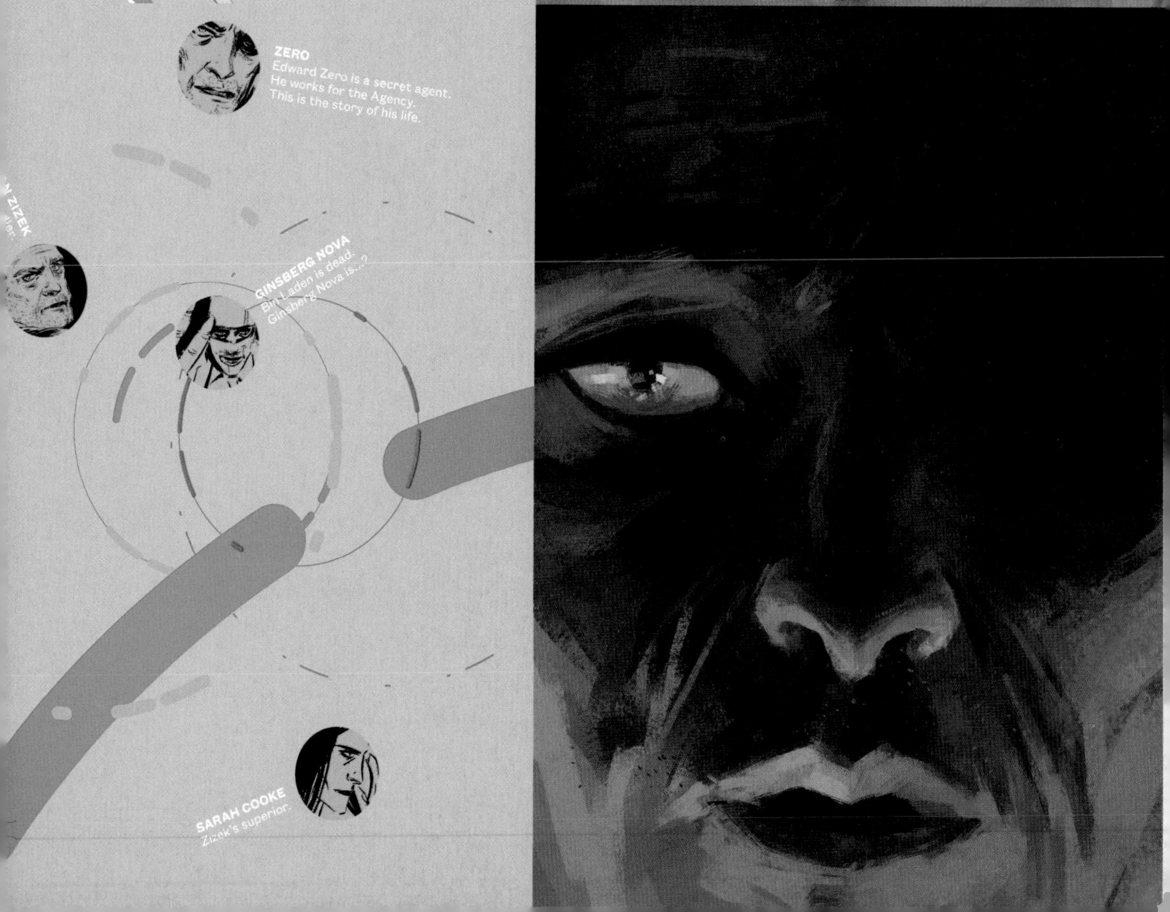

ZERO
Edward Zero is a secret agent.
He works for the Agency.
This is the story of his life.
GINSBERG NOVA
Bin Laden is dead.
Ginsberg Nova is...?
SARAH COOKE
Zizek's superior.

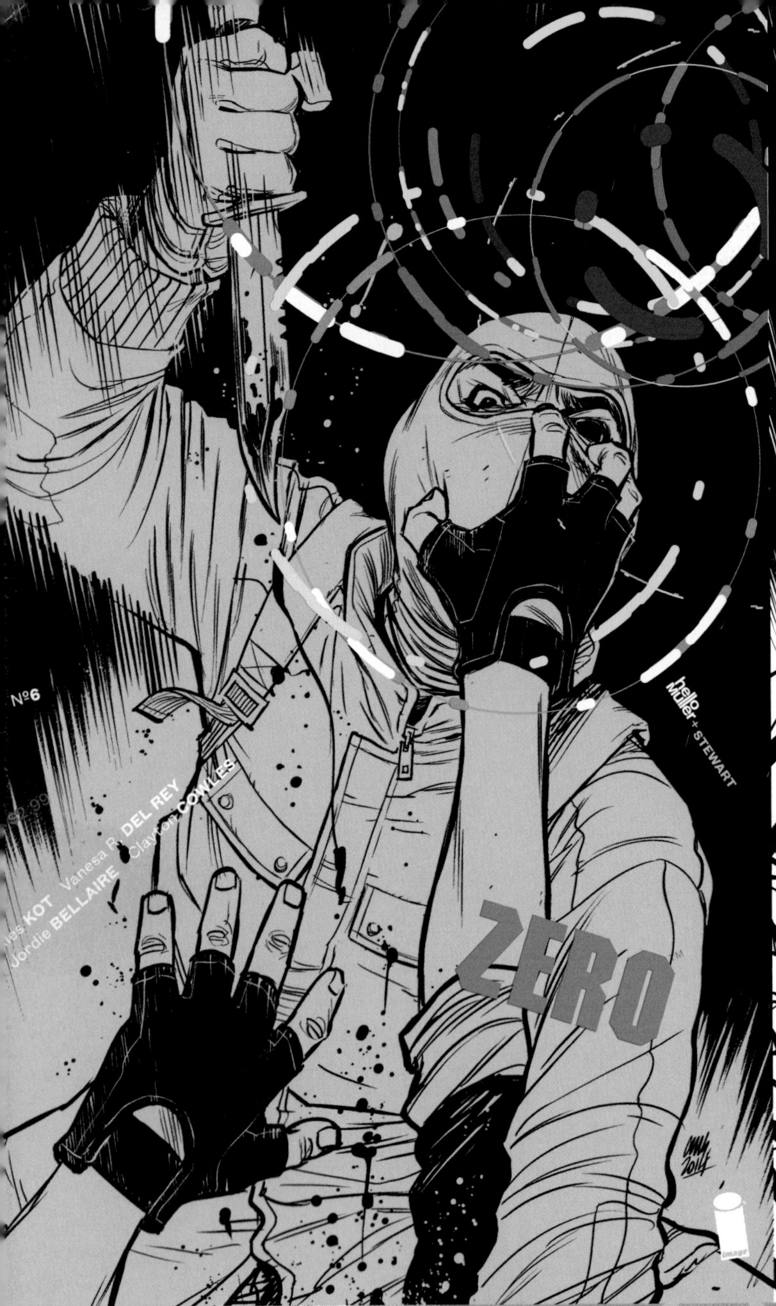
Nº6
KOT Vanesa R. DEL REY
Jordie BELLAIRE Clayton COWLES
ZERO
hello Müller + STEWART
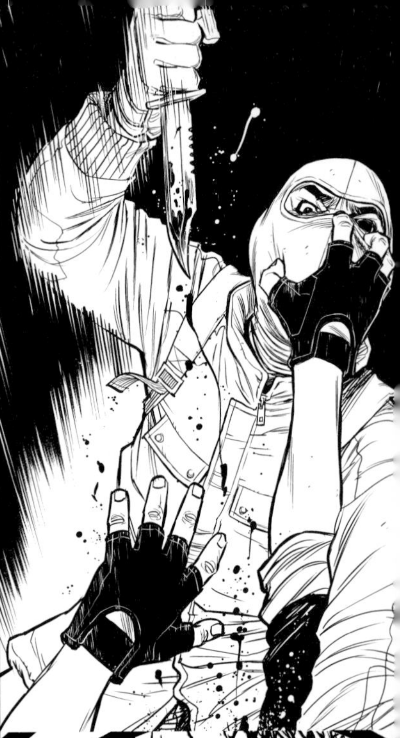
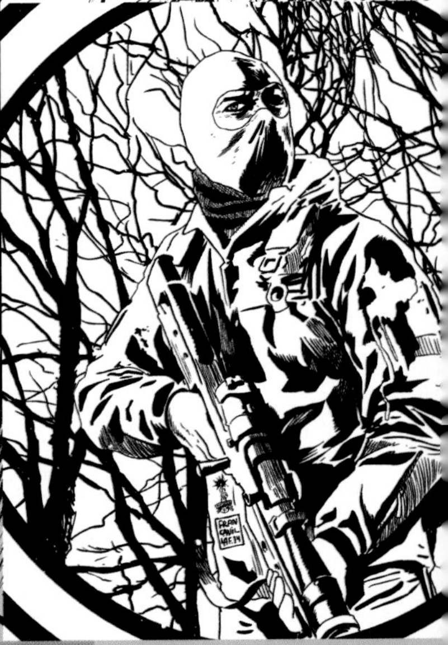
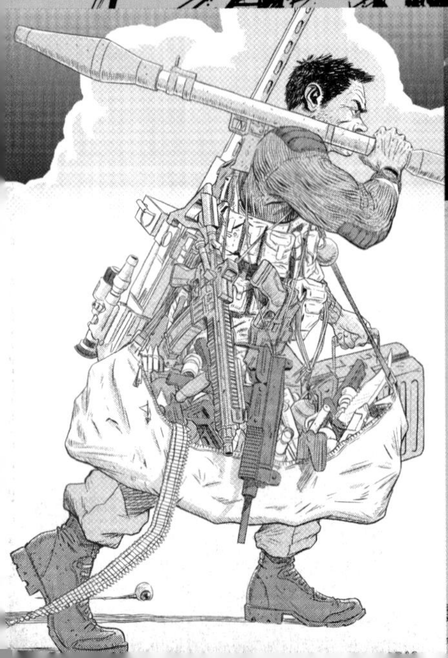
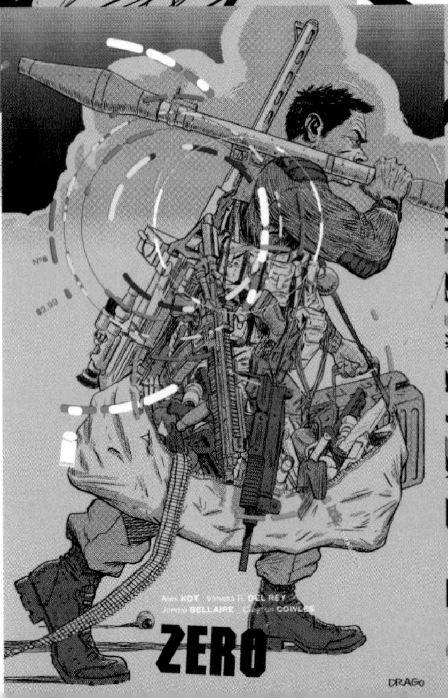
Nº6
$2.99
Ales KOT Vanesa R. DEL REY
Jordie BELLAIRE Clayton COWLES
ZERO
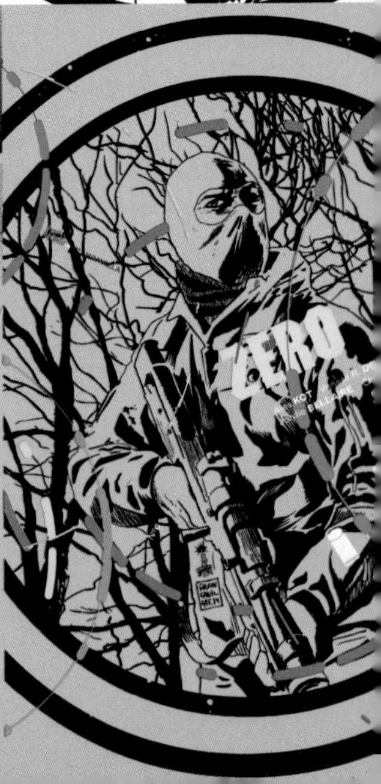
ZERO
DRAGO

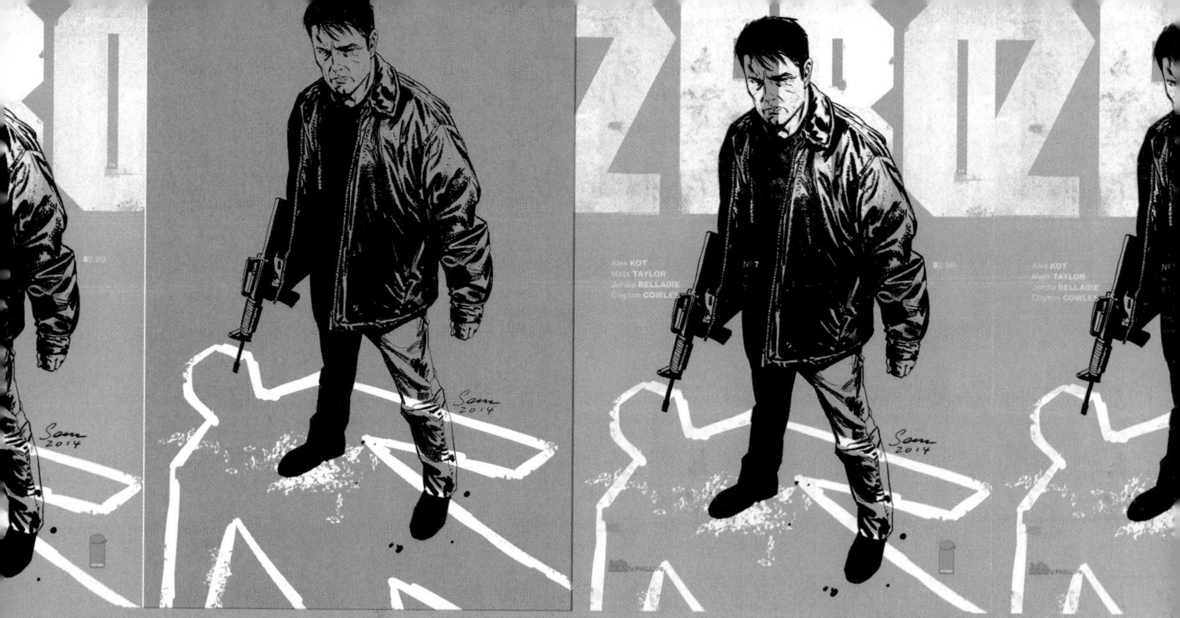
$2.99
Ales KOT
Matt TAYLOR
Jordie BELLAIRE
Clayton COWLES
Nº 7
$2.99
Ales KOT
Matt TAYLOR
Jordie BELLAIRE
Clayton COWLES

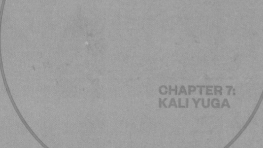

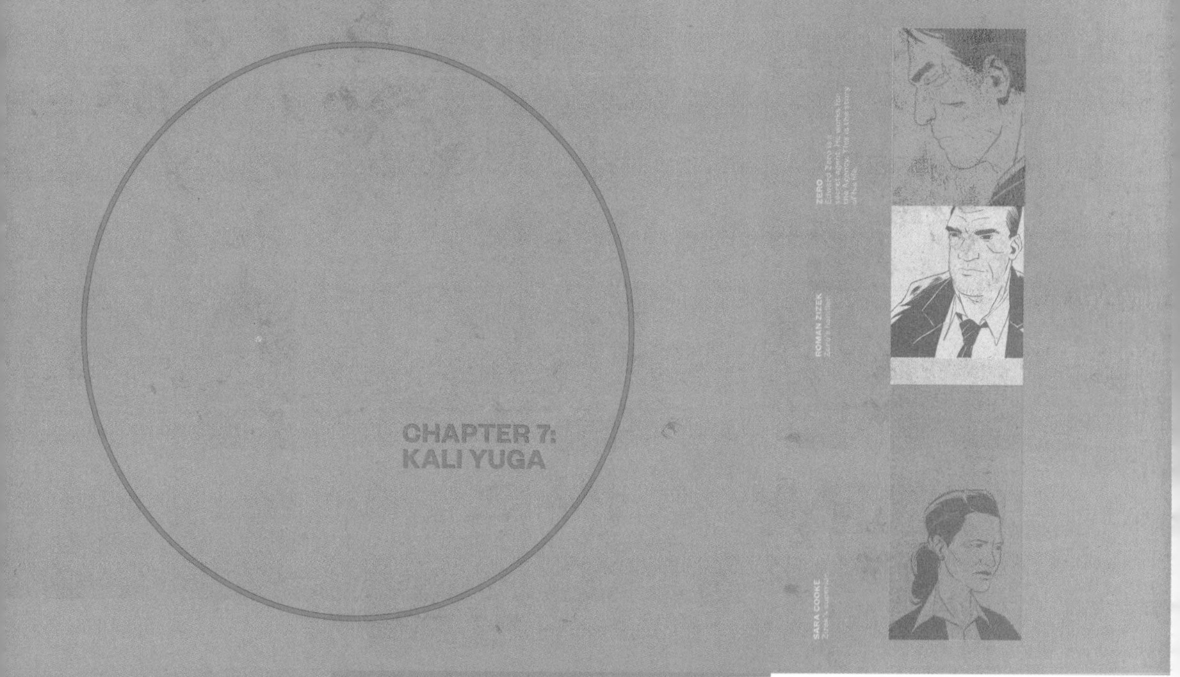
CHAPTER 7:
KALI YUGA
ZERO
ROMAN ZIZEK
SARA COOKE

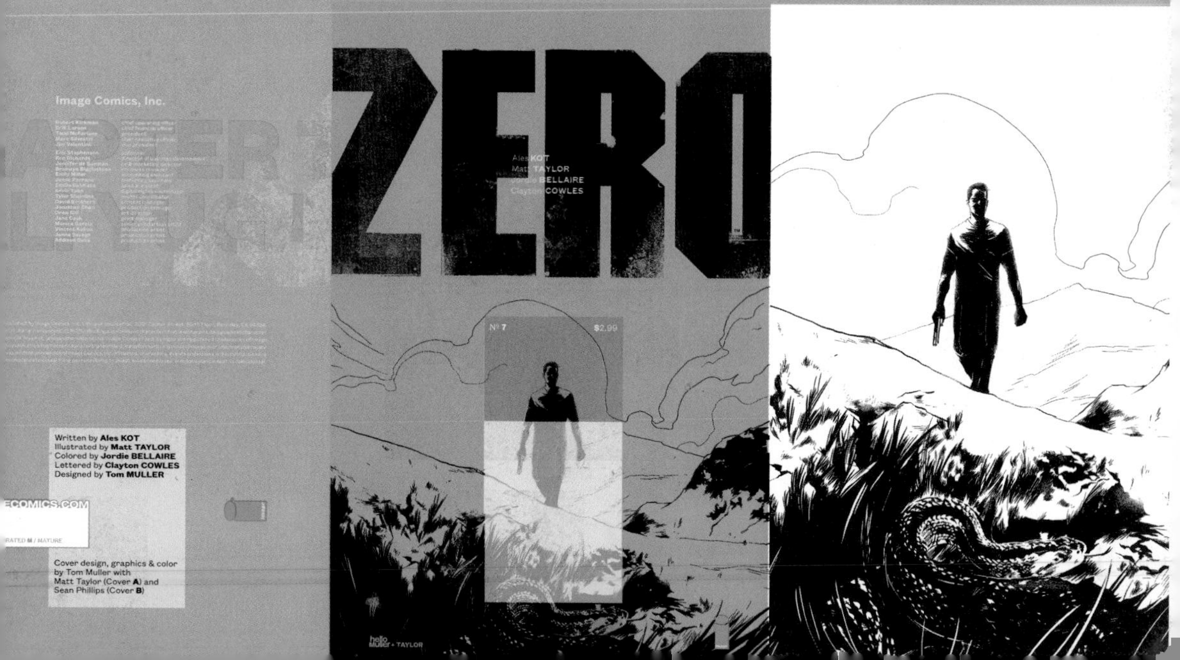
Image Comics, Inc.
ZERO
Ales KOT
Matt TAYLOR
Jordie BELLAIRE
Clayton COWLES
Nº 7
$2.99
Written by Ales KOT
Illustrated by Matt TAYLOR
Colored by Jordie BELLAIRE
Lettered by Clayton COWLES
Designed by Tom MULLER
ECOMICS.COM
RATED M / MATURE
Cover design, graphics & color
by Tom Muller with
Matt Taylor (Cover A) and
Sean Phillips (Cover B)

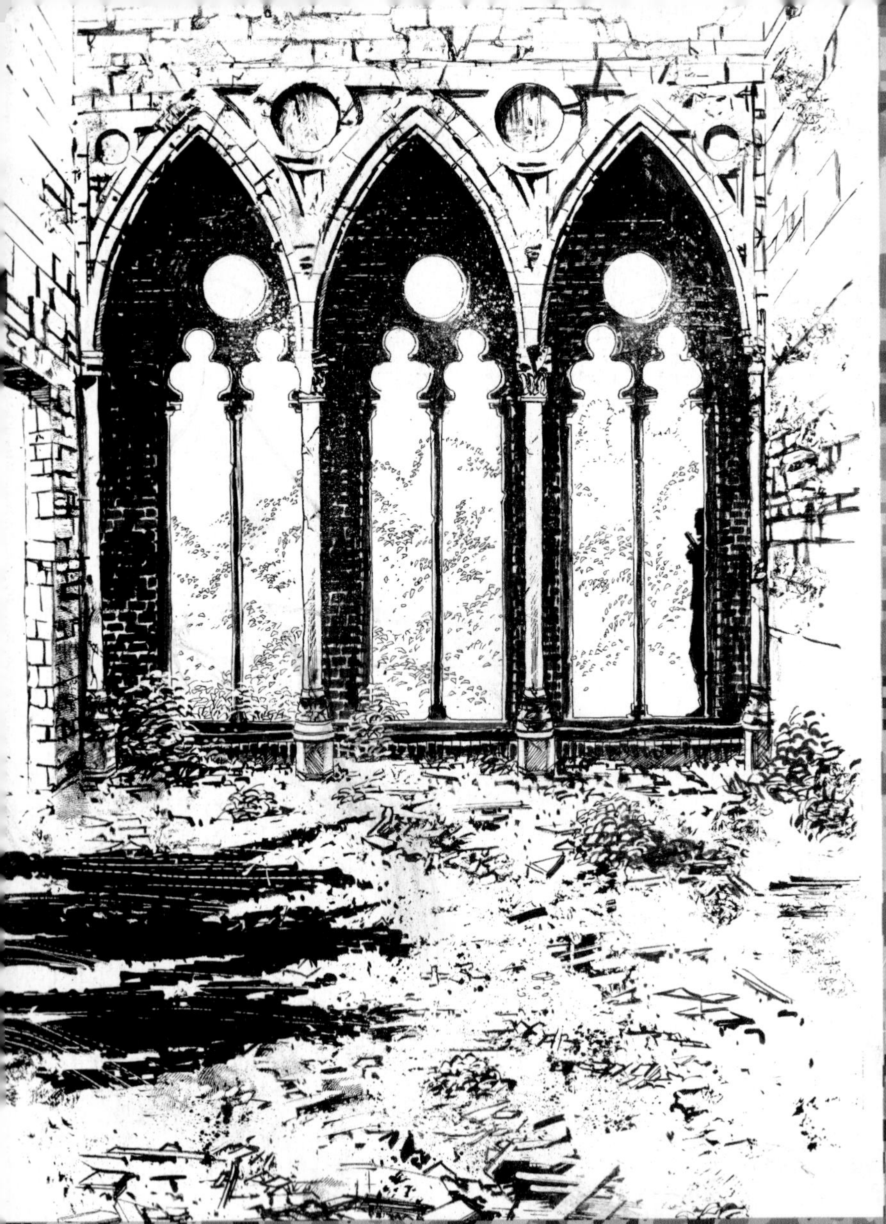

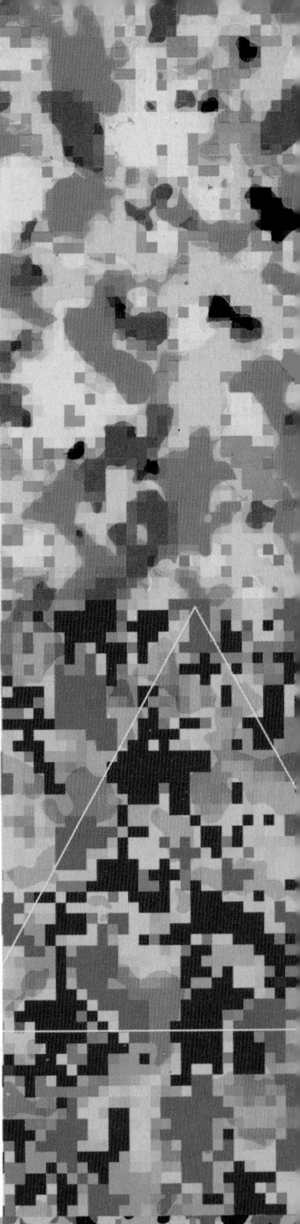

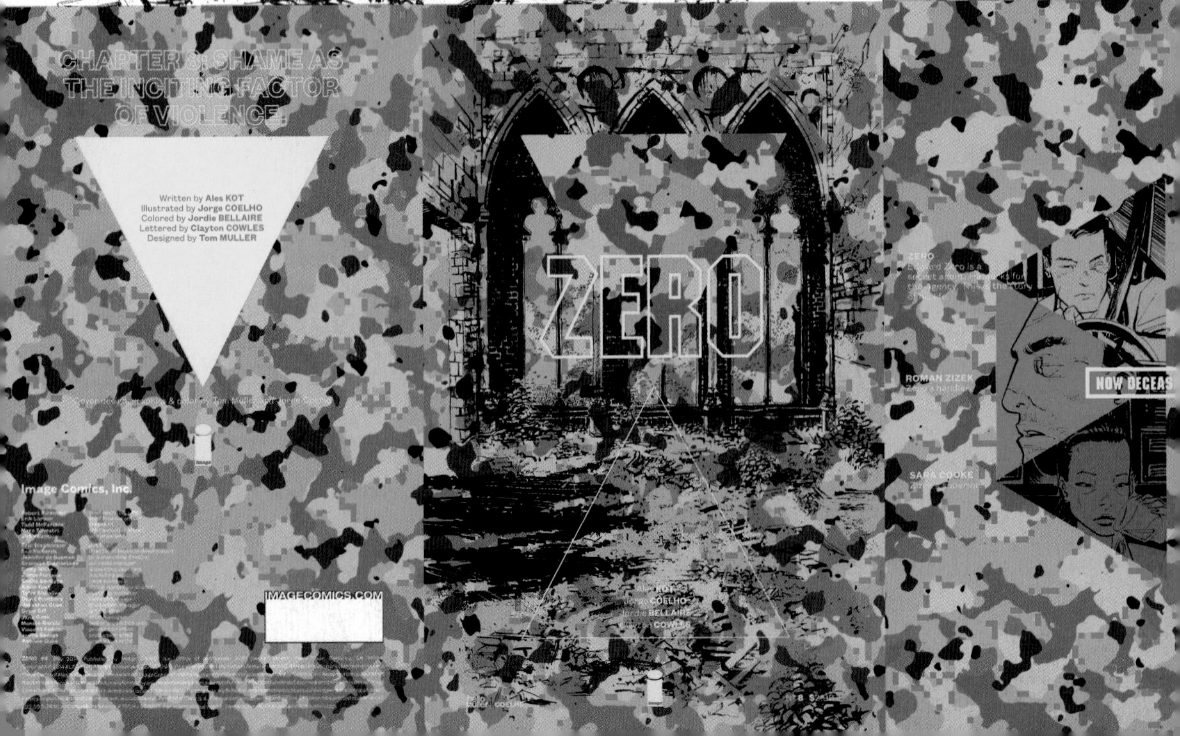
CHAPTER 8: SHAME AS THE INCITING FACTOR OF VIOLENCE.
Written by Ales KOT
Illustrated by Jorge COELHO
Colored by Jordie BELLAIRE
Lettered by Clayton COWLES
Designed by Tom MULLER
Image Comics, Inc.
IMAGECOMICS.COM
ZERO
ZERO
ROMAN ZIZEK
SARA COOKE
NOW DECEAS

HAPTER 9:

ARINA

ttan by **Ales KOT**, illustrated by **Tonči ZONJIĆ**, colored by **Jordie BELLAIRE**,
ered by **Clayton COWLES**, designed by **Tom MULLER**

er design, graphics & color by Tom Muller and Tonči Zonjić

ZERO™

Nº **9** / Ales **KOT** / Tonči **ZONJIĆ** / Jordie **BELLAIRE** / Clayton **COWLES** / **$2.99**

age Comics, Inc.

rt Kirkman — chief operating officer
Larsen — chief financial officer
McFarlane — president
Silvestri — chief executive officer
Valentino — vice president

Stephenson — publisher
Richards — director of business development
ifer de Guzman — pr & marketing director
wyn Bigglestone — accounts manager
y Miller — accounting assistant
e Parrano — marketing assistant
o Bautista — sales assistant
n Yuen — digital rights coordinator
Shainline — events coordinator
d Brothers — content manager
than Chan — production manager
Gill — art director
Cook — print manager
ca Garcia — senior production artist
ent Kukua — production artist
a Savage — production artist
son Duke — production artist

O #9. July 2014. Published by Image Comics, Inc. Office of publication: 2001 Center Street, Sixth Floor, Berkeley, CA 94704.

AGECOMICS.COM

hello Muller +

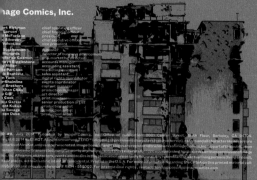

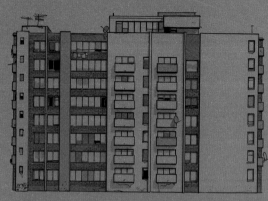

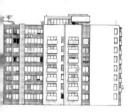

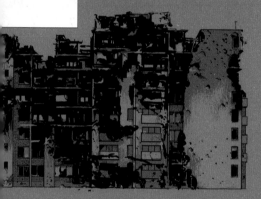

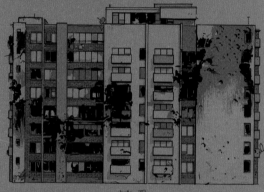

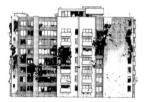

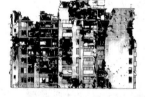

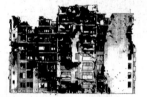

ROMAN ZIZEK
Zero's handler.

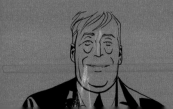

ESTIMATES FOR THE TOTAL NUMBER OF WOMEN RAPED DURING THE BOSNIAN WAR RANGES FROM **20,000** TO **50,000.**

CHAPTER 10: **WHO TOLD YOU THIS ROOM EXISTS**

Written by **Ales KOT**, illustrated by **Michael GAYDOS**, colored by **Jordie BELLAIRE**, lettered by **Clayton COWLES**, designed by **Tom MULLER**.

Cover design, graphics & color by Tom Muller and Michael Gaydos

ZERO #10. August 2014. Published by Image Comics, Inc. Office of publication: 2001 Center Street, Sixth Floor, Berkeley, CA 94704.

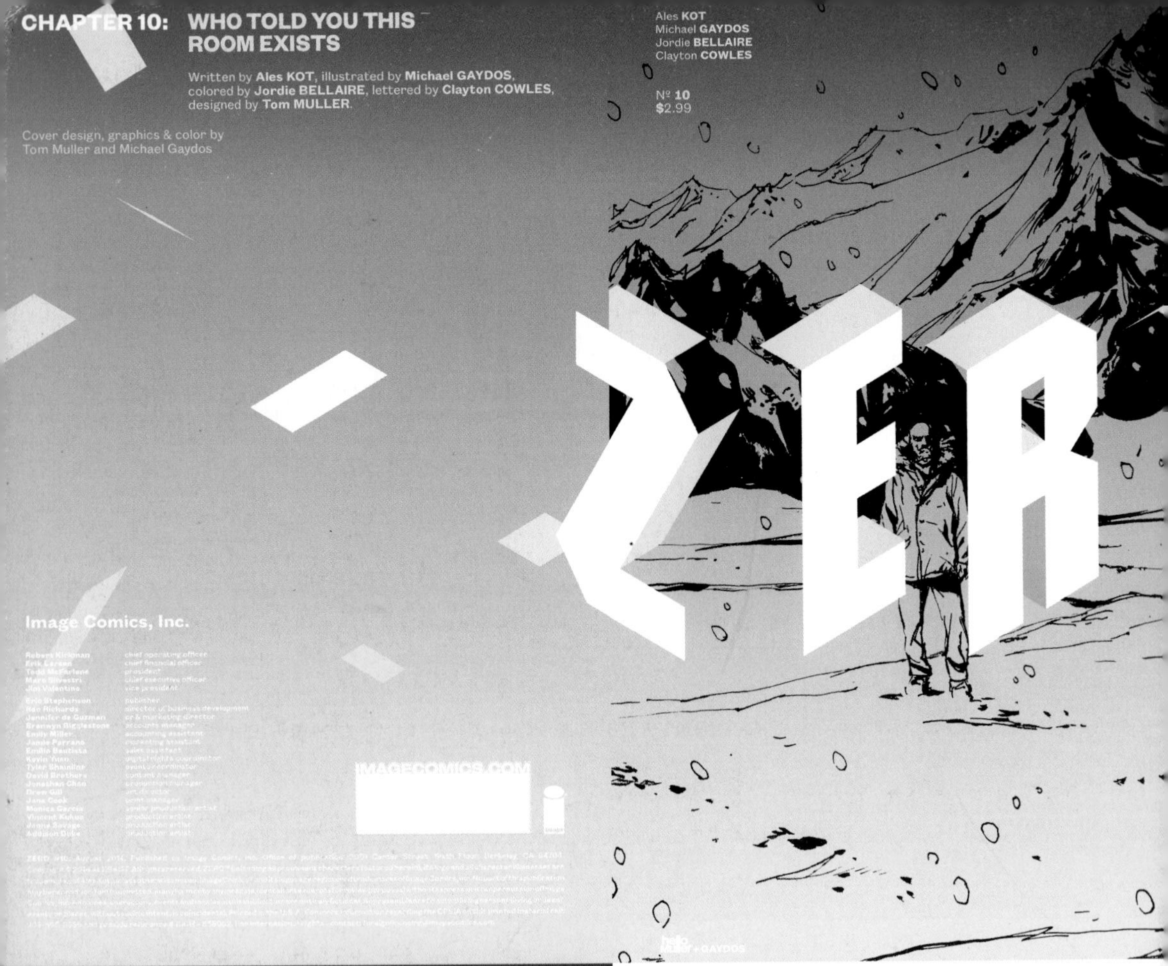

Ales KOT
Michael GAYDOS
Jordie BELLAIRE
Clayton COWLES
Nº 10
$2.99
ZER

ZERO

Edward Zero is a secret agent.
He quit the Agency. This is the story of his life.

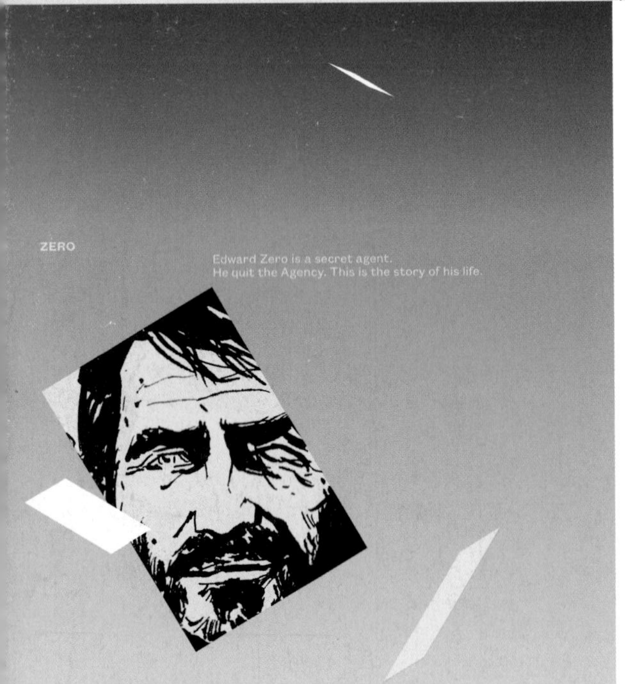

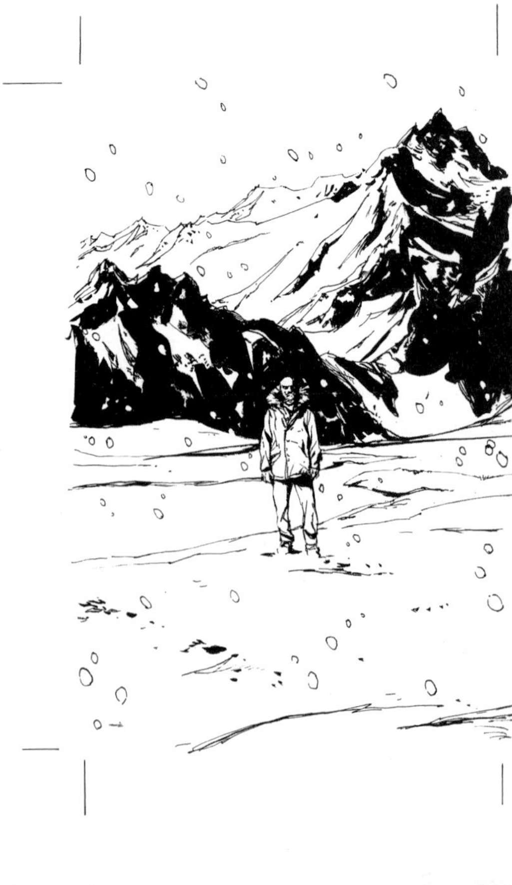